SEXY LIKE US

SEXY LIKE US

Disability, Humor, and Sexuality

Teresa Milbrodt

University Press of Mississippi / Jackson

The University Press of Mississippi is the scholarly publishing agency of
the Mississippi Institutions of Higher Learning: Alcorn State University,
Delta State University, Jackson State University, Mississippi State University,
Mississippi University for Women, Mississippi Valley State University,
University of Mississippi, and University of Southern Mississippi.

www.upress.state.ms.us

The University Press of Mississippi is a member of
the Association of University Presses.

Some names and identifying details have been changed to protect the privacy of
individuals.

First printing 2022

∞

Library of Congress Cataloging-in-Publication Data

Names: Milbrodt, Teresa, 1978– author.
Title: Sexy like us : disability, humor, and sexuality / Teresa Milbrodt.
Description: Jackson : University Press of Mississippi, 2022. | Includes bibliographical
references and index. |
Identifiers: LCCN 2022019886 (print) | LCCN 2022019887 (ebook) | ISBN
9781496838919 (hardback) | ISBN 9781496838926 (trade paperback) | ISBN
9781496838933 (epub) | ISBN 9781496838940 (epub) | ISBN 9781496838957 (pdf) |
ISBN 9781496838964 (pdf)
Subjects: LCSH: People with disabilities. | People with disabilities—Sexual behavior. |
Blind. | Wit and humor.
Classification: LCC HV1568 .M546 2022 (print) | LCC HV1568 (ebook) | DDC
362.4002/07—dc23/eng/20220613
LC record available at https://lccn.loc.gov/2022019886
LC ebook record available at https://lccn.loc.gov/2022019887

British Library Cataloging-in-Publication Data available

For all those who gleefully spread crip humor,
knowing community and solidarity can be found in a smile

CONTENTS

ACKNOWLEDGMENTS

Creating this book has been a process of engaging with scholarship and expanding my thinking and my community. Such would not have been possible without the many people who helped guide me along the way and shared their many forms of knowledge. I am extremely grateful to Anand Prahlad and Julie Elman for their reflections and advice, as well as their encouragement. Thanks as well to Matthew Gordon, Carsten Strathausen, and Mary Natvig for their helpful feedback on early drafts of these chapters.

I deeply appreciate my editor Katie Keene, who saw this book through several stages of development, the readers whose comments were invaluable to revising and expanding the final manuscript, and the journal editors who published sections of this book and offered helpful critiques, including Kim Nielsen, Allyson Day, David Bolt, Peter Grimes, and the creative nonfiction staff of *Booth Journal*.

Many friends, colleagues, and mentors have supported me through conversations about writing, disability, and writing about disability, as well as emergency coffee chats and the occasional pep talk. Maurine Pfuhl, Kelly Waston, Em Rabelais, Jessica Stokes, Natalie Phillips, Sean Ironman, Jake Young, Jeff Wasserboehr, Trudy Lewis, Angela Branson, and Barb Hammer, thank you for helping me to better understand and cherish my interdependence with others.

This book would not have been possible without my collaborators, who were willing to have extended conversations, share stories and jokes, and delve into the hilarious and painful. Thank you for welcoming me into your communities. I'm extremely proud to call you my friends.

Finally, endless gratitude to my partner Tristan Palmgren for their understanding, support, and words of wisdom at high and low points. I'm so glad we can lean on and learn from each other.

Sections of chapter 1 ("The Funny, the Fraught, and Forms of Foreplay") and "Meditation 5: On Sexuality" first appeared in *Booth Journal* in the essay "Helen Keller's Manicure."

An earlier draft of chapter 3 ("'Today I Had an Eye Appointment, and I'm Still Blind': Crip Humor, Storytelling, and Narrative Positioning of the Disabled Self") first appeared in *Disability Studies Quarterly*.

A section of "Meditation 3: On Sight" first appeared in *Pembroke Magazine* in "You May Mistake This for a Love Story."

A more condensed version of chapter 6 ("Sexy like Us: Expanding Notions of Disability and Sexuality through Burlesque Performance") first appeared in the *Journal of Literary and Cultural Disability Studies*, published by Liverpool University Press.

INVITATION/INVOCATION

For Words

In the introduction to her book *Sight Unseen*, disability scholar Georgina Kleege explains, "Writing this book made me blind" (1999, 1). She goes on to describe how, biologically speaking, her vision didn't change, but the book's creation both "made me understand for the first time how little I actually see" and "made me recognize how sighted I am" (2).

Along similar lines, writing this book made me disabled, or rather, led me to explore the creative, contentious, and ever-expanding space of disability and disability cultures. This journey has been a process of rethinking conversations, finding camaraderie, and framing the world in ways I hadn't considered until I discovered my own disability communities and contexts.

Like many people who grew up with a disability, in my case a visual disability, I spent years without a disability community to call my own. My first exposure to disability studies was through studying the folklore of disability. Perhaps folklore might seem an odd place to begin, but it was one that proved extremely fruitful. Folkloric studies focus on creative practices among everyday people—the folk—including music, foodways, clothing, humor, language, narrative, and crafts. The discipline encompasses all forms of artistic, material, and verbal expression, from memes to slang to local legends, and jump rope rhymes to casseroles concocted from Thanksgiving dinner leftovers.

During my research I found that most of the scholarship on folklore and disability had focused on perceptions of disability from outside disability communities. Fleets of fairy tales suggest that disabled bodies must be healed or destroyed for the protagonist to find a happy ending (Schmiesing 2014). Studies of community interactions discuss how people with disabilities are often marginalized and pitied (Gwaltney 1970). Jokes reveal cultural anxieties and resentments toward people with disabilities (Barrick 1980). Traditional curers try to uncover the causes of and proper ways to treat disability and illness (Ferrari 2015). While some folklorists have examined healing and illness narratives (True 1998), and narratives by people with disabilities or their family members (Shuman 2011), there was little work regarding the creative practices of folks with disabilities. How were disabled people using folklore to interpret their diverse forms of embodiment, and times in their lives when disability did and did not matter? This question spurred my interest to study joking among people with disabilities. Humor is perhaps my favorite form of folklore, due to my love of wit and language, and the fragility of finding something funny. I'm fascinated by the alchemy of the joke, how the same story can lead people to laugh or groan, and how close-knit groups can form an intimate jargon of refrains, snubs, and snickers. But how would I find a group of disabled folks who'd be willing to chat about what might seem to outsiders to be the most cheerless of subjects?

My quest began at a celebration of the twenty-fifth anniversary of the Americans with Disabilities Act, where I met two members of a wheelchair basketball team. I figured athletes would be ragging on each other constantly, so I explained my quest for in-group disability humor and asked if maybe a few players might be willing to chat with me. The floodgates opened. From there my network of folks with disabilities branched out in various directions, online and off. As many of us engaged with folkloric research discover, the line between collaborator and friend grew increasingly hazy. What else to expect when asking someone to sit down and tell you a story? Three hours later, you're refilling your coffee cup for the fourth time and swapping childhood memories.

It's not surprising that my entry into disability studies was my entry into disability stories, to disability communities, to thinking more concretely of myself as a person with a disability. That particular flag with the capital "D" had been more difficult to fly before I had this collection of friends, people who made me part of their in-group, privy to legless jokes and cheerful details about bowel obstruction.

Part of community membership means embracing the knowledge that I can't understand everything about my friends' embodiment—if I careened around the world in a wheelchair for a week, went about with earplugs, or had a patch over my sighted eye, I would not know what it means to be in their bodies. But even in the space of realizing that our experiences can't be simulated, that we shouldn't even try, we understand something important about each other and the shifting nature of bodies.

I started my writing career in fiction. I have always been a storyteller, someone who cherishes the importance of being heard, and finding meaning in one's experiences. Stories connect us to other people, help us locate common ground, and certainly this is the case when it comes to the novels of our bodies, those sacred and profane spaces of adaptation and adjustment.

In his book *The Wounded Storyteller*, Arthur Frank suggests that personal stories about the body explore what it means to be fragile, and telling such stories is a way "to touch others and perhaps to make a difference in the unfolding of their stories" (2013, 127). Yet this is not an easy task, since stories about sickness and disability are often related to pain and loss, as well as adaptation. Frank notes that "human illness . . . always returns to mourning. The boon is gaining the ability to mourn not for oneself only, but for others" (136). In sharing and listening to such tales, we can find layers of emotional resonance and connection tied to the experience of physical vulnerability. Yet this is not only a space of sadness. Humor is present as well, always in different flavors, through tales that are long and bawdy, and others that elicit the dark snicker, wry smile, or knowing nod.

But why did I choose to pair jokes and jests and comic narratives by people with disabilities with a subject so tantalizing and taboo as sexuality? Perhaps it was because in my first interviews with members of the wheelchair basketball team, joking about sex was a frequent topic. My collaborators related how some of their friends, guys in their twenties who were wheelchair users, made a point of looking away from women when they passed by on the sidewalk or in a hallway. People who used wheelchairs weren't supposed to watch anyone "that way." During the conversation, my collaborators went on to explain how other people constantly desexualized wheelchair users. The question they were asked most frequently in bars was if their dicks worked. They were prepared with a number of creative responses.

As I continued collecting jokes and anecdotes, listening to stories that were funny and frustrating, the tales wove a collective narrative to counter notions of disability as tragedy. Popular movies such as *Me Before You* and *Million Dollar Baby* construct disability to signify an end to life, an end to hope, an end.[1] That idea couldn't be further from the truth. Yes, having a disability often isn't easy. It can mean pain, procedures, and endless adjustments, but it can be a space of creativity and flexibility. A space of joy.

This book endeavors to expand the definitions of disability, humor, and sexuality in ways that help us reconsider what it means to be in a body. The text is neither a pity party nor an "easy celebration [of disability] without grounding in lived reality" (Kuppers 2013, 153). Our labyrinth path will be far more complicated than that, winding through words and wit and wisdom.

When interacting with this book, I hope you will find a sentence or joke or story worth repeating, texting, tweeting, integrating into your collective knowledge for that is the space of folklore, to never be a static surface but one of shift. This book is not one of set definitions, but of ever-opening doors. Meditate in the margins. Murmur in the white spaces. Touch the possibilities.

SEXY LIKE US

Chapter 1

THE FUNNY, THE FRAUGHT,
AND FORMS OF FOREPLAY

Since I was little, my blind eye has had its own agenda. It's a solo adventurer. I don't have control over its movements, so we've led somewhat independent lives. I was born three months premature, and my retina almost fully detached from the back of my eye when I was a baby due to retinopathy of prematurity. An infant's eyes develop the most during the last three months before birth, time I didn't have, and cells are less likely to cooperate if you want out early. (My mother says I have always been impatient to get things done.) A few retinal cells must have stayed connected, though, since if my left eye is covered, the right eye can see light and dark and a waving hand. It's difficult to describe how this looks, not black or white but presence where there is usually absence, the Morse code of movement.

Que verra verra. What will see will see.

When I was a kid, I thought being blind in one eye was cool. It made me different. It was something I could tell other kids at school: "Hey, I'm blind in one eye." But this revelation led to the inevitable test. The kid I'd told would hold up their hand in front of my right eye and say, "How many fingers am I holding up?"

"I don't know," I'd say, "it's blind."

Even when I was eight, I didn't understand their logic. If my eye weren't blind, I could've lied and told them the wrong number. Other kids didn't notice the blindness so much as the way I held books closely when I read. I also needed glasses to see things that were far away, and to protect my sighted eye. That was something my mother and my ophthalmologist drilled into my head from a young age: No contacts. Ever.

YOU DON'T LOOK DISABLED

This is a book about disability, humor, and sexuality, and the ways these three subjects twist and twine and twirl together like words and bodies often do. But before the joke, the turn of phrase or slow reveal, we must talk politics. The setup precedes the punch line. Over the past several decades, disability has emerged as a political identity in certain countries and cultures, a turn that has marked an important shift in identity politics. Before the disability rights movement, an individual being told that they didn't "seem disabled" was supposed to be a compliment (Shapiro 1994, 3; Garland-Thomson 2017, 374). The label of disability has long been a stigmatizing slap used to devalue people and minority groups (Dolmage 2014, 4). Disabled persons are often barred from being considered full members of society, leading some groups to deny or denounce the idea that they are disabled. Even now, the label is often used to discount women, people of color, and queer people (Baynton 2017, 18).[1] Disability is assumed to be an identity that must be swept under the rug, concealed, and/or derided in favor of the mythological "normal" body (McRuer 2017, 398–99). We cannot underestimate how long the sardonic stare of doctors may linger in one's soul, or for how many years someone could feel the painful slap of stigma from being categorized as defective. Considering an individual to be an "able" human being has personal and political repercussions. As disability scholar Tobin Siebers suggests, persons with bodies that are considered "unfit" for a myriad of reasons can be "dis-qualified . . . found lacking, inept, incompetent, inferior, in need, incapable, degenerate, uneducated, weak, ugly, underdeveloped" (2010, 23). Not being regarded as a "quality" person means someone can be shunted to the margins and lose part of their humanity, and sometimes the right to be alive (23). Siebers notes that bodies "invite judgements about whether they should be accepted or rejected in the human community" based on the "feelings of pleasure or pain" that these bodies create in other people (25). This category includes bodies that need wheelchairs, white canes, and leg braces, bodies with eyes that don't always track in the same direction, bodies that make temporarily able-bodied (TAB) individuals feels uncomfortable.[2] Disability is the phantom reminder of human fragility, the fact we can break (Shakespeare 1999, 49). It's easier for those who assume themselves "able" to turn away, put up fences, gaze over the heads of people who may force that blunt recognition of limitations, the whiff of mortality.

I'm disabled and not. From my perspective, this blind eye isn't a disability, because I've always had it. "Disability" suggests a more severe limitation, impediment, adjustment you must make partway through life. What I have is a way of living. I must be careful on stairs and when descending rocky slopes on hikes. I don't think I have depth perception, but it's like missing snow when you've never caught flakes on your tongue. I position myself at the far right corner of the table when I go out to eat with a group of people, and when walking with friends I stay on their right so they don't get lost in my empty space. These are things I do automatically, adjustments I never realize I'm making. I am awful at sports that involve catching or throwing or kicking a ball. This may be due to that mysterious quality called depth perception. It may also be due to the fact I'm awful at sports.

KNOCKING ABOUT WITH NORMALITY

The idea that variation isn't a negative trait but simply part of being alive has long been acknowledged by (scattered) scientists and theorists who realized the innate nature of biological variability. As medical philosopher George Canguilhiem writes, "Nothing can be lacking to a living being once we accept that there are a thousand and one different ways of living" (2008, 126). Canguilhiem notes that such differences aren't problems in and of themselves, but only "in relation to a milieu of life and a kind of life . . . for human activity, work, and culture have the immediate effect of constantly altering the milieu of human life. The history proper to man modifies problems" (128). In the sparkling spectrum of bodyminds,[3] many ways of living aren't inherently disabling—it simply depends on what someone needs to do at a particular time in a particular space.

The steps to the grocery store. The basketball coming toward me in gym class. The volume of a microphone. The presence of odors—cleaning products, colognes, perfumes. The availability of elevators. The height and width of a chair, and presence or absence of cushions. The brightness of lighting. The ebb and flow of brain chemicals. The chatter of voices, tapping pens, squeaking chairs, clearing throats. The millions of tiny details in the physical world that are ignored by many people, yet can be (are) disabling to others.

Everyone molds their own sense of normal. Of necessity.

When I was a kid, I didn't pause to wonder why no one else sat at their desk and rested their chin on the page when reading. I was doing the logical thing, keeping the book where I could see it.

But disability is more multifaceted than appearance and function—it involves bodies in pain, the tight muscles, the aching joints, the all-over weariness of limbs. It involves the ways bodies are interpreted and treated by others—the sideways glances, the sometimes-excessive courtesy of running ahead to open a door, the outright stare across the street or while passing someone on the sidewalk. It involves how bodies move, or are allowed to move, or are prevented from moving, through the environment. It involves the disclosures people give, or withhold, to others at certain times. It involves the words people use to describe their bodymind, to situate themselves in a world where so many bodily attributes cannot be perceived visually, though many people assume the opposite.[4]

As Siebers notes, being in a certain kind of body influences how an individual interprets the world, and the facets of themselves they reveal and conceal (2017, 324), the disabilities they flash in the form of prosthetics and white canes, the ones they hide in medication bottles in the bottom of a bag, the pain clenched through gritted teeth, the all-over body tired that may be defeated for snatches of time with enough caffeine. Siebers argues that while people often try to hide disability and "pass" as normal, they should refuse to disguise their limp, or hearing aid, or stoma bag, instead greeting the eyes of others as proud of their embodiment (326). But embracing one's shiftable self in a bear hug of love for their brittle bones and network of nesting nerves isn't always an easy task, especially when the self must be poked and prodded and molded into submission to better fit the requirements of the physical world.

I'm accustomed to the ritual of eye appointments, to people shining bright lights in my face and telling me to look up, right, down, left. I like my new optometrist, who's pleased to learn that my research involves disability studies. I explain that when you have a blind eye, it's hard not to be drawn to that field. Some part of me has always recognized that I see things differently than many people. My optometrist says the things that happen to us in life often drive our interests.

"Mine, too," he adds, and then he explains he was a preemie and has a lazy eye because of it. It wasn't retinopathy of prematurity—I have to ask that question—but his eye didn't develop as it should. One day when he was six or seven, he discovered he could read much better if he covered one eye. He asked his mom if it was supposed to work that way. After that he started therapy to strengthen the lazy eye, so now both his eyes track together. I envy the fact they can agree on a direction, but essentially, he is a person like me, half-sighted. That's part of the reason why he decided to go into medicine.

"I tried working in a hospital during my undergraduate years, but it was too intense," he says. "I feel too much for other people." Empathy. I can understand that.

"How big were you?" he asks.

"Twenty-six weeks. Two pounds, thirteen ounces," I say.

"You were smaller than me," he says, but doctors are saving babies at twenty-one weeks now. They know how to treat retinopathy of prematurity more effectively than when we were born, monitoring oxygen levels. A few decades ago, they hadn't realized that higher oxygen levels put babies at risk for retinopathy. Now more preemies grow up to have retinal detachment in later life, losing their sight in their twenties and thirties (Quiram and Capone 2007). That would feel like a disability to me. My fear of delayed retinopathy is why I made this eye appointment.

SMILE FOR THE CAMERA

Disability theorist Rosemarie Garland-Thomson notes how children are taught not to stare at other people—it is considered impolite, and individuals do not want to be the subject of such attention (2009, 5). At the same time, Kleege argues that the averted gaze implies that when a TAB individual sees a person who is a wheelchair user or has a white cane, that person can be ignored as if they don't matter. Kleege suggests that looking away creates a different kind of impairment for TABs: "What you can't see can't hurt you, can't matter, doesn't exist . . . it's also why I now carry a white cane as a nonverbal sign that I do not see as much as I seem to" (1999, 39). This is something else I understand—how a visual impairment affects the way I move, and how others need to move when around me. People must realize the disabilities of others to enable communication and comfort. They must turn when speaking if someone needs to read their lips. Not meet in a room with fluorescent lighting. Provide closed captioning on film presentations. Make copies of the meeting agenda in twenty-four-point font. Find venues with ramps and chairs with cushions and one-person gender-neutral wheelchair-accessible bathrooms.

See? There are things I can't see. People usually can't tell I'm blind in one eye, my invisible disability that makes things invisible until I hit someone in the grocery store because they were lost in my empty space. I say I'm sorry, sometimes to a gracious smile, other times to a frown. It makes me consider wearing a bright purple pirate eye patch. It makes me consider carrying a small informational card entitled "Apologies: Why I Just Ran into You." It makes me think about how people don't look away from those with invisible disabilities whose fragility is hidden, people who have asthma or diabetes or fibromyalgia, depression or anxiety. My friends with chronic conditions have told me it's easier to pass as able-bodied and able-minded—why have employers or coworkers question your fitness for the job, worry about the time you might need off from work, your higher insurance costs, if you can tuck those concerns in medical files and hold them tightly to your chest? But I wonder what would happen if people went into the world waving their inhalers and insulin kits, their bottles of extra-strength pain medications and antidepressants: Hey! I'm impaired! Look at me! Not as healthy as you thought, eh? Would we start to question our idea of health? Would we start to question our idea of fitness? Would we start to question our idea of normal?

As Garland-Thomson writes, dominant culture does not prepare individuals to look at others who do not look as they do—people with body variations—which leads to staring (2009, 38). This phenomenon means that some people with disabilities learn how to artfully direct the eyes of others, a kind of social choreography that Garland-Thomson suggests can "help starers maintain face by relieving them of their anxiety, understanding their motivations, working with them to overcome their limited understanding of human variation . . . a seasoned staree evaluates when to turn away, stare back, or further extend the stare" (87).[5] It is a delicate dance that can work toward easing others' fear of bodily difference, but not everyone wants to be the target of such a gaze.

As Siebers notes, people with disabilities often pass as less disabled to help ease their way through the social sphere, but they may also perform a "masquerade," which involves "exaggerating" their impairments so other people believe they are disabled (2008, 96, 100–2). The prevalence of both passing as nondisabled and disability masquerade reveals how easy it may be for individuals to conceal or enhance certain disabilities, to casually (or tooth-grittingly) float under the radar (100–1). At the same time, there is a dominant cultural assumption that disability should be visually evident, an idea that disability theorist Ellen Samuels terms a "fantasy of identification." Samuels explains that this belief suggests that "disability is [a] knowable, obvious, and unchanging category . . . even as it is repeatedly and routinely disproved by the actual realities of these bodies and minds fluctuating abilities" (2014, 121). Sometimes individuals must use disability masquerade to "prove" they have a disability and receive federal assistance, since people with disabilities are under "perpetual suspicion" of lying (13–14). Yet the many tedious tests required to demonstrate disability suggest "the fundamental instability of the term" (123). Often individuals will not be considered disabled unless they use a wheelchair or white cane, meaning disability can be a closeted identity, one people hide to preserve their social status and protect themselves from stigma or their own seeping sense of shame (Siebers 2008, 96–97, 101; Cox 2013, 101).

As Steve Kuusisto writes in his memoir, *Planet of the Blind*, he spent years masking his visual impairment, only to pass as able-bodied and cranky. Embarrassed by the notion of blindness, when he was in college, he grumped around campus so people would leave him alone and read only in private with a magnifying glass (1998, 63–64). He couldn't admit his weakening vision to his parents, his friends, himself; he couldn't be a person who carried a white cane. As Garland-Thomson suggests, when individuals are in public, they must "perform" a version of self, and people feel compelled to "present high status" through their dress, speech, and how they move through their surroundings (2009, 35, 37). Revealing disability may put their value into question since dominant culture teaches that people with disabilities won't amount to much (Garland-Thomson 2009, 38; Kafer 2013, 1–3), and they are not worthy of being taken seriously or treated with due respect.[6] Passing as nondisabled can also be a necessity when individuals feel the need to protect themselves from the potentially dangerous diagnoses of medical practitioners. As disability theorist Eli Clare writes, being identified as disabled has caused people to be taken from their loved ones and trapped in group homes or institutions, perilous places where they were subjected to "head cages and straitjackets, [and] drugging with psychotropic meds." Anyone who tried to fight back was in danger of further restraint and abuse (2017, 46–47).

Passing can be a means to protect personhood.

Whether or not we realize it, we are always performing different aspects of self (Goffman 1956, 15), often in the name of preservation. We perform gender. Health. Independence. The myth called normality.[7] Insert the category of your anxiety here. In his memoir, *Laughing at My Nightmare*, Shane Burcaw reflects on his performance as a wheelchair user when he went to a summer camp for children with disabilities. Many of the other kids had atrophied feet and no shoes, but Burcaw realized that wearing shoes marked him as different, more worthy of respect. He reflects that the episode "ingrained in my mind the idea that physical appearance has a big effect on how others treat me" (2016, 84–85). Wearing shoes meant he was less subject to the smack of stigma, indicative of how a simple visual cue could represent status and value.

But even that statement I must amend, expand, explode, since many disability studies scholars have recognized that seeing is but one way of knowing, and one that is too often privileged and prone to provide false assurances (Kleege 1999, 97–98; Healey 2017, 92–94, 101–2; Samuels 2014,

11–12, 17). I do not mean for this book to supply answers but to keep asking questions,[8] poking down odd alleys, posing reminders that definitions must always be amended with another "and" or "but" or "maybe."

This is Drew, the person I know who best embodies an East Coast don't-fuck-with-me attitude, combined with a sense of Southern politeness that means he holds the door for women. Drew has spina bifida and has used a wheelchair since he was a kid. When we're walking somewhere together, he says, "Remind me which side I need to be on. I always forget." Few of my other friends ask this question, but some of them don't know I'm blind in one eye. I met Drew through Eric, another wheelchair-using friend. Drew is not a person for casual chatter, so in our first ten minutes of conversation, we were discussing sex jokes and losing one's virginity. It's one way to skip the small talk.

"So you can't do as much as people think you can," he said at the end of our three-hour-long chat, "and we [people who use wheelchairs] can do a lot more than people think we can."

"Pretty much," I said.

That was after he'd explained he liked rock climbing and wanted to be in a marathon. He said he probably worked his joints too hard, but he'd resigned himself to early arthritis. I'd given him a general account of half blindness and bumping into people who were lost in the empty space on my right. I didn't tell him how I won't drive in large cities because I don't know who I won't see and how I seem to be looking in a different direction than everyone else in group photos.

CLAIMING DISABILITY AS POLITICAL IDENTITY

As Siebers writes, the "ideology of ability" suggests that individuals who have "lesser" abilities are "lesser" as people, but disabled individuals can challenge that idea when they "claim the value and variety of disability" (2017, 315–16). Yet disability communities are diverse, a complex collage of individuals with impairments that are congenital and acquired, people who want to own a disability identity, people who want to find a "cure," and many others who float on the spectrum in between. Some may claim their right to be proud crips, others want to pass as nondisabled, and still others are willing to sign up for the latest experimental treatments to make living in their shifting-drifting bodies a little more bearable (Shuttleworth and Meekosha 2017, 186).[9]

Garland-Thomson admits that it is easier to identify as nondisabled and not gamble with one's social status, but if few people are willing to come out as disabled, antidisability stigmas will persist (2017, 374–75). Yet shaping a strong disability identity can be a trying task without an equally strong community to lean on for support. When connected with others through linked hands and elbows, wheels and walkers, prescriptions and prosthetics, disabled people can more easily find pride in their disability, fight ableism, and work against a historic perception of disability that has been "soaked in shame" and "rooted in isolation" (Clare 1999, 90–91). The battle is more difficult for those who have another stigmatized identity. Not all forms of disability have equal social and physical weight, and not all disabled people have equal power or risk the same level of discrimination if their disability is apparent (Shuttleworth and Meekosha 2017, 184, 186). This variability is why it is easier for some people with disabilities to reveal themselves in virtual communities, where they are granted the shield of a computer monitor. As research by scholar Ryan Miller suggests, in these spaces, disabled individuals can more safely locate "others online with shared [experiences]," communities that grant them "a sense of support and validation that may have been difficult to achieve [in] the physical [environment]" (2017, 517).

There is a tension between the need to protect oneself and Garland-Thomson's contention that, to create a shift in the dominant culture's way of thinking about bodies, it is important for disabled people to be seen, even stared at. She argues this type of "performance" can become a creative act to normalize body variability: "[The viewer's] eyes will work toward reducing the strangeness . . . by giving it a story . . . not the same one that started them staring" (2009, 7). Meeting the stare suggests bodily pride and unabashedness that TABs might not expect from someone with a disability. As disability and queer theorist Robert McRuer argues, people with disabilities must fight against the idea that they should be disappointed with their bodies (2017, 400–2), which is why he and Garland-Thomson, among other disability scholars, have launched the call for people with disabilities to greet the stare and be prepared to tell the story of their bodyminds with pride and matter-of-factness. Along similar lines, disability scholars Sharon Snyder and David Mitchell write that disabled people have not been able to make their stories heard due to "silencing" in hospitals or institutions. For decades only treatment professionals could tell the legitimate stories about such individuals (2006, 144). But now some people with disabilities are reclaiming their stories and owning their voices. And sometimes they're doing it with humor.

Drew doesn't have an internal editor. He often damns himself for saying too much, telling too many secrets, getting too personal, but the next time we chat he does the same thing. This is a Drew story: On Tinder he connected with a woman who was married and wanted to meet up for sex because her husband was disabled. Drew said he'd be up for that, but he was also disabled, though the important parts still worked. She didn't respond.

Mostly Drew and I talk about religion and the Hitchhiker's Guide to the Galaxy *series and how he's turned on by punk girls with piercings and tats. We talk about Judith Butler, how everything is a construction, and how he hates Freud, but he's allowed to hate Freud because he was a psychology major. We talk about painful breakups and* Saturday Night Live *sketches and adaptive sports and writing as therapy. We are huggers. He's always looking for love. I tell him that love is really about best friendship since that keeps you with your beloved even when you're feeling more pissed than loving. Romance never put up with much shit. Drew knows that whoever he dates will have to put up with his shit, literal and figurative, and understand his bowel routine. He's anticipating two and three and four decades down the road, when he might not be able to do things for himself, and how his life partner may have a duty of care. Love means the possibility of wiping the ass of your beloved. I wonder if the "In sickness and in health" part of marriage vows should endeavor to be that graphic. Love me, love my body: its tingles and caresses as well as its leakings and failings.*

DISABILITY AND HUMOR

Disabled people have long been cast as the object of humor in dominant culture, the "butt" that is ripe for ridicule in blindness jokes, deafness jokes, and jokes about wheelchair users (Barrick 1980; Dundes 1987, 15–18). Yet disabled people have proven themselves adept at comic cultural critiques of dominant society, using the same rhetorical barbs of joking to jab back at assumptions, assert their political identity, and reveal the ways that disability is both lived experience and social construction (Shakespeare 1999, 49–51).

Through joking, people can shape their identity in the minds of others and work with or against preconceived ideas about who they are. As sociologist Erving Goffman notes, people tend to make assumptions about others based on very little information, yet they don't realize their assumptions until the person in question does something to counter those perceptions. When communicating, Goffman argues, people are implicitly trying to reflect a positive status and "place in the social world" (1967, 7). Yet his writings on stigma note that when individuals belong to a stigmatized group, that identity can be used to discredit or dismiss them as "not quite human" and less deserving of respect (2017, 134–35).

Disabled people can use humor to push against these negative stereotypes, arguing for their social worth and performing jokes as a means of reshaping themselves in the minds of audience members. At least that's the dream. Goffman also notes that individuals do not perform the same self in all spaces, picking and choosing the points of personality they wish to bring to the fore (1956, 49). This type of performance and humor is contextual, alluding to the fact that joke-tellers must plot their stories and sayings according to the social situation.

As disability theorist Tom Shakespeare writes, disabled people are often the targets of jokes by TABs, particularly "when social sanctioning is temporarily suspended—for example, when people are drunk together and encounter a physically different other" (1999, 48). Yet disabled people can wield humor for various political purposes, which may include sparking or easing a sense of discomfort between themselves and TABs. Often, joking can be a means to ease the way into conversations with uptight TABs, who Shakespeare notes are often "anxious about saying the right thing" around disabled people (49). This wariness "is fundamentally undermining of successful interaction. . . . Disabled people, if they are to enter the everyday world of social engagement, must develop skills of interactional management in order to put the other at their ease" (49). While it might seem unfair to hand the task of "normalizing" relations to the disabled person, Shakespeare suggests that people can joke about their disability as a playful "way of acknowledging the difference, showing that it is not important, and that the interaction can now progress" (50). This maneuver lets TABs know they do not need to have disability in the forefront of their minds when interacting with a disabled person. Sometimes those of us with disabilities are thinking about our bodies. Much of the time we aren't.

My friend Eric, a double amputee who sometimes uses a wheelchair and other times his prosthetic legs, has met other disabled people who he says have no comic filter. They don't care when you had your accident; they'll joke even if it was last week. One of his wheelchair basketball coaches was like that. On one occasion, there was a new player on the team who had recently been paralyzed from the waist down by a gunshot wound. He'd been playing piano and a stray bullet from a gang fight went through his window.

"My coach didn't give a crap," says Eric. "He said, 'You are forever known as Piano Man.' He made up a story that Steve played piano so horribly that his neighbor had to shoot a bullet to stop him. I remember everyone on the team was cracking up, and Steve was laughing the hardest. It was absurd, but fun, and fit the situation, but it goes over the barrier [of good taste] between getting over the accident.

"Another time we were on a road trip, and my coach told a story about one of his old friends from the Paralympics. He got run over by a lawnmower and was paralyzed from the waist down. They were at an airport and [the friend] suddenly had a big smile and went into a mini mall store. A few minutes later he comes back out with a shirt that says, 'I fought the lawn, and the lawn won.'"

AUDIENCE AWARENESS

Joking is nothing if not complex, a tangled yarn of words and gestures, subject to mixed and multiple interpretations based on the teller, audience, and occasion for telling the joke. Jokes about disability may break down stereotypes, yet they also run the risk of re-creating those stereotypes based on how the joke is "read" by audience members (Shakespeare 1999, 52). Jokes, like bodies, are shifting entities, explaining why Mairian Corker argues that disability humor must reside with disabled tellers: "As with most forms of humour, the key to our 'comedy' lies in solidarity and context . . . [T]he humour of disability is in its inscription by disabled people and the particular way in which it jokes with 'disability'" (1999, 81). Since joke telling is a performative and embodied act, a joke told by a TAB teller will not hold the same meaning for audience members as the same joke told by a disabled teller. Further, since comedy is subject to personal taste, not all disabled tellers will be comfortable joking about similar things, and various audience members may laugh (or not laugh) at different aspects of a joke.

In her memoir *Too Late to Die Young*, Harriet McBryde Johnson writes of how she recruited an aspiring lawyer as a co-protestor in her work against the fundraising efforts of the Muscular Dystrophy Association. Johnson was decrying the organization's portrayal of wheelchair users such as herself as having insufferable lives. As an incentive for her collaborator, she offered to buy his lunch and write a letter of recommendation for law school (2006, 56). Observing his tactics when chatting with passersby, she notes that "in the face of opposition, he stays cool; when he finds an opening, he grabs it, leads them along. Every word seems straight from the heart. No one would suspect he is motivated by free food or any secondary gain. He'll make a fine lawyer. I'll recommend him without hesitation" (60). Her obvious jab is at the mock sincerity of lawyers who may have mixed and mangled motivations, but hidden in layers of laughter is a sad chuckle that she can only find help for the cause of disability rights with the offer of a letter and lunch.

Later, when visiting a school for disabled kids in Cuba, Johnson feels a connection with the young students when remembering her own school days:

"We, too, used to act cute and engage visiting dignitaries in conversation. But when the visitors left, we had a contest among ourselves: Who'd met the stupidest visitor? Bonus points for a pat on the head" (2006, 159). Even as children, she and her friends knew that they had to perform a version of disability for eager adults who wanted to ooh and aah as if they were at a petting zoo for the plucky and partially paralyzed. Yet the kids were laughing behind too-wide smiles; they knew they were not a pity party but savvy puppeteers.

Think of Jokes as Rorschach Inkblot Tests: The Art Is in Perception

Humor scholar Joanne Gilbert examines the complexities of joking and performing minority identity, suggesting that while some jokes have the political goal of playing with stereotypes to reveal their constructed nature, "the audience must recognize the strategy undergirding of their use . . . [W]e must ignore the fact that stereotypes are inherently reductionistic; to humanize the Other, they must become multidimensional and hence no longer stereotypes" (2004, 152). During the course of a performance, joke-tellers cannot know if the stereotypes they are attempting to parody are shown to be false, supported, or even enhanced (152). It is always a question if these jokes turn harmful constructions on their heads, or if they are shape-shifted into another stereotype. Those who try to use comedy as a weapon or tool must be aware of the fluidity of interpretation of jokes and bodies since that plays into audience members' readings of the joke. We cannot peer into their minds and discover what sort of collage has been created, why jokes spark smiles or guffaws or frowns. Such is the mysterious and delicate art of humor, equally dangerous and delightful, but this is the craft of social change, (re)forming the sculpture again and again.

Some of Eric's best stories come from being part of a wheelchair basketball team. He says, "There was one time I was on a road trip with my coach and he had a broomstick by his side in the van. We drove for three hours and I realized he was using the broomstick as hand controls.

I said, 'Is this the best fix?'
He said, 'Well, it works.'
'We could crash,' I said.
'You'd better hang on,' he said."
Then there was the birthday when Eric's roommate gave him athlete's foot powder, the movies Happy Feet *and* Happy Feet 2, *and two rulers that measured two feet. At a Christmas gift exchange with the rest of the basketball*

team, he was the last person to open a present, and he received several pairs of Christmas socks. No one would trade with him. He lost count of the number of times that his teammates hid his legs in the Student Union. When Eric tells these stories, he laughs long and loud.

STEPPING BACK FROM THE SELF

Disabled people can use joking not only to moderate audience expectations, but also to critique their past actions and attitudes toward disability through the lens of hindsight. In her memoir, *Mean Little deaf Queer*,[10] Terry Galloway writes of herself as a young adult, and how she believed the dominant cultural assumption that disabled people should be dowdy and distinctively unattractive. When she was a college student in New York City and low on funds, she went to the state rehabilitation office to request new hearing aids. Galloway had trained as an actor and determined she'd play the part of a disabled person, wearing unfashionable clothing and not doing her hair as she usually did. She assumed she didn't look disabled in everyday life since "I had a great haircut, a sex life, and interesting shoes" (2010, 169). Before going to her command performance, she "practiced many faces of despair in the mirror and settled on the one that seemed vaguely baby seal like," but after her appointment at the rehab office and being granted new hearing aids, Galloway was soon "morphing back into my sunny skipping self" (170). In her comic language, Galloway mocks not only perceptions of how disabled people should look, but how easy it is to buy into those stereotypes.

Disabled people can also use humor to lend a tinge of comedy to their experiences and broach topics that might otherwise be too painful to discuss. In her graphic essay collection *Hyperbole and a Half*, Allie Brosh writes of her depression in a comic format, explaining how annoying it is when people try to convince her that she should be happy (2013, 128–32). Brosh illustrates how depression isn't something she can fight with hope, explaining, "It would be like having a bunch of dead fish, but nobody around you will acknowledge that the fish are dead. Instead they offer to help you look for the fish or try to help you figure out why they disappeared" (135). Yet there is no solution to the problem of dead fish, so these gestures fall flat. Brosh reflects, "You're maybe just looking for someone to say, 'Sorry about how dead your fish are,' or 'Wow, those are super dead, I still like you though'" (135). Sometimes one's most painful vulnerabilities are best introduced with a jest, making them easier to acknowledge. Far preferable to laugh, rather than stuff such secrets underneath an (already lumpy) rug. A smile can allow us to express the generally inexpressible, to start the conversation.

When we cross the street together, Drew rolls ahead of me.
  "They're not going to hit the crippled kid in the wheelchair," he says.
  "They will hit the half-blind girl who they don't realize is half-blind," I say.
  At the curb we grin at each other like we do when we joke about our frailties.

HUMOR THAT HARMS

Humor is a weapon that can disarm, dispel, distance, demystify, or divide. Within disability communities, its functions are far from set and straightforward. Disabled people are not exempt from telling jokes that are disabling, spiked with horizontal hostilities that can maintain disability hierarchies, implying that some disabilities are "worse" than others (Dolmage 2014, 46). In his memoir, Burcaw teases people with intellectual disabilities who rode the "short bus" with him in high school, including Brandon, a kid who smelled "like he always had a large pile of poop in his pants, which might have been because he always had a large pile of poop in his pants" (2016, 103). In his joking, Burcaw derides and does violence against people with intellectual disabilities,[11] yet he also reveals his frustrations with people who fall prey to the notion of "disability drift" and assume that because he is a wheelchair user, he also has an intellectual disability (46).[12]

But just as humor may do harm to people with disabilities, it can also be used to challenge the cultural meaning of disability as negative, sparking questions and explorations. Disability scholar Jay Dolmage argues that, rather than refuse the label of disability, people must "affirm disability as a shared and positive identity, while challenging the use of disability as a wide brush for the application of degradation" (2014, 20). He further suggests that bodies are "rhetorical" and that people can employ their bodies to pose arguments through performance (89). What better canvas than the joke to begin such dialogues?

Over the past months, my world has become fuzzier, even though I got a stronger glasses prescription last fall—much stronger, according to my optometrist. I go to see my optician for a glasses adjustment and to make sure my eye is really losing focus. A month later, I return for another eye exam. After holding twenty-odd lenses in front of my face while I try to note minute differences in letter charts, my optometrist cheerfully tells me that I always pose an "interesting challenge." He dilates my left eye, shines more lights, and hypothesizes that I might be getting a cataract, which may or may not have been exacerbated by my retinopathy of prematurity. I'm gifted a new glasses prescription that will hopefully make the world less blurry.

"Well," he says before I leave, "the good news is that cataracts are something we know how to fix really well." I depart with that bit of sideways reassurance and my older glasses prescription, since the lens is being replaced in my newer frames. Outside the office, I enter a surreal world of doubled vision and shadowed objects, realizing just how much my sight has worsened over the past year.

The following week I travel to give a reading in Pennsylvania, forgetting that my book has small type. I hold the page four inches from my face, and even then, it's tough to make out all the words. I keep thinking, God, this probably looks weird. Let's read emphatically to compensate. *I don't look up to see how anyone is regarding my performance since I'm afraid of losing my place on the page. I probably couldn't see their expressions, anyway.*

I've always read with my face too close to the page, at least according to the kids in my fourth-grade class, but I've never before gotten headaches from reading, or had to stop because of eyestrain. The standard advice for cataracts is to let them keep getting worse, and worse, and worse, until you need surgery. On the way home from Pennsylvania I think, I can't have surgery now. I'm entirely too young to have a cataract, and there are too many books to read. Doesn't this cataract understand timing?

DISABILITY AND COMIC NARRATIVE

Frank suggests that storytelling can be a way to create the self, shape one's body, and change how others interpret it (2013, 58, 127, 134). *I have a story. My body has a story. Therefore I am.* Through personal narrative, people can also redefine what it means to heal, to recover, and to lead a "good" life in a way that is not defined by medical practitioners (205). Humor may lend a further potency to storytelling, allowing a teller to twist tales into social critiques when a standard lecture would not have the same impact. As Sigmund Freud suggests, jokes often do a kind of political work to convince listeners of the "truth" of their message, even when that idea would have been rejected "in a non-joking form" (1960, 123). Jokes are the wink, the sugar shell over social critique, the smile that coaxes listeners to pay attention. Comic stories can present people with disabilities as "victims" whose problems sprout not from their bodies, but from misguided perceptions embedded in dominant society (Gilbert 2004, 137, 160–61).

Comic narratives about disability are not tales of triumph over adversity, but rather a poking back at confining social norms of what it means to be disabled. The teller can recapture their story, revise the narrative to express their truth, refuse to seek a "cure" for some aspect of their bodymind. These stories can also be a means to address disability scholar Alison Kafer's call to rethink disabilities: what it means to be disabled, how we decide who is disabled, and how we can shape a future in which disability is appreciated rather than a target for eradication (2013, 3–7).

The blurry person down the hall is likely someone I know, so I wave to be polite. They wave back. It might not be someone I'd normally wave to, so perhaps this fuzzing of the world is making me a kinder individual. Shouldn't I wave hello to everyone all the time? Is this a form of disability gain, a positive turn to the twists of my tenuous vision (Barker 2014)? When I get another headache after hours of reading, I wonder how long it will take the cataract to sneak away my sight, how long I'll be able to read at one sitting in a few more months. If I'd worn my sunglasses all the time like I was supposed to, would my vision blur this quickly? I figured I'd castigate myself for going without sunglasses when I was "older" and more deserving of cataracts.

I meant older than this.

I hope my new glasses prescription will resolve the world into crisp shapes, but the lens only makes it blurry in a different way. Damned dear vision, quit sliding so quickly.

This lack of resolution heralds another visit to my optometrist. He says my corneas look "a little weird," which he assures me is a technical term, and I might need to get a very large contact. I balk, recalling the words of Dr. Neville, my first ophthalmologist, and the decree I heard year after year after year. No contacts. Ever.

I have been raised on a healthy dose of fear:

What if I'm not wearing glasses and something I can't see pokes my sighted or blind eye?

What if the contact gives me an eye infection?

And yet the world continues to lose definition, everything going soft about the edges, words hazing to smears.

ACCESSING THE JOKE

When most people consider accessible societies, they imagine aspects of the physical environment: elevators, large-print or braille menus, parking spaces near building entrances, sign language interpreters standing to one side of the stage at public events, scent-free or quiet spaces that are not saturated with stimuli, and online spaces that are compatible with screen reader programs. People may not often ponder access to jokes. Not everyone can find disability humorous. We can't simply consider the topics of jokes, but we should also contemplate why some subject materials may be carefully skirted, labeled as too serious, touchy, or taboo to be mediated with a laugh. Sometimes these topics involve how one's disability was acquired, such as through a form of trauma or violence.[13]

Joking interacts with multilayered intersectional identities and the many facets of self: gender, race, social class, ability, sexual preference, and age, to name but a few. The social expectations and interpretations of one's performance of disability depend on the intricate patchwork of a person's being (Kafer and Kim 2017, 123–24).[14] For example, the combination of race and disability has often been used to justify violence against individuals, marking them as disposable "nonpersons" who can be beaten, shot, or trapped in classrooms for "special needs" children.[15] This persecution may be part of the reason why the prevalence of disability has also been erased from African American history. As disability scholar Chris Bell notes, textbooks have long omitted Harriet Tubman's seizures, which stemmed from a concussion she received from an overseer, or Emmett Till's difficultly speaking, which caused him to whistle so that his voice would return, a tactic that led to his brutal murder for supposedly whistling at a white girl (2012, 2–4). Bell faults disability studies for focusing on "whiteness" to the exclusion of people of color, while in African American studies disability has been "relegated to the margins" (3). This erasure suggests that even among minority groups, there can be power imbalances and stigma when it comes to admitting disability (Coleman-Brown 2017, 151). Fear of further oppression has created resistance to accepting mental illness diagnoses in African American families, since people of color can be in danger if they are labeled "crazy." Passing as able-minded can therefore be a necessary survival strategy (Jarman 2012a, 20–21).

A similar refusal of disability diagnoses has been widespread in queer communities, which bear a historic trauma from the medicalization of queer identity as a mental defect. The lasting scars have caused some queer people to remain closeted in their gender and sexual orientation, as well as their disability (Brownsworth 1999, xix). Being disabled and being queer are too often considered undesirable aspects of self that must be erased if someone is to be truly "healthy" in mind and body. As McRuer argues, people with such identities are expected to deny them or be dissatisfied, not embrace those aspects with a punch of defiant pride (2017, 397–402).

Individuals in queer communities have also felt pressured to hide their disability if it does not fit with their self-reliant image. As Lizard Jones writes, her MS clashed with her perception of self as an independent lesbian, a person who "[doesn't] need anybody, [and] can't expect much, [but] we've learned to take this as a strength" (1999, 53). Vicky D'aoust relates a similar struggle to find acceptance in Deaf communities. A wheelchair user and lesbian, she has been ostracized due to homophobia and stigmas against people with physical disabilities (1999, 115–17). In the face of such prejudice, when it is difficult to come out as either queer or crip, it is far simpler to slide by as "normal" and avoid questions, the potential loss of social standing, and the drawn-out explanations of one's identity (Samuels 2017, 346).

Through the lens of dominant culture, disability can signal that someone may be dismissed, derided, or doted upon or that they might pose a danger, so it's clear why some people find themselves caught in a space where this identity can't be a laughing matter.

The blurring of words and fear of more headaches leads me to call an ophthalmologist and schedule an appointment. I explain to the receptionist that I have a referral from my optometrist, who says the ophthalmologist has more specialized equipment to measure and photograph and shine additional lights in my face, and hopefully determine my overall level of cataract severity and corneal weirdness.

The receptionist says, "You're too young to have cataracts. You're my age."

"Yeah," I say with a verbal shrug, "I know it's kind of young." I explain that I have retinopathy of prematurity, so I'm blind in my right eye, and my optometrist thinks that might be why the cataract is coming on this early.

"And now I have this little black floater in my left eye," I add, "so I figured it was time to see an ophthalmologist."

"You poor thing," she says, making me wince. I don't want to be considered a poor thing. I don't feel like a poor thing. I feel like a somewhat frustrated thing.

"You get used to stuff like this," I say. "I've never known anything different. It's normal for me."

She said, "I guess so. You have a good attitude."

So now I'm not only a poor thing, but a disabled person with a good attitude. I wonder if her responses are shorthand for "I would feel like a poor thing in your shoes." I don't ask, just make my appointment, and we remind each other to have a nice day.

I don't tell her my floater's name is Mike, not short for "Michael," not named for anyone I know, I just want it to have a name so when it gets in the way of my reading, I can think, Mike, quit that. *Not that the floater will listen, but it feels more like a relationship.*

PAIN, PERFORMANCE, AND COMEDY

Accessing the joke also implies that an individual can access a larger disability community where joking thrives and is encouraged, and where disability is a political identity that can be used with pride. Yet not all people with disabilities may want to form such alliances, and not all disability communities may welcome all people. Such groups must always be alert to those whom they may leave out, since it's too easy to unwittingly exclude individuals (Kuppers 2013, 4–6; Kafer 2013, 6–8, 11–12). Creating a more accessible world also means opening disability communities to discussions about race, class, and ability levels and how disability may be both a social construction and a physical reality of pain. As disability scholar and performance artist Petra Kuppers suggests, an individual can "take pride in their difference" as a disabled person and exhausted by the aches that don't let them leave bed in the morning (2013, 95). She argues that art should not provide an "easy celebration" of disability "without grounding in lived reality" (153), yet creative spaces can be a place to have comic and convoluted conversation about bodily pride, physical pain, and emotional pain that wrap together in the knot of one's personhood.

But how do we discuss pain in the twisting tales of disability comedy, particularly when no one wants to hear stories of aches, and when people with disabilities feel socially pressured to be little chips of sunshine and say they're just fine, thank you for asking? As poet and memoirist Lucia Perillo notes, "Pain does not make for good conversation material because the purpose of good conversation is to elicit more conversation, and if you tell someone you want to chop off your legs the talk will come to a halt" (2009, 46). Pain can be the only thing some people want to hear about disability— the expected thing—so those with disabilities become reluctant to speak of it at all, fearing it's the only subject that will stick in the TAB listener's mind.[16]

Perhaps this is one reason why we have in-group disability comedy, jokes that can be shared with those in the know, who understand the pleasures and downfalls of certain types of embodiment, the way that joy can merge with sorrow.[17] Other jokes are out-group comedy, stories to share with the rest of the world, yet there will always be disagreements within disability communities about which jokes fall into which category. The aim of such humor raises a question: When should jokes work toward the integration of people with disabilities into dominant society, emphasize their separateness as cultural groups, or settle in a space that floats between the two?[18]

This is a date: When I was in college, I met a guy through an online personal ad. We exchanged a couple emails and arranged to meet for coffee. He had dark hair, was kind of stocky, no glasses. It must have been the weekend because there weren't many other people in the campus coffee shop. He was terse, cool, hard to talk with, like playing catch with someone who keeps his hands in his pockets and doesn't go for the ball. I tried to make smiling conversation like you're supposed to do when on a date with someone you've never met. I wondered why I was doing all the work.

"You didn't mention you had a lazy eye," he said five minutes into the "chat."

"Oh," I said, "it's not a lazy eye, it's blind. It's been that way since I was born. I don't think about it much."

"You should have said something before," he said.

"I'm sorry," I said. Did he think I was trying to pull something over on him? Was I supposed to explain every physical detail?

I have retrospectively made a list of all the brilliant, cutting things I could have said/done in return, like telling him, "You didn't say you were an asshole," then leaving. But I had my cup of coffee and had walked fifteen minutes in the chill autumn weather, and hopeful objects at rest tend to stay at rest, talking to the asshole and thinking some pleasant spark of personality may emerge. We might have shaken hands at the end of the conversation, but I don't think he ever smiled.

DISABILITY AND SEXUALITY

People often joke about the things that make them most anxious, which includes sex and sexuality, desire and desirability, and fitness to pass on your genetic material. Since disabled bodies are often regarded in dominant culture as deformed, deviant, and unfit for sexual contact, disabled people have been the target of a slew of sex jokes, cast as sexually desperate, desexualized, and unworthy of reproduction.[19] These attitudes are apparent in the way disabled people may be relegated to the "friend zone" by TABs whom they'd like to have as intimate partners (Shuttleworth 2012, 56–58).[20]

This topic has long been a source of frustration for people with disabilities, but for years, it was scooted to one side of the disability political agenda in favor of other issues such as public transportation and job accommodations. Economic oppression is easier to discuss than sexual oppression, as it involves less blushing on the part of politicians unwilling to speak of the bedroom (or couch, or top of the washing machine, or back seat of the car) (Waxman 1994, 87). Yet people with disabilities have found platforms to position themselves as sexual beings on social media and in memoirs, through performance and on the comedy club stage. These are forums to discuss performing sexuality in bodies that are subject to change, to shift, to limitation.

Dominant society crimps and cramps the definition of sexuality until nobody and no body can fit into its narrow confines, leaving disability theorists to call for exploding the definitions of disability and sexuality to allow for more play with both ideas (McRuer and Mallow 2012, 13). Sometimes the most sensual act can be understanding the body of one's lover: how they move, what they need to feel safe, sexual, and cared for. In his memoir, *Born on a Blue Day*, Daniel Tammet explains the ways his boyfriend has adapted to his unique rhythms. Tammet is on the autism spectrum, and it can be difficult for him to adjust when friends stop by and pause his daily routine. On such occasions his boyfriend helps to calm him down. He's accustomed to repeating words when Tammet misses something that was said, and he helps Tammet shave with an electric razor, which can be a challenge due to his skin sensitivity (2006, 156–57). In these small acts, there is a sexy and intimate knowledge of a lover and the ways of their bodymind.

Artist and writer Riva Lehrer uncovers another kind of sexuality found in a lover's attention and stories told in scars. She writes of being in bed with her beloved, how their "hands trace the pampliest of forty-three surgeons' signatures and the imprint of three hundred hospital bracelets" on Lehrer's skin (2012, 250). While her body reveals painful stories, she reflects that "skin is not a shell, it reverberates in me like ringing a bell. My skin sings in one dense chorus. . . . Now my fingers speak to your skin . . . my body surprises us both with its ability to be joyous" (250). In this moment, the reminders of procedures past become a sexy and sensual form of knowledge. Even in public, Lehrer suggests how the mark of disability can be transformed from one of stigma to sexuality, a revelation made intimate in its shared nature: "Sometimes when we were out on the street together you let your disability show. That made me so happy. It freed me, too; we weren't running from anyone's scrutiny" (250). Lehrer explores the erotic possibilities of vulnerability, letting one's guard down, not struggling to hide the limp, the stitches, the sockets. It is the sexuality of stripping off social sanctions.

In her memoir, Perillo explores another dimension of sensuality in forgoing the controls people are supposed to maintain over their bodies. She suggests that individuals feel pressured to hold everything in, spilling neither fluids nor feelings: "When it comes to sex, though, what we want is leakage: for the essence of self to get through to somebody else somehow. And this applies not just to body but to mental essence as well. We want to experience the same ecstatic goop that's packed inside the person with whom we're trying to fuse. . . . I want my faulty neural circuits to be overridden and overwritten" (2009, 146). In her world, sexuality translates to all manner of release, opening mind and body to the lover, finding space to merge.

Given that this exploration must be corporeal and cerebral, how better to investigate the nexus of disability and sexuality than through the well-placed sex joke, the twirl of words and bodies that can break boundaries and show them to be a farce. People with disabilities still skirt the edges, fringes, communities on the outskirts of dominant society. This space, neither in nor out, is the space of the joke-teller, the observer, the place from which to comically criticize cultural beliefs (Gilbert 2004, xi). While disability performance and humor may not be able to create change on its own, these liminal areas may be fertile soil to plant ideas, pose questions, and suggest alternate ways of interpreting the world. Blessed are the joke-tellers, the mirth-makers, the boundary-breakers, the ones who make us laugh until we're crying.

THE BOUNDS OF THIS BOOK

This text is a playful and provocative perusal of cultural expressions developed by disabled people and in disability communities. The chapters explore ways that disabled people perceive their bodyminds, and how their creative and comic acts crash, collide, or collaborate with perceptions of disability and sexuality in literature and dominant culture. My analyses of their narratives, performances, and other forms of expression suggest such practices have the potential to break down dominant cultural assumptions about disability and sexuality, but they also risk repeating harmful stereotypes.

The book draws from a range of disability studies texts and memoirs, in which authors slide personal stories together with scholarly pursuits and fit those narratives into the struggle of larger disability communities. Perhaps unsurprisingly, many disability studies texts include elements of memoir, in which scholars relate their own experiences with disability back to the discipline, molding theory into the largest of mirrors.[21]

The text also addresses the diversity of disability, which Kafer suggests is a "site of questions rather than firm definitions" (2013, 11), a space that is continually counterconforming as it grows more complex. Yet Kafer argues that disabled people have a "collective affinity" because they are considered "disabled or sick and have faced discrimination as a result" (11). Disability cannot be paved with a single definition since the experiences of disabled people are so wide-ranging, dependent on numerous aspects of one's intersectional identity, type of disability, and the time and place in which one lives. While recognizing that all bodies are inherently vulnerable to disability, Kafer asserts that we must pay "more attention to how different bodies/minds are treated differently, not less" (2013, 13).

As Kuppers notes, disability involves points of identification with and separation from other disabled people, tales that twine together and diverge again. She writes that she can "take pride in my difference," but there are other times when she may "feel unable to speak of the nature of my discomfort, cannot find the words, but find comfort in the company of others whose pain might be different, but who somehow feel simpatico" (2013, 95). Disabilities cannot be distilled to a single experience: they are multiple and varied, even within forms of disability stigma and oppression (Kuppers 2013, 96–97; Garland-Thomson 1996, 13; Kafer and Kim 2017, 123–24, Shuttleworth and Meekosha, 2017, 186). This variability makes disability studies a delightfully diverse yet daunting discipline for scholars who fear leaving anybody, or any body, out of the frame.

While reading this book, it is important to recall the drifting definition of disability, as well as where and when and why people are willing to accept disability as their label, their checkbox, their mantle of pride. Not everyone feels free to reveal disability in public or private, to families or friends or at work, because they may fear repercussions or the loss of social power (Shuttleworth and Meekosha 2017, 186). People will spin their own stories of pride and pain or prejudice, and some will never call themselves disabled because of the ball of fear hiding (rightfully) in their stomachs.

So perhaps you will not mind if I slide back to the refrain of how disability can contribute to an individual being labeled a nonperson, particularly if they have a marginalized status as poor or queer or a person of color, particularly if they are older or a woman or happen to meet the wrong person on the wrong day and act in a way that can be considered "misbehaving." How many times have I seen headlines about gunshots, protests, or court trials, only to be reminded that many actions considered "misbehaving" might be interpreted otherwise if the person(s) in question appeared to be well-to-do and straight and white and (temporarily) able-bodied in a society that rewards such identities (Erevelles and Minear 2017, 382–83). As Clare writes, it is too easy for disability to detract from one's humanity in the minds of others, leading them to assume that the individual in question doesn't have a life worth living (2017, 30).

How telling that researchers and doctors who work with disabled clients often deny their own disabilities, stuffing that segment of identity into a file cabinet drawer for fear it will be discovered by colleagues.[22] Where else but in these professional realms of diagnoses and drugs would the stigma of disability be so feared, as individuals worry that their credibility and credentials could be put at risk. Yet where else but in the medical field would it be so critical that those diagnoses be made, so that people treating others could themselves receive proper treatment (Jamison 1996, 207–8)?

All of this is to emphasize how it can be difficult/daunting/socially impossible for many individuals to identify as persons with disabilities, let alone explore disability through creative practice. Sometimes one must do endless calculations, calibrations, and speculations about the risks of waving the flag with that capital "D." This defining and delineating of disability identity has effects on representation in disability communities in both face-to-face interactions and online. Who is allowed to speak or sign or type, and in which spaces? Who lacks access to a place where they can be heard? Who can bear the consequences of communicating their truth? Those are the questions woven throughout this book, as we ask whose stories still whirl in their minds, who finds themselves unable to claim a proud disability identity due to gender or race, class or place, time or trauma or countless other reasons (Kafer and Kim 2017, 128). Sometimes people cannot allow another label on their bruised and battle-scarred body, sick of classification and category and being slotted into spaces (Clare 2017, 144). Sometimes those who are willing to identify as disabled have a level of social privilege, the skin color or sexual orientation or other form of social status that assures they will not slip too far, risk too much, lose their personhood.

The following chapters explore these topics more deeply through narratives of and performances by people with disabilities. Yet when contemplating the quips, philosophies, and creative expressions of those who feel comfortable speaking, writing, and dancing their truths, we must recall those whose tales are whispered to a single ear, whose jokes are silent but for a smile, whose performances are staged in the corner of a bedroom since (for now) that is the safest space.

ON HOLES

I attend a reading and lecture by Pulitzer Prize–winning poet Natasha Trethewey, and am surprised to hear about the violence that echoes in her past. Her mother was killed by her abusive stepfather when Trethewey was nineteen, a terrible moment that shaped her life and her writing. Trethewey has been asked if she would want to have her mother back if she could, and explains that she pauses when answering, and says no. The questioners are surprised, but she has realized that the tragedy shaped her to be the person who she is today.

I catch my breath. I can't compare our losses, but I am familiar with the sentiment around loss, which I have heard from many other people with disabilities: Who would I be if not for this? Not being able to see on my right side has never felt like a loss, but a not-having, a never-having, not even a problem until those snatches of seconds when I almost get hit by a car when a driver doesn't see me not seeing them.

This is not the same sentiment as Trethewey has since she feels her loss deeply. The similarity is in realizing how we have been molded by absence. She recalls that the poet Rumi wrote, "The wound is the place where the light enters you."

My body hums to those words.

Trethewey also quotes poet Federico Lorca, who suggested that writers are always trying to heal the wound that never heals, the awareness of death.

What am I trying to heal when I write about my disability but do not feel like my disability is a wound? Or perhaps I know my disability is a wound, an indication of fragility, but it does not have the same meaning for me that other people think it might. Perhaps some writing about disability is not about healing the wound but living with the wound, with the awareness of being wounded, the awareness of the finite nature of bodies. The wound does not always sting. Sometimes it just is. The place where the light comes in.

My vision with this cataract is often like an impressionist scene. Monet and Renoir and Degas depicted a similarly hazed landscape, so perhaps my sight embodies their artistry, and maybe their sight as well.

I think of Monet and his paintings of the Japanese bridge in his garden at Giverny, how those images changed as he developed cataracts over ten years. The image shifted from a bright pink and green garden to one rendered in dark olive, burgundy, and beige. He composed letters lamenting that he could no longer see his palette or distinguish one hue from another. For a painter whose world was based on the play of light and dark, it was devastating. But in 1923 he had cataract surgery, and his canvases shimmered again.

Monet abandoned most of the paintings he did in his decade with cataracts, but a few survived (White 2007). Those works are the most alluring to me now: a world transformed into darkness, then returned to light. Adapt, adjust, paint what you see.

Some scientists think Degas might have had a problem that affected his retinas, couldn't be fixed, and slowly made the world blur. A few of his acquaintances noted that his paintings were softening their edges, becoming less distinct. Degas continued to mix paint upon palette, creating works without crisp lines, those dreamy ballerinas whom he might have glimpsed through his own auras of fog (White 2007).

Kleege writes, "I have trouble imagining myself as sighted, just as I have trouble imagining myself as Swiss" (1999, 4). This reflection reminds me of times when people have asked if I'd want to have surgery to restore the sight in my right eye if I could. I explain that it doesn't matter. My brain might not be able to process those images since it hasn't done so for four decades. The questioner always presses me with a what if, what if, what if, then seems perplexed when I say no, I'd skip the surgery. Part of me knows what they (unconsciously) want, a confirmation that two-eyedness is better than having one eye, but I disagree. Half blindness has shaped how I see the world both literally and metaphorically. If I'd had two sighted eyes, maybe I would have been better at basketball and tennis and volleyball, or maybe not. If I'd had two sighted eyes, would I have been so aware of my differences, and those of others?

But I'd be lying if I left you with the passive impression that my blind eye has never been a problem. There are stories I've kept hidden that go beyond bumping people in crowds because they get lost in my empty space. This is one time when my right eye mattered: I was maybe twenty years old, getting milk from a cooler in the college cafeteria, when I shut the door and heard a loud "Ouch" on my right. I'd pinched the fingers of an invisible girl next to me who'd been reaching for juice, but I only saw her when I turned my head.

"You slammed the door on my hand," she said, glaring at me.

I must have seemed like a malicious bitch.

"I'm sorry," I said, and I tried to explain what didn't seem logical, that I hadn't seen her.

"My hand was right there," she said.

I told her I was blind in my right eye, that I really hadn't seen her. I felt like shit. She wasn't soothed. She shouldn't have been soothed. Her hand hurt like hell.

I might have followed her to the cashier, still apologizing. She might have said it was okay in a hard tone that suggested the opposite. I don't remember, but I hope I apologized until it got annoying. I hope she thought I sounded sincere.

I don't mean to pass as fully sighted. Again, I consider that bright purple pirate eye patch to make the invisible visible, so that even I might remember my difference during the twenty-three hours and fifty minutes of every day (on average) when my disability does not matter, and the ten minutes when the sighted and nonsighted worlds collide. I forget I'm in both of them.

I've also not told my parents about the time I was bumped by a minivan while crossing the street. I was living in Arlington, Virginia, that summer, taking a morning walk before I went to my internship in Washington, DC. Halfway through the intersection, I felt a light tap on my hip. The driver braked but I went down on the pavement, an involuntarily action as I thought, *I have just been hit by a vehicle. That means I should fall.*

A young woman bulleted out of the driver's seat and said something along the lines of, "Oh my God, are you okay?"

"Yeah," I said and took her hand even though I didn't need to be helped up. "It was just a bump on my hip. I'll be fine."

"But I hit you with my car," she said.

I spent the next five minutes trying to comfort her. She had two little kids strapped in car seats in the back of the minivan.

"Really, it's okay," I said. "I'm fine." My hip smarted a little.

"But I hit you with my car," she said again.

I said it was more of a tap, but she made me come home with her and asked if I wanted to go to the hospital. I said I was fine, and I called my boss at the internship to explain I'd had a problem and would be a little late to work. I don't think I said I was hit by a car. I might have said I was bumped by a car. I didn't want her to worry.

The young mother was far more shaken, fretting over how much worse I could have been injured. My Midwestern instinct was to remind her that

I wasn't hurt too badly, I might just have a little bruise. I could walk back to my apartment on my own. She made me exchange contact information with her, in case some injury surfaced, and I needed treatment.

I felt bad about being late to work—I was twenty-two, and it was my first job that felt like a nine-to-five version of reality—but yes, I was reminded of how easy it was not to see something important. Now I wonder how often that lady thought of me in later years and looked once, twice, three times for pedestrians before turning. I wonder if she thought of me when teaching her kids how to drive: *Remember that time, with that girl, when you were very young?*

Now when a car emerges from the empty space on my right and whizzes past me in a left turn, I want to scream at them. *Can't you see that I can't see?* But they're too far down the road to hear me.

My story is not everyone's. In many ways, it is a health care fairy tale. I've lived in towns with excellent medical facilities and do not have to drive far for specialized care. I have support at school to do my work, my teaching, and go through the motions of life mostly uninterrupted. I have friends and a partner who give me rides and hugs and remind that this cataract, too, shall pass. I have enough money to cover the expense of vision care after health insurance has paid their due percentage. I have health insurance. Yes, a first-world disability story.

I am a very lucky person. I cannot write this loudly enough.

I know my unearned privilege as a white cisgendered straight-passing girl whose disability is mostly invisible, a person who has skirted past many of the economic and access worries that would have blocked other people who were not in my shoes, my glasses, my body.

And I know my story isn't over.

Chapter 2

CRIP TALK

Humor and Reclaiming "Cripple" and "Crip" in Disability Communities

I don't remember when I first found myself in a conversation in which people cheerfully referred to themselves as "cripples" and "crips." Probably it was during one of my chats with members of the wheelchair basketball team, who intuited that I wouldn't raise an eyebrow when they used insider language. But the experience was new for me. I knew these words were not terms that everyone could broadcast so freely, as a form of tenuous teasing and a mark of pride. Given the ambivalent status of "crip" and "cripple," it seemed important to dig more deeply into their history and significance inside and outside of disability communities.

Lucia Perillo discusses the mutability of language in her memoir, *I Have Heard the Vultures Singing*. She writes about wrangling not only with her multiple sclerosis and need to use a wheelchair, but how to describe her embodiment to others and herself. She notes, "I'm given some latitude in my use of *cripple* as an aggressive form of self-description. In doing so I may tend to suggest that I have become hardened to its connotations, or that I am a realist about my body's state, or that I am using the word to announce my affinity with a subculture that aspires to outlaw status. Each of these meanings enshrines some sort of little fib" (2009, 24). Her use of the word *cripple* signifies belonging to a community she doesn't want to join, but the lack of adequate language to situate her body status leaves her in search of another term.

Perillo doesn't like the word "disabled" since it suggests an inability to do things, so she gravitates to "handicapped." She connects this word to Kurt Vonnegut's story "Harrison Bergeron," about a world in which talented people are artificially "handicapped" by various devices, such as graceful dancers who must wear bags of shot pellets around their necks. This is how Perillo feels in her changing body—handicapped (2009, 27, 29). While I appreciate Perillo's suggestion that she feels weighed down, we cannot forget that the word "handicapped" raises eyebrows and hackles among some members of disability communities. The term was coined by social workers in the early 1900s and came from the idea of cap-in-hand, or begging for coins. Thus, the term that Perillo finds most fitting for her body is one that many others feel is deeply offensive (Johnson 1994a, 27).

Names have power—that is evident from both of these examples—and they are highly fluid in their meaning. Such labels can serve as a mark of pride, a term of derision, a word for groups of people to unite behind or fight against when shaping a collective identity. This power is also evident when we consider terms used to label groups that have been historically marginalized. Social and political activists have often made it a priority to fight for their group's right to name itself or to push for reclaiming words that were previously used as derogatory terms and redefine them to express pride.

In this chapter, I examine how a similar controversy formed around the terms "crip" and "cripple," and the search for a word to connote "disability" that does not provoke controversy and consternation in disability communities. The quest for the "perfect" phrase is endless since every linguistic candidate has a variety of connotations, denotations, and assorted meanings depending on context and individuals' past experiences. This long-standing argument also reflects the diversity of disability communities, where spaces of agreement may be present yet tenuous (Kuppers 2013, 109).

Through an analysis of online message boards and personal interviews, I discuss some of the ways "crip" and "cripple" are used by people with disabilities and how meanings can shift and meld and fold in on each other, multiplying and morphing in various social situations. Examining how and when these words are deployed reveals significant information about the nature of disability communities and attitudes toward disability, including how the terms reflect individuals' attitudes toward disability, and their relationships with other disabled people. These terms can have expressly positive or negative meanings, create community and connote belonging, or cast a pall over one's character. I discuss why some people choose not to use these words, how that decision reflects their beliefs on cultural perceptions of disability, and how meanings that mock can leave too strong a sting.

While I primarily focus on the use of these terms among people who use wheelchairs or have a mobility impairment, it is important to note that "crip" is employed by people with a wide range of disabilities who wish to express a political disability identity.[1] As Kafer suggests, this word is meant to "jolt people out of their everyday understandings of bodies and minds" (2013, 15). She further writes that "claiming crip" as a political stance can be "a way of acknowledging that we all have bodies and minds with shifting abilities," while not ignoring differences among identities and forms of embodiment (13). The political and social definitions of the words "crip" and "cripple" highlight the power of language to communicate pride, prejudice, and anxiety in a single term. This weight is indicative of complicated history surrounding disability communities and disabled people, the constantly shifting cultural significance of disability, and the struggle to accept the ever-changing nature of the human body.

THE NAME GAME

"Reclaiming" a name is rarely without the push and pull of controversy from inside and outside a given community. For instance, the term "queer" has been embraced by many people in LGBTQ communities during the past several years, yet the shift has been gradual (Johnson 1994a, 39). Words are not stable—they slip and slide within the lexicon, they are loaded and emptied of venom, and they float or fall from the tongue. While the term "cripple" has often been used to refer to a person who needs to use a cane, wheelchair, or other mobility aid and has had a negative connotation, the breadth of its possible interpretations is far more complex (41–42). As Eli Clare notes, "Queer and cripple are cousins; words to shock, words to infuse with pride and self-love, words to resist internalized hatred." But he also suggests that they "have come to sit on a cusp. For some of us, they carry too much grief. For others, they can be chosen with glee and pride" (1999, 70). These words are infused with memory, from schoolyard taunts to doctors' diagnosing darts. Many disabled people who use the word "cripple" understand that its history is fraught, shot through with shattered smiles—and for some it still bears barbs. As memoirist Nancy Mairs writes, "I prefer to call myself a cripple . . . because it is a word many people with disabilities find deeply offensive, I apply it only to myself, and so it reminds me that I am not speaking for others . . . [but] it lets you know what my condition is: I can't use my limbs as I once could" (1996, 12). For Mairs the term is practical and political, one of coming to terms with the shifts in her body, though for Perillo it draws a wince. Regardless of one's feelings about "cripple" and its colloquial cousin "crip," both draw strong emotions inside and outside disability communities and can be deployed in ways hostile and humorous.

One of the most emotionally hurtful methods that oppressors have used to deny power to those in marginalized groups is through refusing them the power to name themselves. While this phenomenon seems like a colonial-era occurrence, disability writer and activist Mary Johnson discusses a debate over terminology that occurred during the late 1980s and early 1990s. The

National Cristina Foundation had a contest in 1991 to find a new word to replace "disabled." This contest was initiated by TABs who were seeking a more "positive" term than "disability," and the judges chose the phrase "people of differing abilities." The notion of a naming contest raised the ire of many people in disability communities, who were again smacked with the knowledge that well-meaning TABs thought them incapable of naming themselves. While those who ran the contest assumed that "disabled" was a negative word, people who proudly claimed the label did not agree (Johnson 1994a, 25–26; Snyder and Mitchell 2006, 190).

Johnson notes other debates regarding labels for disability communities, citing a 1987 poll from the newspaper the *Disability Rag*. Respondents rejected the term "handicapped" and preferred "disabled" since it "did not mark them as people who could not function in society" (1994a, 27–28). Still others favored the phrase "person with a disability" since it "[puts] the person first" (29).[2] The *Disability Rag* also found dissent around the term "physically challenged," which was rejected as "condescending" and also because it "plays into the myth of the disabled person as being responsible, somehow, for surmounting the barriers, individually" (31). Yet others argued for the term "survivor" since disabled people have "survived lack of respect," expensive rehabilitation treatments, "confinement," and "deplorable economic conditions" (Rosen 1994, 20–21).

When it comes to naming conventions, one person's mark of pride will be another person's put-down, but Johnson points to a larger problem regarding the way dominant society conceptualizes disability and disabled people. She argues, "Until the perception of disability changes, any word saddled with the meaning of disability—retarded[3] or cripple or deaf—eventually will acquire a stigma of its own" (1994a, 39). She suggests that disabled people should use "the same [tactics] other oppressed groups have found: reclaim the negative and use it with pride. The pride, and the power, make the word a proud one" (39).

Along similar lines, psychologist and linguist Steven Pinker has described the "euphemism treadmill" effect that occurs when a society tries to find new phrases to describe groups of people who have been historically devalued. He notes, "People invent new 'polite' terms to refer to emotionally laden or distasteful things, but the euphemism becomes tainted by association and the new one that must be found acquires its own negative connotations" (1994). The only way out of this loop, he suggests, is through changing societal thought patterns, so the subjects in question are no longer considered inferior.

Many people within disability communities have expressed disgust and exasperation at attempts to use "prettifying euphemisms" that suggest disability is a shameful state of embodiment (Shapiro 1994, 33). Clare contributes two more terms to the list, suggesting that "'differently abled' and 'physi-cally challenged'" are phrases designed to "cushion us from the cruelty of language" (1999, 68), while the word "special" has a tone that "drips conde-scension. It's no better than being labeled defective" (2017, 6).[4] He echoes Pinker's point about the cultural associations attached to certain groups of people as being the heart of the problem since disabled people have long been cast as "out-of-control, excessive, incapable" and "courage, metaphor, cautionary tale, downfall" (2017, 7). We should not fault the term, the label, the mishmash of syllables used as a marker, but much deeper stigmas that sit heavy on whatever words are chosen to signify disabled bodies.

Pushing back on a culture that loves to label, there is little wonder why Mairs desires to take control of such markers: "Whoever gets to define ability puts everyone else in place. . . . When I have occasion to refer to a class with a broader spectrum of impairments, I use the more conventional 'people with disabilities,' or 'the disabled' for short, and people who lack them I call 'the nondisabled,' since in relation to me, they are the deficient ones. Already, in this way, I begin to reconstruct the world" (1996, 14). Johnson finds a similar world-shaping power in the word "cripple." While many respondents to the *Disability Rag* poll said the term was "politically passé," Johnson notes that it was being used by "avant garde" disability rights activists in the early 1990s (1994a, 41). The problem with all words, however, and particularly ones with such historical weight, is that their meaning is contextual, dependent on who is using the word, the meaning the word holds for them, and the social setting in which they are using the word. Johnson suggests that "cripple" may "be used only by those in the know" (41), as it holds a derisive bite when used by those outside the community in question.

Tom Shakespeare also emphasizes setting and audience when using "crip" and "cripple" with humorous intent. Even though such language is often employed in joking contexts within disability communities, the labels are still fraught with a multiplicity of meanings, as are other forms of joking behavior. We must continually ask who might get the joke, who will take offense, and who will offer a half smile, unsure whether it's okay to laugh. Along these lines, Shakespeare writes, "There is an understanding about the irony with which formerly hostile terms are deployed, so disabled people, in certain contexts, will use words like 'cripple.' . . . Because of their dangerous resonance, such words have the relish of taboo and the reclamation of identity" (1999, 50). This risk is apparent when one considers the continued flexibility of these words. Disability theorist Gary Albrecht notes that the language of disability can easily be misinterpreted by those who are not in disability communities, especially when the words are incorporated into joking behavior: "Inside jokes add to disability culture by providing a bond to this minority or marginalized group; hence 'crip humor.' What they accept from their peer they may not tolerate from others because of the perceived intent of the language or joke. Conversely . . . people in the outside world easily misread the lives and texts of insiders" (1999, 73).

One example of this misreading comes from a study by researchers Harold Burbach and Charles Babbitt on humor among college students who use wheelchairs. They conducted a phone survey of approximately one hundred individuals and found that students used "humor as a means of building in-group solidarity" and that they had a "pervasive use of insider nicknames" such as "crip" (1993, 7). The researchers further suggest that this kind of humor is a "form of social aggression" since some of students called each other "crip" in front of TAB students to watch them squirm (7). In interpreting their results, Burbach and Babbitt argue that there is an overall negative tone to the in-group humor:

> The problem is that physical disfigurements are so disruptive to the normal flow of communication that humor is used to alleviate the tension that arises from their intrusion upon interpersonal exchanges. The resultant humor is thus used to disguise the real message of the communication which, in the case of people with physical handicaps, is often a combination of discomfort, confusion, insecurity, and embarrassment. (9)

Since they are not members of this disability community, it is debatable whether Burbach and Babbitt could determine the "real message" of in-group communication. Based on their interpretations, it seems likely that they attached a negative stigma to disability and to the term "crip," which they could only read in a darkly comic context. This is not to say that joking cannot have a hostile intent, but their interpretation doesn't appreciate the multiplicity of meanings possible in joking behavior. Their reading also points to the complexity of reclaiming any historically fraught word. Using such language as a form of joking behavior is powerful and perilous, since as the researchers suggest, the terms can be interpreted in a variety of ways when couched as a jest.

COLLECTING CRIP TALK, MESSING WITH MEANING

To gain a wider perspective on the multiplicity of meanings these words hold, I studied two wheelchair-user message boards: Apparalyzed and

WheelchairJunkie.com. In both forums I searched for the word "crip," finding posts that included "crip" and/or "cripple." The posts on Wheelchairjunkie .com were made between 2008 and 2016, and the posts on Apparalyzed.com were made between 2013 and 2016. I reviewed approximately fifty discussion threads on each site, noting linguistic contexts and social attitudes regarding the use of both words, as well as comments that suggested why the words were being reclaimed or rejected by individuals.

I chose to analyze posts on these boards due to the number of participants and threads on each board, which covered a range of discussion topics and conversations. Each community had been in existence for a number of years, and this longevity led to greater diversity in the conversations related to disability and wheelchair use. Both message boards involved individuals with congenital disabilities and others with acquired disabilities, some of whom were still adjusting to a disability identity, so participants' attitudes toward disability were wide-ranging. While those who commented on Wheelchairjunkie.com indicated that they lived in the United States, the Apparalyzed board involved individuals from both the United Kingdom and the United States. Locational and cultural differences may have led to greater variety in the function and meanings behind "crip" and "cripple," though I found similar uses on both boards.

In addition to examining message boards, I interviewed three individuals regarding the use of these terms. My collaborators included Drew, a white male wheelchair user in his early twenties, Eric, a Black male wheelchair user also in his early twenties, and Amy, a young professional white female in her late twenties, who is an amputee and uses a prosthetic. These individuals had been part of various disability communities for a number of years, including in high school and college adaptive sports and work environments. While my collaborators have congenital disabilities, they have friends and acquaintances with congenital and acquired disabilities, and they are comfortable reflecting on their experiences with disability communities and people with newly acquired disabilities. Our discussions focused on their observations of the (in)appropriateness of "crip" and "cripple" in different social contexts, revealing both creativity and controversy around these words.

I hoped to gain a better understanding of the meanings these words can have in various contexts, but humor was always at the edge of the conversation, showing how often "crip" and "cripple" are employed as a form of in-group joking, sometimes with a gentle smile and sometimes as a hard punch. Words are as prone to shift as the bodies they describe, as I suggest when discussing the multiplicity of functions.

"Crip" and "Cripple" Can Have Interchangeable Meanings (or Not)

In the online forums "crip" is used more frequently than "cripple," perhaps because it lends itself to a more casual context, though in terms of meaning the words seem interchangeable. Among my collaborators only Amy notes a distinction between the two words, but she suggests a comic lightheartedness is more often associated with "crip." She says, " 'Crip' is a more of a subverted version of 'cripple.' It's even more like a term of affection, and I've heard it used like that. 'Crip girls got to stick together,' stuff like that." For her, "crip" is a word for friends and affiliation, a word of belonging. At the same time, Drew reflects that for him there is little distinction in meaning between the two: "I use 'cripple' more often than 'crip' because it's just fluent to me. I haven't really seen a difference between 'crip' and 'cripple,' although there might be something different . . . I just don't use crip as often." For him it is a matter of preference and familiarity, the word that comes more naturally to mind, though the meanings don't shift. Eric also remarks that he doesn't consider the two terms to have different meanings, adding: "I've heard 'cripple' used more often. 'Crip' is used occasionally, and I sometimes wonder if it's not used as often because it might bring up ideas of the Crips [gang], but honestly I can't think of a difference other than one is used more than the other." These language preferences may be part of one's dialect, and different disability communities prefer one to the other, so their members adjust their speech patterns to fit the company. Clare makes a similar observation, writing that "many of us call each other crip, practicing the art of refashioning and reclaiming language full of hurt, but typically we veer away from crippled. It's too much." Yet he also suggests that this isn't the case for everyone since "my friend uses that riskier word with affection" (2017, 131). While the meaning of the two words may be contextual and group-specific among close friends, an individual's word choice may depend on personal preference, comic context, audience, and whichever term seems more appropriate to them when flying from the tongue or floating from fingers across the keyboard.

Functions as Identity Markers and Comic Screen Names

On the Apparalyzed forum, a number of members incorporate "crip" or "cripple" into their screen names, using the words as a form of self-identification. Often these screen names have a comic intent, such as Supercrip 13, Cripwalk, Cripplezilla, and Crapple.[5] Using the words so freely hints to an individual's willingness not only to reclaim the terms, but also to adopt a political disability identity as a way of expressing disability pride and playfulness. In this way, the terms fulfill Clare's call for disabled people to "develop a self-image full of pride" and "be at the center of defining disability," shaping communities that can combat discrimination (1999, 90–91). Language is one part of this effort to create solidarity, and these words are often used as a form of in-group joking and camaraderie, as in the following:

> Megatrig on Apparalyzed writes in a thread about terms related to disability: "If more time was spent building ramps, etc for us cripples to get into places I would prefer that to be sorted out before deciding what to call me!!"

> Crappler on Apparalyzed replies: "This made me LMCAO (that's Laugh My Crippled Ass Off. See how I stayed on topic there?)."

> Stephen D on Apparalyzed, who posted the original question about disability terminology, asks another question but then adds: "However, please feel free to go off-topic . . . because . . . you gimpy cripples are da' best!"

In this thread the words are employed with a dash of political commentary, which makes sense when one is using disability to mark a personal and political identity. The sentiment is particularly true with Megatrig in his suggestion of how people with disabilities often have their needs overlooked or not prioritized in dominant society, a theme other members of the group would understand. In these posts, using the word "cripple" to define the community implies that everyone is fighting for the same cause, battling those who refuse to give them wheelchair ramps.

Along similar lines, Amy notes that she has heard both "crip" and "cripple" used to make in-group jokes and as terms of endearment. She explains, "It's something that, in my experience, we say a lot of times with each other. It's used as a joke. I can use it, but somebody without a disability can't." Her remarks point not only to the exclusivity of such terms, but also to the way individuals can situate themselves in the in-group or out-group by using or refusing to use these words. In this way, employing "crip" and "cripple" can suggest that someone is comfortable having a political disability identity and being affiliated with disability communities, which includes some aspects of shared culture and concerns.

Notably, one way that Perillo expresses her lack of interest in being associated with disability communities is her distaste for "crip." Instead of adopting the word, she mocks its use: "To make the label more aggressive and maybe chummier, the brotherhood of those foiled by bad body luck sometimes shortens it to *crip*, as in: *the crip community*. Never having been much of a club-joiner, however, I find myself too aloof for the bonhomie of *crip*" (2009, 27). Throughout her memoir, Perillo often expresses her frustrations through this kind of hostile joking, refusing to conceal her anger at having to adjust to life with MS. It is not surprising that some of this disappointment is directed at people within disability communities whom she perceives have adapted to their bodies in ways she has not (at least at the time of her writing). Perillo continually remarks on her "bad body-luck," which some people in disability communities would find offensive, since she is devaluing the disabled body. She directs these barbs not only at her own embodiment but also at the terms that might be used to describe it. In contrast to Perillo, all three of my collaborators have congenital disabilities and are accustomed to their modes of mobility. My collaborators' use of the words "crip" and "cripple" suggests a kind of comfort with their bodies that Perillo doesn't possess, having acquired a disability in midlife and making adjustments whether she wants to or not.[6] Accepting these terms would mean accepting this new version of her body and situating herself with similarly embodied people whom she wants to ground firmly as "them," instead of making herself part of "us."

Neutral or Positive Connotation When Used with In-Group Members to Describe Embodiment

In the online forums, "crip" and "cripple" are often used as positive or neutral shorthand terms instead of writing the more drawn-out "person with a disability," "disabled person," or "wheelchair user." People who refer to themselves as "crips" also use the term when discussing their level of independence and the ways they assert their autonomy.

When discussing his financial status, Sully on WheelchairJunkie.com writes: "To be a crip, at 51 looking for a job, can be a tough thing to overcome. I took a truck driving job delivering municipal supplies (Interstate)."

Reflecting on electric wheelchair speed, McLauren87 on Apparalyzed notes: "15 mph would of come in handy when I drove my crip ass 2 miles home from a bone density scan, after getting fed up on waiting for a cab."

Commenting on how individuals define autonomy and independence, Supercrip 13 on Apparalyzed states: "What I mean is that so far in my half century as a crip, Ive needed very little assistance with any aspect of personal care, and certainly nothing regular."

In these instances, "crip" is paired with statements regarding the individual's self-sufficiency. This use could be interpreted as ironic, since these individuals subvert the connotation of "crip" as referring to someone requiring assistance, instead deploying the term to work against the stereotype of people with disabilities as helpless. Their insistence on independence and the right to use the word "crip" also suggests pride in the fact that they can negotiate a landscape built for TABs with greater facility than many TABs might imagine. Here "crip" refers to people who find ways to work around and within the system and get things done. They are often faced with environments that are riddled with social and physical barriers, so they need stamina and creativity to make it through.

Along these lines, Kuppers discusses how words such as "cripple" can be powerful and have the flexibility to accumulate new meanings: "One of the ways to mark the shift of the signifier over its ground, the non-fit of language and lived reality, is to mark the play we can engage in with words" (2013, 23). Reimagining the uses of language within disability communities can be another way to flex the meanings of words, allowing individuals to creatively find alternate definitions and layer different meanings.

As my collaborators suggest, people who use "crip" and "cripple" have acquired a comfort level with the terms because they have participated in conversations in disability communities. The causal use of these words among friends may remove the sting of their historically derogatory use and render them to be a simple shorthand for the embodied self. At the same time, Eric observes that some people tend to be "more cautious with the terminology when they're new to the discussion [on disability], but after they become accustomed to it and they have experience with disabled individuals, they can use simple terms like crippled, which is a replacement for disability." Similar to joking about disability, Eric notes that using "crip" and "cripple" must be done with careful regard for one's audience and their background. The words can suggest that individuals are familiar with their community and know they're in a space where like-minded people will interpret "crip" as liberatory as opposed to offensive. Yet Eric is aware that while some may feel they have wrung all the venom from "cripple," there will always be others like Perillo who wince at the term.

Negative Meaning When Paired with a Negative Modifier

In the online forums, "crip" is used as a pejorative to make fun of other disabled people but usually only holds that meaning when it is paired with a negative modifier, such as "angry crip," "ugly crip," "whiny crip," "crip with an attitude," or the bitingly sarcastic "good little crip" (WheelchairJunkie .com). "Crip" in this context is an in-group term, but one that can be used to reference people with disabilities whom the individual posting the comment wants to mock. Often the persons who use "crip" in this manner are complaining about wheelchair users who they perceive as reinforcing negative stereotypes about disabled people, suggesting it's important to promote a positive political group identity:

Commenting on the parking violations of another person on the forum, Windjammer on WheelchairJunkie.com writes: "Just because a person is a crip, it does not mean he is above the law. Comply with what every other person does and obey the law. Unless you think you are entitled becuase your a crip."

Supercrip 13 on Apparalyzed starts a thread titled "Lazy crips infuriate me" to detail her frustration during a hospital stay:

Now, I've been here five days, am in severe pain, and not once have I asked the staff to help me with my personal care . . . I don't understand people that lay back and let others do this stuff! Where is the dignity? I'm having all-on not to shout "get out of bed you lazy trollop" I'm sitting here thinking "how many quads would love your level of injury; it's wasted on you!" She gives cripdom a bad name, and it is making my blood boil.

In this post Supercrip 13 also refers to "cripdom" as a collective culture for people who use wheelchairs. This illustration suggests her belief that wheelchair users have a stake in promoting an image of independence to people who do not use wheelchairs. Both posters are invested in everyone "doing their part" to project a law-abiding, self-sufficient crip identity, and both maintain that being a "crip" is a label that they want to protect from those who might sully the image.

At the same time, this anger suggests an unspoken acknowledgment that TABs often perceive disabled people as entitled and slothful. These posters want other wheelchair users to combat those stereotypes and maintain the positive image of cripdom, which explains their use of "crip" when writing about people with disabilities "behaving badly," and suggesting they need to shape up. However, this condemnation does not take into account varying ability levels among crips or what constitutes "necessary help." These posts may promote independence and autonomy over interdependence, which can have a negative effect on the psychological well-being of disabled people who feel pressured to do everything on their own (Watermeyer and Swartz 2016,

271, 274). I will discuss this debate among members of disability communities in later chapters, but it suggests that some people with disabilities have an investment in the word "crip" as promoting membership in a group of people who look out for each other and their political and social interests, and who share a stake in the way people with disabilities are perceived in the larger world.

Adjective to Denote Something That Is Part of In-Group Culture or Community

On the discussion boards, objects or concepts that are unique to disability communities and wheelchair users are sometimes given the adjective "crip" to coin a term that has special meaning for the in-group and/or is part of in-group culture. These pairings can also be comic, drawing a wry smile because of the wordplay. Using "crip" also attaches a type of ownership to things that are "exclusively" for crips, even in ironic contexts. For example:

Supercrip 13 on Apparalyzed calls the hospital a "crip prison" when discussing an especially long stay.

Paraguy1 on Apparalyzed refers to the community of wheelchair users as "the crip club" when explaining how he acquired his disability: "I joined the crip club back in 2001 from a bad accident."

Supercrip 13 on Apparalyzed discusses wheelchair names, noting: "In typical black crip/teenage humour we had nicknames for our chairs in general—spaz wagon and crip cart were two I remember."

Apparalyzed on Apparalyzed begins a discussion thread with the question: "What 'Crip Swag' have you been given or offered, and how did you feel at the time of being offered it, were you embarrassed or grateful?"

Using "crip" as an adjective provides a window into experiences that are common among those within this community, including hospital stays with a long duration, making up names for wheelchairs and other mobility devices, being offered "perks" because one uses a wheelchair, and having to decide whether or not to accept those benefits. In this way, people shape the meaning of the word to acknowledge a shared culture, cultural understanding, and cultural experiences, deepening the sense of community individuals may feel with one another. Many people have been there, done that, and marking these experiences with "crip" also suggests that they are unique to disability communities.

Another instance of "crip" being used as an adjective is in a post about the "Crip Posse," a group of wheelchair users whose job is to enforce parking regulations.

Wheelie on WheelchairJunkie.com suggests: "Texas should consider 'A Crip Posse' certified to issue citations for violations of downtown parking violations. . . . Its been proven before in other communities in other states that the 'Crip Posse' are very effective and issue 2–3 times as many citations as the Police." This word pairing has the lovely relish of the ironic, since a "posse" is a group of people who serve as formal or informal law enforcement or social control, whether sanctioned or a renegade force. Pairing it with "crip" is another way to reshape the meaning of the term and give a sense of power to formerly maligned words. On the other hand, the imagined power of a "crip posse" is still contextual and audience-dependent, as it could be interpreted by the listener or reader as an impossibility, farce, or a statement of the strength of a group of people with disabilities. In all these instances, community members find meanings in the word "crip" that suggest shared knowledge, experiences, and empowerment. These pairings may at first seem comic, but underneath that layer of humor is a deeper understanding of how people with disabilities are regarded in dominant culture, and the affiliations formed to fight stigma.

Term Used to Distinguish In-Group Members from TAB Individuals

While some members of the disability communities I studied call themselves crips, they may also refer to TABs as "ABs" (short for "able-bodied") or "walkies." This is another form of in-group language, but one meant to differentiate non-group members. In the examples I found on the discussion boards, these terms are used in a pejorative context to express frustration and comment on how often TABs use facilities that are meant for disabled people or instances in which TABs "masquerade" as crips. Using "AB" and "walkie" to mock TABs shows how easily disabled individuals can employ words those in the dominant culture may assume to be positive modifiers into ones with a negative connotation.

Commenting on Lady Gaga's use of a wheelchair during a stage performance, Windjammer on WheelchairJunkie.com writes: "I think GA GA took the liberty in using a chair because [the television show] Glee has a fake Crip rolling on stage every week. I am offended by that little AB as well."[7]

Amy provides another example of similar in-group language, explaining the experience of one of her friends who was a university student and used a wheelchair: "She went to the Student Center and there was one Mac that's accessible that's on a lowered table, and someone who was able-bodied was at that one. She sent me a text and said, 'The walkies are at the cripple Mac, what's up with that?'" This ironic turn demonstrates how people with disabilities can find new meanings for words that connote ability and use them as pejoratives that suggest an individual's dismay at TAB entitlement. In this case, disabled people use humor to reject what McRuer terms compulsory able-bodiedness, the idea that everyone should want a "normal" and able body (2017, 398–400). The individuals posting on these message boards demonstrate how easily "ABs" and "walkies" can become words of derision, labeling individuals who ignore the realities and needs of disabled people. Using the terms in this way also twists the notion that disabled people have a sense of entitlement, revealing that is instead true of TABs.

It is equally important to note the number of people who have invisible disabilities and may at times need to sit or use a wheelchair due to pain, exhaustion, or other impairments. Since her wheelchair stage performance, Lady Gaga has revealed that she has fibromyalgia, an invisible disability that causes chronic pain and fatigue, bringing the question of who needs and does not need to use a wheelchair to the fore.[8] Her story also reveals the social pressure to hide disability and appear able-bodied, gesturing again to the state of disability as a devalued condition.

In-Group Members May Reject These Words Due to Personal Preference, Historical Connotations, and Changes in Joking Behavior

Because "crip" and "cripple" have often been used as pejoratives, they have a negative resonance for some people with disabilities. As Amy reflects, "'Cripple' is a word that carries a lot of history with it, and some of that history is really bad. It's like 'queer' or the n-word in a lot of ways, though not to that degree. Some people in disability communities hear it and react negatively, whereas some people don't." Along these lines, while several individuals on both wheelchair forums embrace "crip" and "cripple," others express sentiments similar to Perillo in reflecting their distaste for those words:

Bulldog on WheelchairJunkie.com rejects the idea of using the term "AB" to refer to able-bodied people, and further explains his refusal to use words that connote one's embodiment: "If you and others want to go on labeling people, according to their physical condition, don't whine when you're referred to as a gimp, crip, etc., which merely describes your physical condition."

Softball Dad on Apparalyzed also comments on a thread regarding terms used to connote disability, writing: "I do not like either word 'cripple' or 'gimp.' My friends call me by my first name as I do them. When I'm not around I'm sure they say something like 'He's in a wheelchair' or 'he's the guy in the wheelchair' at least I hope. When I'm on the phone with people I have to meet I say 'I use a wheelchair' so I'll be easy to spot/find. There was a day when I use to use 'cripple' but it's not funny or humorous to me any longer."

Reflecting on his post, it's important to consider how an individual's sense of humor, and the meanings they may give to these terms, can change over time. Just as some people may gain a comfort with the words in a comic or in-group context, others such as Softball Dad may feel the words are no longer appropriate for them to use. These preferences are often subject to shift based on one's life experiences, age, and social groups, among other factors. Both posters object strongly to the idea of labeling people based on an aspect of their embodiment. More than refusing to use any particular term, they didn't want to emphasize the physicality of their identity as opposed to their personhood. For them, the meaning of words may have felt too constricting or suggested a slippery slope in terms of judging people based on appearance.

At the same time, other members of disability communities consider their embodied status as an important, positive part of their political identity, one that they want to acknowledge and that affects how they interpret the world (Dolmage 2014, 140–41; Longmore 2003, 110; Siebers 2017, 315–16). These individuals insist that embodiment can't be ignored since it plays into identity through how people experience their environment and how they are treated by others. While they reject the notion that disability is the sole feature of their identity, the debate remains as to how much individuals want to emphasize their disability in the construction of a multifaceted self. Perhaps in making meaning for these words, a question at play is how much an individual wishes to engage in a political discussion about bodies and assumptions around ability, rather than swiveling around the issue and allowing their actions to (re)define themselves.

Meanings Given to the Words "Crip" and "Cripple" May Reflect an Individual's Age and Gender, but Not Necessarily

My collaborators agree that whether or not someone chooses to use the words "crip" and "cripple" depends on personal associations with those terms. Meaning-making has much to do with the meanings these words have been given in an individual's experiences to date. This idea connects back to the question of whether someone has access to disability humor or if they consider disability to be such a serious matter that it can't be regarded in a lighthearted or comic context. An individual's opinions can also be shaped by prevalent attitudes toward disability while they were growing up and by gender expectations. In essence, while the meaning someone gives to these words is personal, it's cultural as well. As Eric comments, "Even in the older age group there's a diverse group of individuals. . . . It's one of those things where older generations will stick with the terms they have used."

Along similar lines, Amy suggests that attitudes toward disability at the time a person was coming of age will greatly affect their opinions on the subject: "Everything is generational. Even identifying as a person with a disability is generational, since historically that was a very bad thing to do. You were seen as helpless." Drew provides an example of that idea, explaining that his great-grandfather was injured in WWII and later had his leg amputated. Despite this impairment, he refused to call himself disabled. Applying for disability assistance at the time would not have provided a high enough income to support his family, and he had to confront the stigma that disabled people could not work and were excluded from the economy. Due to these financial and social pressures, he made a prosthetic leg for himself and continued to be employed as a carpenter until he reached retirement age.

Perhaps because of the pervasive nature of stereotypes that suggest disabled people are helpless, Amy notes that some of the men she has met have a more difficult time accepting a disabled identity than women. She says, "Women are more likely to own being disabled, and men are less likely to own it. Every single man I have ever worked with, it has been like pulling teeth for them to call themselves disabled and in need of accommodations." Amy remarks that one of the earliest proponents of reclaiming the word "crippled" was Harriet McBryde Johnson, a lawyer and activist for disability rights. Given Amy's comments on gender and claiming disability identity, it is interesting to note that on WheelchairJunkie.com and Apparalyzed, two of the posters who use "crip" and "cripple" most frequently are Supercrip 13 and Windjammer, both of whom identify as middle-aged women. In this context, the question of gender expectations might affect who is willing to own a disability identity and employ these terms in a positive light. In many social contexts, men are expected to be independent breadwinners, and not reliant on others. The idea of being disabled and a "crip" seems to run counter to the idea of masculine strength and self-sufficiency (Manderson and Peake 2005, 231–32), possibly leading more men to reject the term.

Meanings Are Always Sensitive and Unstable

My collaborators and those on the online forums acknowledge that "crip" and "cripple" can be highly charged, and not everyone will agree on how and when to use them. The connection between these words and joke telling is clear, since both must be done with great care and social awareness, or the speaker risks coming off as crass and insensitive. The consensus seems to be that, before using these terms, it is important to know how comfortable the disabled individuals in a particular conversation are with their disability and their stance on terminology. As Drew comments, "With people who are more active in disability rights and who are sensitive to actual physical disability, 'cripple' is a term you don't want to use. Freshly disabled people are also a little concerning with that. . . . Usually they're okay with it unless they have an extreme issue with their disability." Using "crip" may suggest that someone is more comfortable with their embodiment in general, lending the word a positive meaning that suggests adaptability and pride. Perillo illustrates this felt tension when she writes of her adjustment to having multiple sclerosis. For her, "cripple" describes a changed body that feels limited and not like her own. She is a nature-lover who enjoyed hiking and camping alone, and she's upset because disability has restricted her from enjoying those pleasures in the same way she had been accustomed to for many years (2009, 3–23). Perillo realizes that she must be considered disabled to have the social permission to use words such as "cripple," but she doesn't like people to see her in her wheelchair because they will either stare or look away and confirm that she has changed physically (26). In Perillo's case, not using the words means avoiding a part of her embodied reality that she wants to reject. Finding a positive meaning in the words is thus dependent on one's comfort with the terms, their body, and the perceived comfort level of their audience.

As Megatrig on Apparalyzed remarks on a thread about disability terminology: "I joke about 'the cripple in the corner' when the timing is right . . . I refer to myself usually as 'a wheelchair user.' But when booking tables, etc, etc. I usually say I'm 'confined' to a wheelchair. It gets the message across and saves any hassle." He demonstrates a high level of situational awareness in his observations about the words that audience members will understand most readily, and he shapes his language accordingly. It's also apparent from his reflections that he considers vocabulary to be as much of a matter of efficiency as social context. For him, "cripple" is a term used for joking, one that has comic meaning and isn't for serious contexts, since he is likewise aware of the language that TABs are more likely to accept.

Words Used in Familiar Contexts with Family and Friends and to "Acculturate" New In-Group Members

Several individuals on the forums comment that they tend to use "crip" and "cripple" more often with friends, family, and close members of their social groups. While these people may not belong to disability communities per se, they are still part of the individual's in-group. Since this type of joking can create tensions or miscommunications if one isn't familiar with the use of such terms (as exemplified by Burbach and Babbitt), those posting on the message boards also defined the words as ones they wouldn't use around people who would find them more awkward and insulting than comic.

As Big D on Apparalyzed notes: "As a matter of preference I refer to myself as 'cripple' or 'gimp,' and I allow this for people who are close to me. I find regular people I encounter just call me disabled or 'in a wheelchair' which is fine." Those posting on the forums also mention that they "educate" people who are not in their in-group by using words such as "crip" and "cripple" to make these individuals aware of their attitudes toward disability. The terms could be shocking in some situations, such as when the audience members weren't accustomed to them being used casually and as a positive identifier. Because the words still possess a negative meaning in much of dominant culture, this reaction is understandable. At the same time, people with disabilities who use these terms note that they often find the initial reactions of others to be comic.

MTB John on Apparalyzed writes: "My wife has just started a new job—whole new bunch of people in her life. When they ask about me she started out saying—'Oh, he's busy being a cripple.' And then THEY would cringe as though she had just insulted me. So she stopped saying it, at least until they had become friends and knew it wasn't offensive in our view."

Along similar lines, Ackrin on Apparalyzed reflects: "My friends, family, and I use cripple. It wouldn't bother me at all if others used it. It's all about the context it's used in. I actually find it hilarious to see peoples reaction when if I'm out with my mom and she asks where the crippled seating is. People get so offended FOR me."

These individuals find the words helpful to bring people into their in-group, realizing how their casual use of these terms can shift the meaning of "crip" and "cripple" in the minds of others and convey their attitude toward disability. Employing these terms can help individuals emphasize that, to them, disability is no big deal. Yet not everyone will understand or appreciate the joking manner in which these words can be used, and others may never feel comfortable giving them such a meaning. Drew comments that his mother would allow him to use "cripple" in certain circumstances but not in others, saying:

> Whenever my mother heard the word "cripple," she took it to be a derogatory comment towards me, unless I was hanging out with my other crippled friends. To my mom, "crippled" was the n-word. If she heard anyone else use it around me, she would throw a fit, and she would tell me to stop using that word. If I was around my own people, she would be okay with it, but she didn't want me to fall into the self-fulfilling prophecy of the word. She didn't want me to think I was more helpless than I am.

In this case Drew's mother considered the word as having different meanings, or levels of permissibility, depending on the audience and whether her son was with friends. While it was fine for him to use the word with those in his in-group, there were still overwhelmingly negative social connotations related to dependence that she attached to the word, meanings that she did not want Drew to associate with himself.

Another complication with these words is how they are interpreted when they are used by individuals who are not part of one's in-group of family and friends. When the social context is ambiguous, the words may create uncomfortable situations when individuals use the terms but do not have the permission to do so. As with other forms of joking behavior, those in the out-group can sometimes assume they have more leeway to joke about disability than they do in actuality (Rosqvist 2012, 242). For example, Stephen D on Apparalyzed writes:

> I had a new acquaintance refer to me as gimpy. For a moment, I felt weird because we didn't know each other. After a second though I realized that we were just talking like the casual smartasses that we are. My response, "I find that term offensive. At this point in history, I demand to be referred to as a Gimp American, godamnit." We had a good laugh about it. And I got to mess with someone. Win-win if you ask me.

Stephen D was able to turn a moment that could have been considered offensive into a comic occasion since he paused, considered the meanings that they were giving to the word, and realized they could both use the term in a similar joking manner. At the same time, the anecdote suggests his acknowledgment that "crip" and "gimpy" can become charged when the permissions to use the terms are unclear. It may be difficult to discern an individual's meaning as affable, aggressive, or somewhere in between when they are not part of one's social circle.

"Crip" and "Cripple" Take on a Negative Meaning When Used by Those Who Are Outside the In-Group or Community

When individuals outside of disability communities who are not part of a disabled person's social circle use "crip" and "cripple," they often lend the words a pejorative connotation, even if the context is somewhat ambiguous. This facet is acknowledged by members of the online forums, such as Zen12many on Apparalyzed, who reflects on his use of disability terminology. He writes: "I do use a double standard re gimp, etc. If I overheard a waiter in a restaurant say 'I just served the wheelchair gimp crip,' I think I would find that offensive. But if one of you wheelchair gimp crips calls me that, I probably wouldn't think anything about it. I give wheelchair gimp crips a little slack."

Along similar lines, MoMo on Apparalyzed tells a story about a confrontation that involved these words being used in a hostile joking manner. She explains:

> I don't think I have a problem with being called any particular term, unless its used it a derogatory or cruel way. For instance, there was an incident on a sidewalk in Miami one evening, where my sister asked a guy to please move for a moment because he and his friends were blocking the sidewalk . . . He said in a very sarcastic tone "Oh EVERYBODY stop what you're doing because this crippled girl has to get through!" He made some other comments and his friends told him to shut up and move. My sister wanted to kill him.

As Eric suggests, often it's not difficult to discern whether "cripple" is used in a way that is chummy or cutting: "Like any other mixed word, it can be considered derogatory. Given the English language and body language, it is easy to identity if someone really means it to be offensive and derogatory."

One person who posted on the forums is less concerned about the use of the term "cripple" than the meaning she believes the word has outside disability communities. Island girl on Apparalyzed worries about assumptions made by TABs that wheelchair users are uniformly unhappy. In some contexts, she found that the word "cripple" became a comment on her physical *and* emotional state:

A few months ago I had a very unpleasant encounter with a woman who parked illegally beside my van blocking the lift. She said among other things I was just a unhappy cripple. I do not think I am a unhappy or happy go lucky person I think I am a person like every one else with good days and bad. If I seam always unhappy they will in fact treat me like the unhappy cripple. . . . For those of you who take offence at my use of the cripple sorry but face it its not a bad word its what we are. I took offence when it was used by that woman but in hind sight I see I should not have. Yes she meant it to be nasty. But its only nasty if we let it be.

Island girl suggests that for her, "cripple" doesn't have a negative meaning. It's a neutral word she uses to describe her body. The fact that the woman in the parking lot blamed her attitude on the fact that she was in a wheelchair was a much bigger concern. The woman paired the concept of being a "cripple" with unhappiness, implying that Island girl's wheelchair must be the cause of her emotional state (as opposed to being irked by someone blocking the lift on her van). This idea points back to Johnson and Pinker's contention that words assume a negative social connotation if what they name also has a negative social connotation—for example, that being crippled means being helpless, unhappy, and envious of TABs.

This illustration returns us to the idea that "crip" and "cripple" have many layered and conflicting possible meanings, yet some disability activists have suggested that "cripple" may also be more powerful because of this fluidity, especially in ways that connote resistance. Johnson quotes disabled poet and performer Cheryl Wade asserting the word is "visual, strong, feels good—like a gnarled fist," while poet Mark O'Brien writes, "It packs a punch" (1994a, 41). While "cripple" and "crip" may have expanded their use in disability communities since the *Disability Rag* poll, the controversy around their use has not ended. The positive, negative, and politically charged impact of these words is clear, along with the range of definitions and connotations individuals can employ when using these terms.

Wider Use of "Crip" and "Cripple" Exemplifies a Trend in Disability In-Group Language

Eric suggests that the increased use of "crip" and "cripple" is part of a linguistic movement in disability communities to find shorthand terms for disabilities. He explains that in his interactions with disabled people, he has noticed that "as knowledge of disability has grown, there has been a development of a list of common terms for the concept of disability that is used in casual conversation, like abbreviations for cerebral palsy. People will say, 'I have CP,' but other terms will be used as well. People with spina bifida will use the term 'biffer.'" In terms of practicality, the words are a time-saver, and employing them in this casual context also suggests that individuals can give the same meaning to their disability, a fact of embodiment that is no big deal.

Amy reflects along similar lines, stating, "Person-first language [identifying as a person with a disability as opposed to a disabled person] is the standard because it feels safe, but it doesn't resonate with individuals. That is where you get a lot of the identity-based language, I am Disabled, with a capital D. A lot of identity-based language is focused on a specific disability, but we are many different disabilities. Some people don't feel a kinship with everyone, just people who have their disability." Amy's comment reiterates how people in disability communities can adopt "crip" or "cripple" as a form of identity-based language, giving them a sense of belonging to and solidarity with a larger group. Along these lines, Dolmage suggests that using common terms can shape a community's perspective of their individual and collective selves: "The shared word allows for the shared body, and vice versa. In this way, discourse shapes embodiment (and the inverse). This shaping is rhetorical" (2014, 114). Here language becomes an argument for a kind of reality, a space to express political and social goals and to resist to dominant cultural ideologies—the "punch" described by O'Brien. Just as words can develop meanings that help solidify communities, communities can solidify around the shared use of words. Kuppers notes how words can gain a positive meaning when groups use them as identifiers in a positive way, yet she suggests that "crip" may work best as a "provisional word: That seems to me important in any discussion of 'crip.' It will serve us, for a while, as so many people are only slowly coming to a political and artistic understanding of what it means to lead a rich disabled life" (2013, 27). Language use is always shifting. Words collect and abandon meanings, as happens in a living lexicon.

REFLECTIONS AND RUMINATIONS
ON MEANING-MAKING

The meanings my collaborators find in these words are shaped by their identities and communities: they are all under thirty, identify as disabled, are part of disability communities, and readily joke about disability among friends who understand such humor. They don't consider their disability to be a negative aspect of who they are, but simply another facet of their identity. All three have college degrees and exposure to the disability rights movement, which affects their thoughts on meaning-making, word choice, and joking about disability.

Likewise, the individuals who participate in the online forums I analyzed are seeking to join conversations within disability communities, sharing experiences and gripes and jokes with like-minded people. This need to affiliate with a larger community also affects the meanings they find in "crip" and "cripple," contrasting with other individuals who may use wheelchairs but don't wish to identify as disabled, such as Perillo. As her sentiments relate, the desire to be part of a disability community can affect how individuals use language, the connotations and denotations they find in these words, and the types of people they associate with using them.

I wasn't able to obtain demographic information from the forum participants, other than through specific comments in their posts. Since opinions on the words "crip" and "cripple" tend to be generational, I may be lacking data from older disabled individuals who may not be involved with disability communities, and who would attach negative meanings to the terms based on their past experiences.

At the same time, "crip" and "cripple" have expanded their use over the past three decades, being embraced by a greater number of people in the disability rights movement, as I found in both my research and fieldwork. These terms have gained wider acceptance among younger people and disability communities as a mark of identity, pride, and shared interests, as a way to differentiate themselves from TAB individuals, and as a form of in-group language and joking.

Disabled people may also shape the meanings they give to these words based on their level of education and the exposure they've had to language that plays with these words in different ways. As Amy suggests, those who have attended college may have thought more deeply about reclaiming words, morphing their meanings, and finding new ways to use the words in collaboration with their communities. She observes, "There is a certain degree of education and unconventionality that comes along with [using those words]. People who are involved with subversive behavior use those terms." Joking behavior is a form of subversion as well, which suggests how both humor and language use can promote a political disability identity, multiply the meanings of words and concepts, and push back against dominant cultural notions of disability as connoting inferiority, replacing these ideas with models that are much more flexible and fluid.

Despite the wider acceptance of these words, there is still conflict about their use within disability communities, as there is about other forms of joking. As Johnson and Amy noted, the terms have a great deal of historical baggage and negative connotations when they are used outside said communities. Individuals may or may not use the terms, depending on how familiar they are with other people in the conversation. The problem with the shifting quality of language is that one never knows how these words may be categorized in someone else's lexicon and the multiple layers of meaning the terms may have for them personally. As I will discuss in the next chapter, the same social considerations come into play when telling comic stories related to disability.

Even when the terms are used with humorous intent, they can still be interpreted as negative by individuals both outside and inside disability communities. As my collaborators and those posting on forums convey, even if individuals understand that these words can have a positive meaning, they may not be able to let that idea override previous negative associations or social sanctions against using the words, especially since "crip" and "cripple" still have a pejorative connotation when used in the abstract sense (such as a crippled economy or infrastructure). As Burbach and Babbitt's remarks imply, those outside disability communities may assume that disabled people use these terms to hide anger, as opposed to accepting and embracing their state of embodiment. This line of logic follows Pinker's euphemism treadmill, suggesting that as long as dominant society regards disabilities as negative traits, words associated with disability will be considered in the same manner. While such stigmas continue to be a pervading ideology, TABs will continue to assume that people who use wheelchairs must be "unhappy" and secretly desire to be made "whole."

Reclaiming and redefining the meanings of "crip" and "cripple" within disability communities will not break the euphemism treadmill, yet twisting and tweaking these words and using them as a form of joking is part of a larger movement to throw a wrench in the gears of dominant cultural perceptions of disability. The right to name oneself is integral to the political fight to have a voice, to have agency, and to define oneself in the social sphere. There is power in a name, but more importantly, as Mairs asserts, there is power in the act of naming, in language play, and in having the ability to shape and reshape the world as one sees fit.

ON BLINDNESS

I call my blind eye my invisible disability since most people don't realize it's blind and since it has the hidden benefit of making things invisible. It's simple to situate objects on my right when I don't want to see them. Being blind in one eye was helpful when I was learning how to drive, and my mother gripped the dashboard so hard she said her knuckles turned white. I didn't have to see that, and a good thing too, since it would have made me more nervous. Monocular as I am, I'm happy with my identity.

But I know I live in a sighted world, sitting at the edge of blindness.

As much as I rail against disability simulations, the idea that one can artificially re-create disability and "understand" what it's like to be in someone else's body (Kafer 2013, 4; Nario-Redmond, Gospodinov, and Cobb 2017), sometimes I'd like to have snap-on body parts like Lego pieces, so I could detach and reattach and learn to adjust to a theoretical life without sight. Or I could get another bright purple eye patch. Just a half-hour at a time, and perhaps I could figure it out, the scenes of sightlessness, preparing myself for that possibility so the prospect would be less scary. Part of the reason my optometrist and ophthalmologist want to delay cataract surgery is that there is a risk of blindness. It's always the monster under my bed, in the closet, around the corner.

I'd be lying if I said I wasn't scared, but the fear also makes me feel guilty. I know I could adapt to less sight, am adapting to less sight, but the process isn't easy. I'm in agreement with Kafer, who suggests, "I am not interested in becoming more disabled than I already am. I realize that position itself is marked by an ableist failure of imagination, but I can't deny holding it" (2013, 4).

Even now the cataract makes me more sensitive to light, more susceptible to eyestrain and headaches. I wear sunglasses more often. Why am I always so tired? Is my body trying to hibernate? I just want to write and teach and cook and read and walk. What's all this needing extra sleep? But even on days when sun sears my vision, I bump around the world passing as fully sighted and so do not often bear the sting of disability stigma.

Rod Michalko, who lost much of his vision due to retinal pigmentosa, explains an occasion when he was not able to get a hotel room because the front desk manager would not allow someone who was blind to make a reservation. A friend of Michalko assumed that the process would have been easier if he'd gone to the hotel to show he could "control" his disability. Michalko reflects, "We often reason that interaction between disabled persons and nondisabled ones would diminish the fear of disability" (2002, 11), yet he argues that on a larger scale we must change dominant cultural perceptions regarding disability that make it permissible to leave disabled people out of the social sphere (12).

As I write this, the world has been swept into a viral pandemic that has caused many disabled people to worry that their lives will not be considered ones worth living if there is a shortage of respirators, and doctors must make difficult decisions about who is granted crucial life-saving equipment.[1] It would not be the first time disabled life has been so devalued.[2] This is a truly terrifying moment, in which I have heard politicians on the radio bandy about terms such as "acceptable losses," as if they were points in a football game as opposed to people. Whose life is more acceptable to forfeit in this play for scarce resources, when the present reality has taken on the tone of a dystopian sci-fi novel?

This is not a new question, but an age-old one repeated at different times, in different flavors. Whose life is worth living, and who gets to make that determination?

This is when compulsory able-bodiedness, and the question of whether someone can be happy living with a disability, has dangerous implications.

Michalko writes that while his job involves the same tasks as those of other professors, he can't ignore how their ease of access diverges from his since he lives in a world designed for sight. It's more challenging for him to find accessible reading material and review and comment on student work, and when applying for the position, he "had to convince some people that blindness does not prevent me, or anyone else, from teaching at a university" (2002, 79–80). There are always doubters, wrinkle-nosed skeptics, people who'll vote for another candidate without explaining why. This is the bane of many people in marginalized groups, the task of proving themselves. And proving themselves. And proving themselves again.

As Michalko "[moves] through the world" with his guide dog, Smokie, he knows he's accompanied by the expectations of others, the connotations and denotations of what blindness signifies culturally, the negative interpretations that are bound to be roadblocks. He writes, "People often grab my arm and offer me help in crossing a street, more often than not a street I do not wish to cross; a few people have offered me money; others offer prayers; still others speak of the good fortune of their 'gift of sight'; and some, of how they have been graced by God, saying, 'There but for the grace of God go I'" (2002, 88). It is another space of smacking against stigma, the sting from statements of wonder that he can move independently, and the exasperating sense of others' pity (88). Given the signs—a dog, a pair of sunglasses—other people figure they understand him in a few symbols. Metaphors and movies have dictated the rest of the cultural cache.

As disability scholar Amy Vidali writes, metaphors around the idea that "seeing is knowing" often appear in everyday communication. One can "look forward to" something, be "shortsighted," "lose sight of" a goal, "be blind to" something obvious, "focus on" important matters, or have a good "outlook" (2010, 40). Sight is not to be questioned, and those without it are met with stark suspicion. How can someone understand the world without vision? This attitude is woven into the English language itself: as disability scholar David Bolt notes, "the dictionary offers thirteen definitions for the adjective *blind*, but twelve are negative, and only one pertains to visual impairment" (2013, 20). Bolt also analyzes the definitions of adverbs related to blindness and finds that "the image that emerges . . . is one of someone who is unprepared, unable to judge or act rationally, someone who is confused" (21). These cultural beliefs ingrained in the language led to Michalko being denied hotel rooms, dragged across streets, and forcibly blessed.

Stereotypes of sightlessness also pervade cinema. Kleege quips, "If I want to have nightmares I go to movies about the blind" (1999, 45). In films, blind people are endlessly cast as "timid, morose, cranky, resentful, socially awkward, and prone to despair" (45). These characters have not "mastered any of the skills that real blind people employ" to adeptly navigate the world, and only lament their blindness. Kleege writes that when encountering such depictions, she must suppress the urge "to run screaming from the theater" (45).

Blind people are rarely asked to explain their reflections on how they have adapted to their environment and their means of perception, as Michalko notes (2002, 93). While he experiences the world visually, he's found that his sight lacks credibility with sighted people who determine that what he's seeing isn't "real": "There are no clouds on the street, standing still, moving, or speaking. . . . These are only distortions, for there are only sign posts and people on the street and only buildings and intersections. . . . Blindness is thrown on the heap of 'useless-difference'" (94).

With my cataract I understand what it means to see a different version of the world than many other people, but it's a version I find beautiful. Objects come in pairs, like telephone poles and traffic lights hanging over streets.

I know the poles are solo sentries, and traffic lights don't need to clutch each other closely but swing alone over passing cars, yet my vision says otherwise. I enlarge the type on my computer screen so letters are bigger and accompanied by a shadow of themselves. Every car has a sibling driving beside it down the street. I try to explain this to my partner, how it looks like there is one car on the road and its close confidant coasting ghostly on the sidewalk, with a rainbow arc connecting the two. The world is full of geminis, and I don't want to make them sway with separation too soon. At night the moon floats in triplicate. Why not have three satellites? Too much has been written about the moon's lonely trek across the sky.

Michalko writes about his chats with Don, a college student who has been blind since birth and developed his own methods of interpreting surroundings. He's discovered that if he " 'kinda brushes up against' someone" while riding a bus, he can be cued to the tension in their bodies and how they might be feeling (Michalko 2002, 125). When navigating the world with his cane, Don must be similarly "vigilant and flexible" to understand the moods of other people that are often perceived through sight, translating their feelings to cues given by sound and touch (126).

I am a novice in the shadow of such expertise, yet I have found myself tuned to different sensory information when my eye is tired of sight. I note the whoosh of traffic slowing and stopping, know it's time to cross without looking to the light. I feel the edges of coins in my purse to distinguish the smooth penny and nickel from rough dimes and quarters. I sniff for the warm odor of browned toast, the deep perfume of chocolate cake when it has almost finished baking, the herbal notes of soup brought to a simmer.

This is not a science but a learned art, though all of our world is molded by sensory information. Everyone's sculpture is different.

Kleege writes of being introduced to a banker in France who had a visual impairment, and he told her that "he had *un probleme* with his eyes," so he could not make eye contact (1999, 18). She noted that his clothing and manner of speech were "calculated to affirm, in the most reassuring way, that he could dispatch even the most distasteful or compromising financial matter with discretion so deft it would seem effortless" (18). He understood the social pressure to prove he was competent, hiding the extent of his blindness for fear it would discount him in the minds of other people. Kleege suggests that this worry leads individuals to mask their diminishing sight through tactical passing: "They walk fast, purposefully; they do not ask directions. Forced to read something, they pat their pockets for reading glasses they do not own. When they make mistakes, they feign absentmindedness, slapping their foreheads and blinking" (18).

The temptation to pass as fully sighted becomes more apparent when we consider how, even in their everyday rhythms, people with visual impairments are disallowed from expressing their stories, indicating preferences, and being granted agency. Bolt observes that "those of us who have visual impairments are often in danger of being left out of our own conversation. Does he take sugar? Does she take sugar? Do they take sugar? The questions are now clichés, but the underpinning attitude is by no means a thing of the past" (2013, 9).

Blind people are trapped in what Bolt terms a "metanarrative of blindness that is shaped by cultural representations" of visual disability, which is "an overriding narrative that seems to displace agency" (2013, 10). For example, the cultural misconception that blind people are beggars is particularly pervasive. Bolt explains that on one occasion when he was standing outside a bar expecting a friend to arrive soon, someone assumed he was collecting change: "It was 2010, but in the mind of this kind stranger, I was reduced to the characteristic of visual impairment and, by extension, keyed to a metanarrative in which the blind beggar and sighted donor have become stock characters" (11). Yet Bolt allows that blind people can recognize these metanarratives and sometimes play with them: "Though reasonably aware of the stereotypical possession of extraordinary senses . . . I cannot help feeling a little pleased when someone notices if I am first to hear the arrival of a taxi at the end of an evening with friends" (11–12). He's generally "listening for the sounds of the engine and closing door," but at the same time, "I may secretly embrace the so-called positive stereotype and all its cool mysteries. What is more, I am then likely to save myself from the internal displacement of identity by nervously cracking some joke about the extraordinary hearing of the blind. In other words, albeit through irony, I invoke the metanarrative of blindness overtly as well as covertly" (12).

I admit my own play in this game of culture and connotation around the metanarratives of blindness. When including characters with visual impairments in my fiction, I may push and pull at the folk beliefs, the legends, the cultural cache, writing over, around, and through them. Why not tell the story of a high school administrative assistant who claims (with a wink) that her blind eye can see into the future? An excerpt:

This is what people used to believe: when you were deprived of one sense, the others would become keener. That was the world of a too-cruel and too-just god (don't think too deeply about it), one who'd smite you in a second or gift you with extraordinary abilities. My right eye has been blind since birth, so it has been blessed for an equally long period of time. It is the eye that Dali would have loved. Malleable. Mutable. It can see anything but mostly the future, an invisible stick-on eye in the middle of my back, my forehead, my knee, under my left breast, over my heart. It is where it needs to be. While my left eye must squint to read the fine print, the right eye sees at a glance that the kid asking for a late pass was making out with his girlfriend in the back of his mom's car during second period. Eye omnipotent. I give him the pass. Sometimes I am kind, even to liars. My right eye sees what it should and what it should not, playing on a separate screen in my mind. Actually, it isn't like that exactly, but the analogy might help you understand.

My eye allows me to see love like a landscape. I take notes when no one is needfully standing beside my desk. The librarian will have an affair with the biology teacher—nice fellow, no kids, broke up with long-time girlfriend two and a half years ago, does laundry on Saturdays, doesn't wear too much aftershave, makes good stir-fry. The affair will last six months, just dinner and movies and sex at his apartment and then he'll move to a different school district in another state because the job pays more. They will both mourn. She'll feel betrayed but shoved by invisible hands to go to marriage counseling. Her husband will never know what happened. She'll think of him as sweet and oblivious. He'll wonder why she's suddenly more creative in the bedroom. (My eye squints to give them privacy.) This is as happy an ending as anyone can expect, and better than most.

I allow myself to twist and twirl the fabled notion of blind "seers" and fortune tellers, though Kleege suggests that these "ancient myths about compensatory powers" can make blind people seem "dangerous" (1999, 28). It's hard to resist the (guilty) pleasure of being potentially diabolical, so I sink into the sentiment of second sight as a kind of tease, though I'm never sure who will get the joke.

As with all disabilities, there is variability in visual impairment, which smacks against the limitations of language to accurately describe one's bodymind. Kleege notes that one complication with the word "blind" is that people who are classified as such have a wide range of visual perception. Only 10 percent of those who are visually impaired have no vision, but should we use the word "blind" only to refer to them (1999, 14)? In my own experiences with visual variability, I have often wrangled with the question of how to explain my embodiment short of a five-minute lecture because there is so much space on the spectrum between fully blind and 20/20 vision. Many people in the dominant culture don't realize such a realm exists and how saying "I'm blind" may also mean "I can see some stuff." Bolt concludes, "It is evident that, wherever we position ourselves in the terminology debate, there can be no denying that the word *blind* causes confusion" (2013, 25).

At the end of fall term, I receive an email from one of the students who is enrolled in a creative writing class I will teach the following semester. I'll call her Dana. She explains she's blind and a braille user and would like to discuss the accommodations she'll need in the spring. I've never had a blind student in one of my classes, but every semester I've quietly wondered when it might happen.

I phone Dana to chat since I want to make sure she'll have access to the PDFs we'll be reading in class and that they'll work with her optical character recognition (OCR) software. She says not to worry, her OCR software has done a great job on PDFs, converting them to documents that she can read using the accessibility features available in Microsoft Word.

Near the end of our conversation, Dana says, "You can use the world 'blind.' It's okay—it's not a bad word."

I blush since I've been using the term "visually impaired" in our conversation, but I explain I've spent time hanging out with folks who had a lot of vision variability, including some who could see shapes and colors and read big type.

"It feels more all-encompassing to me, since I never know how much sight someone is able to use," I explain.

"That makes sense," says Dana, "and you shouldn't worry—I won't be any extra trouble or work for you in class."

"Oh gosh, I didn't think so," I say. "I just wanted to make sure you had everything you needed at the start of the semester."

"Great," Dana says, wishing me a good evening and a happy holiday, and that she looks forward to seeing me soon.

"You, too," I say.

I wonder how often she has this "I won't be a bother" chat with professors. Ten times a year? It's probably part of her usual rhythm, starting a new semester and assuring the sighties that she'll be fine.

We need a means to promote the validity of sensory variability, as disability scholar Devon Healey argues in her narrative about wading through appointments with ophthalmologists and psychiatrists. She wants someone to give credibility to her way of experiencing the world but finds that "when blindness aims to tell sight of its actions, hopes and desires . . . sight makes blindness reflect only what sight can imagine. This is how blindness is made to be a medical problem, understood as outside normal functioning and therefore in need of treatment. . . . When blindness speaks it is only ever heard as yearning sight—angry that it has been denied sensorial functioning not social validation" (2017, 94). Even (especially?) in the medical realm, her perspective has no credibility. Healey's story fits into the larger social narrative of disabled people being dismissed. Too often their narratives are ignored, dubbed over, erased, reinterpreted.

The TAB world does not want to consider the possible benefits that Frank suggests can be found in fragility (2013, 118–19). Investigating those possibilities means we must admit that we are prone to breaking. We have bodies that change and require us to find new forms of interdependence with each other, spaces we can't understand until we inhabit them.

As Healey writes, "my blindness is not bitter. It is full of sights you would not believe. I want to tell you that blindness is sweet, but that is in my imagined time. I have been told that blindness is hard and, to tell you the truth, it is. But, it can be so much more than merely sweet or merely hard" (2017, 102).

I'm back where I began, afraid of blindness, afraid of not getting better, ashamed of being afraid. I want to be someone who doesn't let ableism cloud her thoughts, who is secure in her interdependence, who adapts to new circumstances with wild abandon. I want to be a trooper. I do not want to be afraid of braille. I am very afraid of braille.

Yes, this is more than "merely sweet or merely hard," as Healey suggests. It can be, it always is, complicated.

And I know my story isn't over.

Chapter 3

"TODAY I HAD AN EYE APPOINTMENT, AND I'M STILL BLIND"

Crip Humor, Storytelling, and Narrative Positioning of the Disabled Self

When I embarked on a folkloric mission to collect jokes told by people with disabilities, I collided with a sad research reality: the best way to make anyone forget all the jokes they've ever read or been told is to ask them to tell one to you. What I discovered was that it was much easier for people to remember stories about times when they had made a joke out of their disability. These tales highlighted individuals' creativity in defining what disability means to them and ways that disability does and does not affect their lives and interactions with others.

This sideways approach to my search for jokes made sense in retrospect: by their nature, people are storytellers. Part of the ritual of getting to know someone is discovering their stories and determining which stories of your own to share. Much of this decision about the appropriateness of a story is based on occasion and audience, choosing which sides of yourself to explain, or coaxing friends and family members to tell their most beloved stories to a new or old audience. Performing story means performing self, perhaps bonding through narrative, outdoing each other, or just passing the time.

Stories can serve other functions when it comes to disability since as narrative theorist Thomas Couser notes, people with disabilities are often expected to tell stories of their bodies and "account" for what has happened to them, reassuring TABs that their own bodies are "safe" (2009, 16–17). This need to soothe TABs is tied to McRuer's theory of compulsory able-bodiedness, and the idea that everyone should want an able body (2017, 398–400). Through using due caution, a story may suggest, people should be able to protect themselves from the "horrors" of disability. But storytelling by people with disabilities can also resist that social imperative, while incorporating humor.

As I discussed in the previous chapter, joking can be an important communication tool for disabled people in peer groups, among friends who do not share similar disabilities, and when talking with TABs. As Shakespeare maintains, "Disabled people have discovered and proved that impairment is not the end of the world; that it does not undermine subjectivity or possibility, and they have demonstrated this by developing an alternative comic language around the body" (1999, 51). While this kind of crip humor has an important function, it has not been studied as intensively as disability humor in cartoons, comics, and texts. As disability theorist Albert Robillard notes, little critical attention has been paid to "specific interactional situations where, in the course of interactions in real time, disabled people and able-bodied use humor as a way of integrating the disabled into the ongoing social surround" (1999, 62–63). While some studies have examined joking among groups of disabled people, they tend to focus on how joking can cement group cohesion, distinguish in-group from out-group members, and be a way to poke back at dominant society and assert agency (Burbach and Babbitt 1993; Rosquvist 2012; MacPherson 2008). Further exploration is needed on the function of humorous narratives inside and outside of disability communities, and when shared with TABs.

I started my quest seeking jokes disabled people told that were related to disability, but I found much more complex comic stories disabled people used to narrate aspects of disability. Through examining these tales, we can understand the meanings people give to their disabilities, how they integrate stories into everyday communication, and how humor can do much more than mediate relationships with TABs. The storytellers I interviewed were mindful of both audience and the occasion for the telling, as any joke-teller should be. Many of the narratives address ways that disabled individuals combat awkward moments with a witty remark, find comedy in potentially uncomfortable situations, or otherwise use humor to interact with TABs and challenge ableist perceptions of disability. These tellers also use stories to demonstrate how disability can be a social construction that is dependent on environment and not inherent in the body itself. These narratives illustrate times when the disabled tellers are allowed to "fit" in the world and find places of belonging, and times when others try to impose limits on them due to their disability. The stories reveal ways of seeing and experiencing the world through a disability perspective that may run counter to the listener's expectations. The tales also reflect the tellers' ability to laugh at themselves and not find their mistakes upsetting or tragic, but amusing.

Such comic stories are a means for disabled people to advocate for themselves and their abilities and deconstruct the able-bodied/disabled dichotomy to reveal the shifting nature of all bodies. Finally, these tellers use stories to show how they can be victims of disability stereotypes, teasing TABs about their misguided perceptions. The humorous tales reveal how people with disabilities perceive their bodies and what disability means to them, a perspective that may destabilize how the listener interprets disability through questioning their previous assumptions.

CRIP HUMOR AND PERSONAL NARRATIVES

Telling personal stories can be an effective means to create a space of understanding between individuals. This is certainly true when considering disability narratives. Literary and disability scholar Mark Mossman alludes to this power of storytelling when he states:

> As a person with a disability, I believe that telling stories, both in my scholarship and in the classroom, is doing something, making something happen, for telling stories, in the social context of disability, articulates the rhetoric of social change, enacts the autobiographical process that enables the disabled subjectivity in part to make itself, to take some measure of control and volition in its own construction. (Mossmann 2002, 652)

Storytelling not only forms connections between the teller and listener: it can also be a way for disabled individuals to explain their identity and lived experience. Mossman suggests that telling stories can be a type of activism, as it gives individuals the potential to "resist the oppressive force of a master discourse by taking control of his or her narrative and constructing it as he or she chooses" (2002, 653). While telling one's story doesn't guarantee that an individual will change the way she is perceived by others, it is still a means to express agency and counter dominant cultural notions of disability.

Both storytelling and humor can be methods to debunk commonly held stereotypes about disabled people. Disabled comics in particular unite these two modes of expression in their routines. As Kim Reid, Edy Stoughton, and Robin Smith note in their research, comics with disabilities "counter prevalent ideas that disabled people are unhappy and long to be 'normal' . . . they reveal that their lives are full, rich, and well worth living" (2006, 633). Equally important, their stories can "open a space for dialogue about what it means to be disabled, about relationships with one another, and about the relationships we share. Comedy educates, because it represents disability, potentially leading to changes in social behavior and even social policy" (639). Yet while this kind of crip humor may be socially and politically transgressive, we must remember that, as with joking language in the last chapter, its success or failure depends on both the teller and audience.

Mairian Corker points to the potential of crip humor as "an emancipatory praxis," yet she emphasizes that analysis of this humor can be difficult, since, "as with most forms of humour, the key to our 'comedy' lies in solidarity and context . . . the humour of disability is in its inscription by disabled people and the particular way in which it jokes with 'disability'" (1999, 81). Crip humor can be read in numerous ways, and it's easy to interpret a joke in a manner not intended by the joke-teller. This type of comedy requires a disabled teller, and an audience that understands the teller's perspective and "gets" the joke. As Corker suggests, "Disabled people's comic narratives do not travel well in the non-disabled world when disembodied from this sense of solidarity or when decontextualized" (81). In other words, the humor of a comic story about disability could be read in multiple ways depending on the perspective of the audience member in question. Interpreting crip humor relies on specific contexts: who is telling the joke, who is laughing, why they are laughing, and what those individuals understand about disability. Different people may laugh at the same story for a myriad of reasons, so some people may laugh *with* the disabled person, while others laugh *at* the disabled person. For this reason, crip humor has the potential to simultaneously break and reinforce stereotypes.

This type of comic storytelling may also reveal the ways that disability is not a fact, but a social construction based on expectations of what bodies should be able to do in a particular society. As Kleege notes, "Some days, and in some contexts, my blindness is at the forefront of my consciousness. Other days it is not" (1999, 4). She reflects that many of her regular tasks are not disrupted by her visual impairment, yet many people are afraid of blindness, since it would threaten their ability to drive and be independent. In an environment where driving a car is not an issue, however, a visual impairment might be far less disabling (29–30). Similarly, wheelchair users who spend their days working in an office at a desk may not feel "disabled" until they need to take an inconvenient route around the building to access an elevator.

At the same time, as Clare points out, we must delineate between disability as a social construction and the physical limitations and pain that some people with disabilities experience. Yet Clare also suggests that it can be difficult to separate these two categories. Some limits may be posed by society and others by disability, yet both are equally vexing (1999, 4–7). Joking about disability through narrative can be one way to relieve some of the tension of this frustration, as well as reveal the ways people negotiate disabling environments.

NARRATIVE AND POSITIONING THE SELF

I focus my analysis on the ways the disabled individuals I interviewed use humor to present themselves within their stories. To do this I use a model of narrative discourse suggested by scholar Michael Bamberg, who emphasizes the idea of "positioning" when telling personal stories:

> "Being positioned" and "positioning oneself" are two metaphoric constructs of two very different agent-world relationships: the former with a world-to-agent direction of fit, the latter with an agent-to-world direction of fit. One way to overcome this rift is to argue that both operate concurrently in a kind of dialectic as subjects engage in narratives-in-interaction and make sense of self and others in their stories. (2005, 224)

"Being positioned" relates to how people in a society regard an individual as fitting into the world. For example, can individuals move freely in their surroundings, or do they have difficulty negotiating the physical space? Do they blend in to the social atmosphere, or do they stick out in the crowd? "Positioning oneself" relates to how individuals regard themselves as fitting into the world and whether they perceive their environment as allowing or preventing them from making such a fit possible. It follows that stories by disabled tellers can reveal how the social and physical world permits or bars disabled individuals from finding a good "fit."

Bamberg also explains that when individuals tell stories, "speakers work up a position as complicit with and/or countering dominant discourses (master narratives). It is at this juncture that we come full circle by showing how subjects position themselves in relation to discourses by which they are positioned" (2005, 225). This is an important facet to consider when examining stories about disability since dominant cultural narratives told about disabled people may position disabled individuals as helpless, tragic, bitter, and/or lacking agency (Kafer 2013, 2; Healey 2017, 92–97; Clare 2017, 7–8). These narratives suggest that disabled people are socially as well as physically disabled and unable to function in dominant society. Comic narratives by disabled people often work against these ideas of social and physical disability, suggesting ways that disabled people are "able" and not hindered by disability, and ways that TAB individuals may be physically or socially "disabled" in certain situations. In telling their stories and employing humor, disabled people can position themselves on their own terms, portray themselves as having independence and agency, potentially subvert dominant ableist ideologies, and give multiple meanings to the concept of disability.

THE STORIES

I interviewed seven disabled people over the phone, on Skype, in person, and in one extended email conversation. My collaborators include two people with visual impairments, one with a hearing impairment, three who use wheelchairs, and one who uses a prosthetic foot. These individuals range in age from early twenties to midforties, including two women and five men. One of my collaborators is a Black American, one is a white Canadian, one is Egyptian, and four are white Americans. All have congenital disabilities, are members of various disability communities, and are comfortable discussing issues surrounding disability. They include people who play adaptive sports, ones who work with other disabled people as part of their profession, and ones who contribute to comic blogs about disability and often post funny stories online. Since not all disabled individuals consider disability to be a joking matter, it was important for me to find collaborators who were willing to discuss this potentially sensitive subject, enjoy telling comic narratives, and could reflect on times when such stories were and were not appropriate for a particular audience.

I examine these stories according to the ways in which the joking behavior shapes the meaning of disability in that particular context and helps the teller mediate discussions with TAB individuals. Across these categories, my collaborators generally position themselves as having control of the situation, even if that means the ability to find a story comically absurd as opposed to frustrating. These stories reveal that the world is rarely a good "fit" for people with disabilities, but that predicament is often created by ableist cultural constraints and disabling environments rather than the "disabled" body itself. In these stories, disability takes on multiple and varied meanings as diverse as the tellers and situations themselves, revealing the mutability of disability identities and humor.

Stories and Sitpoint Theory

Comic stories can reveal how disabled individuals interpret their environment and interactions with others differently than a TAB person would in the same situation. Garland-Thomson coined the term "sitpoint theory" to refer to the insights and knowledge people with disabilities gain from having their particular form of embodiment (2017, 373). Many of the stories my collaborators tell are examples of sitpoint theory, showing how disabled people recognize their unique ways of knowing, defining, and making meaning of their world.

Thomas is a college professor who has been hearing-impaired since childhood. For several years he integrated jokes about his disability into a stand-up comedy routine. Thomas reads lips and uses a hearing aid, but he must often explain to TABs why he speaks the way he does. He writes, "My favorite thing to say over and over: People ask me *a lot* where I'm from. 'You have an accent!' they say. 'Oh, I'm from Wisconsin,' I say. 'No,' they say, 'I mean what country are you originally from?' So I say I'm from Deafmark."

The TAB person asking the question becomes the object or butt of the joke since they do not believe Thomas is from the United States. This question also reveals an assumption on the part of TABs that people who don't have a visible disability must be able-bodied. Ironically, when Thomas says he is from "Deafmark," he confirms that he is from a "different place" in terms of his means of communication and how disability has shifted the ways he interprets the world. As Albrecht notes, this kind of crip humor has a social function that "allows us to understand better the lives and trajectories of disabled people; to understand what it is like to span two worlds and cultures. Disjunctions between these two worlds are the basis of humor" (1999, 72). Thomas finds comedy in this separation and maintains control of the situation by answering the question in a teasing way, cuing the questioner to his hearing impairment. He also corrects the misinterpretation that he must be from "somewhere else," yet his creation of the fictitious country of Deafmark both affirms and denies the attempt of TABs to "other" him by situating him as a foreigner. He uses the joke to define his disability as difference, but not the same difference the listener first perceived. Additionally, as Freud noted, jokes can often hide a conscious or unconscious anger on the part of the teller (1960, 122). In this instance, the joke might suggest to the listener, "If you won't believe I'm an American, I'm going to have a little fun with you."

Thomas used this story in his stand-up routine, and he still uses it to combat awkwardness when communicating with hearing people. He writes, "For example, if a student mumbles in class and I have to ask that student to repeat once or twice, I might tell the 'Deafmark' joke to ease the student out of a situation in which he or she might feel embarrassed in front of a group." He constructs his disability as something that might stop dialogue for a moment, but it's nothing to be ashamed about since the conversation can continue after a laugh. As Shakespeare writes, these interactions between disabled and TAB individuals can be muddled by "anxiety and tension," which "prevents communication progressing or rapport developing. Disabled people, if they are to enter the everyday world of social engagement, must develop skills of interactional management in order to put the other at their ease" (1999, 49). While Thomas used comic stories to interact with comedy club audiences that had limited experience with hearing-impaired individuals, he still relies on such stories "occasionally in a situation that requires humor. . . . Usually something instigates me needing to tell such a story." Comedy is also a way for Thomas to suggest that he's in a predominantly hearing world and that this might create a few issues, but he knows how to navigate those spaces with a joke. Disability in this instance becomes an occasion for creativity and flexibility as Thomas explains his form of embodiment.

This story would likely draw sympathetic laughter from the audience, identifying with the teller in his exasperation at not being believed, and at the questioner who demands an answer that fits their presuppositions. In the "Deafmark" story, Thomas both acknowledges his disability and suggests that it is not important since he is accustomed to this mode of interaction and knows how to negotiate misunderstandings. In laughing, the listener may also convey an understanding that while Thomas comes from a different "place" in terms of how he experiences the world, this is not a factor that should stop conversation.

Eric tells a similar story that demonstrates how disability can provide a unique sitpoint. An amputee and wheelchair user, Eric explains that when he was working as an intern in a congressional office, he had to "train" other members of the staff to understand that it was acceptable to joke about disability. He enjoyed making "legless jokes" at work but notes that he was accustomed to his TAB audience back home, one that accepted his humor and found it funny. In contrast, other congressional staffers weren't used to those kinds of jokes and often gave him odd looks. Eric explains, "In the office it was situational things. They would step on my foot and be like, 'Oh I'm really sorry,' and I would be like, 'It's okay, I can't feel it.' And they would pause and say, 'Oh, yeah, that's right.' Then it would be funny." In this instance, the TAB individual is the butt of the joke since they assume they have hurt Eric and apologize unnecessarily. Since they forget that he has no feet, the apology becomes a comic "expenditure" of action "that is too large" (Freud 1960, 235).

In this story, Eric positions himself as being in control of the situation through giving others permission to laugh at disability and defining it as no big deal. To the contrary, he is intentionally creating humor since he wants to joke about disability in a congressional office, a location he finds comically absurd. For him, disability is something that must be joked about so that TABs understand the many ways in which it doesn't matter to him. In essence, he is encouraging the listeners to shift their definition of disability to include something that can be amusing and connote bodily flexibility. Invoking disability becomes an occasion to reconfigure its meaning and find delight in the unexpected body. This story also suggests the power disabled individuals have in turning a potentially tragic situation into something humorous. The person who stepped on his foot is reminded that Eric does not have legs below his knees, yet he wants them to laugh rather than to mourn the situation, and maybe they *can* laugh when they see the huge grin on his face. Some of the laughter this story draws from listeners may come from Eric's performance, including his obvious glee at recalling someone's horror at stepping on his foot. It is the opposite reaction that TABs might expect, and thus has the potential to create a shift in the listener's thinking about disability. More often than not, Eric has found humor in being an amputee because it plays with other's expectations about the necessity of limbs. The joke makes space for a moment of reflection that may sensitize TABs to the comedy of crip humor and potentially allow them to perceive disability as merely another form of embodiment that Eric considers to be mundane.

In this story Eric also reveals the socially constructed nature of disability since he reflects on how he was accustomed to a community in which his disability was "normal" and not considered tragic; then moved to a new social context in which that was not the case. Eric had not often told this story at the time of our interview since it had happened recently, but he explains that the kinds of stories he tells are dependent on audience, since "people in disabled communities are used to this kind of humor, [but] I'll be careful with certain individuals who aren't accustomed to it." While he may take different approaches to disability and humor depending on context, in this story, he encouraged his co-staffers to reconsider their notions of disability and comedy and to revise some of their previous beliefs. Since they were working with him for the entire summer, this aspect of his personality was something Eric wanted his coworkers to adjust to accordingly.

Amanda tells a third story that reveals the value of sitpoint theory to interpreting disability humor. She's a college student whose visual impairment is not always apparent when she meets new people, and she often finds those misunderstandings to be comic. One kind of interaction that makes her laugh is when sighted people want to shake her hand, and patiently hold out their hand without realizing she cannot see it. As Amanda explains, "What

I learned when I met my ex [boyfriend who is blind] is that you should tell a blind person 'Hand out' when you want to shake their hand. Somebody will tell me somebody else has their hand out [for a shake], and I'm like, 'Oh. Oops.'"

In this story, the disabled individual and TAB individual both become the butt of the joke because of their misunderstanding. The narrative reveals two different sets of assumptions about how the world works, yet neither individual realizes the disconnect. As Amanda explains, there is a difference in perception between the visually impaired and TAB worlds since the former often relies on auditory cues, while the latter assumes that everyone uses visual cues. The TAB person is the butt of the joke since they do not realize they need to give Amanda an auditory cue. At the same time, Amanda could be perceived as the butt of the joke since she doesn't realize that she needs to let the TAB individual know about her disability.

Amanda has used this story as a teaching tool and "told the story to sighted people to illustrate the point of why they should hold out their hand. Most of them tell me that they never thought about it before I brought it up." She adds that this technique is probably familiar to many blind people since "the 'hand out' method is something that the NFB [National Federation for the Blind] centers use." This story is an example of disabled people not finding a "fit" in the TAB world, yet Amanda suggests this breach in communication is not a tragedy. She depicts herself as having control of the situation since she can shrug off potential embarrassment. The result is not the fault of either party, but a laughable and ironic moment since information is being assumed but not conveyed. Amanda also defines her disability to involve creativity, flexibility, and a learning process among people with different forms of embodiment, a physical and cultural becoming. This is not a custom she knew but one she was taught, and the comic tale is a means of sharing that knowledge.

Her story does not put fault on either party but suggests a mutual responsibility, yet the resulting laughter may be difficult to interpret. Some audience members might laugh at the "poor blind person" who didn't see the extended hand, yet others would laugh with Amanda at the mutual gaff. The nature of the laughter might depend on the relationship audience members have with the teller, but could also depend on their response to her delivery. Amanda finds the joke quite funny, so it is hard not to laugh with her as she explains this aspect of blind culture. We cannot discount that her telling could shift the attitudes of some listeners to see the comedy of the situation in Amanda's favor. In this way she also shows how her disability has granted her a form of insider knowledge about communication that not everyone may possess. In those situations, other people may be disabled from communicating with her because they don't understand the cues she requires, but she realizes the need for adaptability since bodies work in different ways. Her story also suggests that while using humor may be a helpful tactic to aid communication between disabled and TAB individuals, when this connection is lacking, the result can be quite funny.

FINDING DISABILITY COMIC

Another way that disabled people use comic stories to mediate interactions is through finding comedy in their own actions, taking potentially "tragic" situations and reframing them in a humorous way. Nathan tells one such story. He's a college graduate in his midtwenties who has been blind since birth and is an assistive technology specialist. When he was in eighth grade, playing basketball with friends, he told one of them to tap the net with his cane so he could try to make a basket. Nathan explains, "I threw the ball, and it bounced on the rim and hit my cane and broke it. We were all laughing."

Nathan does not portray himself as embarrassed by the missed shot or broken cane, but he frames the story as a moment of slapstick humor with his friends. The story demonstrates an occasion to share crip humor—his friends knew he would not mind if they laughed—no one needed special "permission," and Nathan allowed himself be the butt of the joke. Though he is in a sense further "disabled" when his cane breaks, he also constructs himself as "abled" since he has the agency to make adaptations to play basketball. The story focuses on that engagement with his TAB friends, as they share the same kind of laughter. Further, Nathan's reaction to this incident suggests that he won't be stopped from being on the court. Similar to Eric, he defines his disability as an opportunity for play, not something that will dissuade him from any activity. Adaptation is experimentation, and not every experiment will prove successful, but that is an occasion to have a good laugh and try something else. The reality of his disability means he's not going out for the NBA, but the point is to have fun, be playful, and creatively find ways to engage in adaptive sports, even if the result is comic.

Nathan tells this story to TAB and disabled friends, family members, and others, and says he has joked about his disability for years. He suggests, "If you can't poke fun at your own disability then you're not very comfortable with yourself. I did it when I was a kid. I would make jokes about not having seen something in years, and people would crack up." Nathan has found emancipatory potential in making himself the butt of the joke, a means to create a shift in the thinking of his listeners as they laugh with Nathan at the shot that was perfectly aimed to break his cane. Reid, Stoughton, and Smith comment on this function of comic stories, writing that disabled individuals can "use self-deprecatory humor positively to dissolve and recreate disability. By shifting from victim to perpetrator, they undermine the power of people who laugh at them. They emerge as capable people who find life's predicaments amusing" (2006, 635). Nathan doesn't feel like the butt of the joke, but a person with the ability to create humor. While this notion may seem counterintuitive, positioning themselves as an object of laughter gives disabled individuals the ability to suggest that these mishaps are funny and not a crisis.

At the same time, while Nathan is very comfortable joking about his disability, we can't assume this is the case for all disabled people. That idea was expressed to me several times by my collaborators since many people acquire disabilities during their lifetimes due to various causes. Individuals must *learn* how to joke about their disabilities and feel comfortable doing so. Further, we must consider that some listeners would find the story to be tragic as opposed to comic since they might focus on Nathan's broken cane and inability to make a basket. This joke could potentially support ableist ideologies, if the listener laughed because of imagining Nathan as a bumbling Mr. Magoo who barely avoids disaster. Told by another individual to a different audience, the same story might be a cause for laughter *at* rather than *with* disabled people, implying that Nathan's idea that he could play basketball without seeing the basket is absurd. At the same time, this stereotype is countered by Nathan's shrug since he is still going to engage in sports. He suggests he's been empowered by his disability to not take himself too seriously and instead find occasions for laughter and connection with others. Nathan shows that bodies and disabilities do not always have to be the subject of serious conversation. Yet as Corker suggests, the inscription by Nathan as a disabled teller is what makes the story crip humor.

Along similar lines, Eric tells a story that reveals the potential of disability to create absurdly comic situations that can reframe the notion of disability. He explains that when he was younger, he often joked with family members about the possibility that he might forget his prosthetic legs somewhere. "It's just the probability of you having to say that [you forgot your legs] is so small," Eric says, "and it's even funnier when you say 'Oh shoot, yeah, I did. I forgot my feet.'" On one occasion when he was in middle school, Eric forgot to take his prosthetic legs home following a wrestling match. He says, "My principal had to call my mom and say, 'We usually don't do this, but we think these are your son's feet, and we don't want to put them in the lost and found box.' My mom said, 'Eric, did you forget something?' and I said 'No, I don't think so,' and my mom said, 'Look down.' And I said 'Crap, I forgot my feet at school.' "

In this story, Eric positions himself as the absentminded butt of the joke, but he retains control of the situation through depicting it as a comic event that challenges normalizing perceptions of the body. While a middle-school student may be more likely to forget a hat or book, Eric suggests that leaving his feet at school was an easy mistake and that his feet were no more or less important than any other item. The story can be read as containing "normalizing" elements since it is a tale of an adolescent kid being forgetful. At the same time, the narrative is transgressive, allowing Eric to reveal the socially constructed nature of disability and questioning the notion that feet are necessary. In this case, he shows how his disability has allowed him to play with the idea of the "normal" body and demonstrate how he could get along fine for hours at home without realizing he'd left a part of himself behind. Disability becomes a way of thinking about bodily flexibility and adaptability.

Eric explains that he tells this story often, both to TAB and disabled audiences, when he needs a funny story to tell, or in social situations when someone else has forgotten something. He notes, "There is nothing that isn't funny about that [story]." At the same time, this story has the potential to create discomfort with some TAB listeners since the prospect of leglessness is brought to the fore. Whether laughter at this story could suggest a change in the listener's thinking about disability might depend on their acceptance of the fact that Eric went home without his legs, then proceeded to go about his evening unimpeded by their absence. Eric's ability to be without feet for several hours points not only to disability as a social construction, but could allow the listener to chuckle at the idea that legs might not be as crucial as they first assumed.

Eric also realizes the tension that TAB listeners might feel at hearing such a joke, and he adjusts his joking behavior according to his audience. He reflects that he is careful not to focus too much on stories and jokes that relate to disability, explaining, "Certain people exclusively use disabled humor, to the point [that it becomes] uncomfortable." Drew, another wheelchair user, agrees with this sentiment, suggesting that when disabled people only use crip humor, their sense of the comic may seem too one-note. He explains, "You try to balance yourself between disabled humor and other outlets of humor. You don't want to be known as the guy who just tells disabled jokes." While both of them enjoy crip humor, their disability is only one facet of their personality, and they realize that needs to be reflected in their storytelling.

In telling these tales, they define their disabilities as an important part of who they are and how they experience the world, yet not the entirety of their being.

ARGUING FOR ABILITY

Another function of comic storytelling among disabled people is to dispel ableist beliefs regarding the limited capabilities of disabled individuals. Drew tells a story about how he often has to confront those misconceptions since he enjoys heavy metal music and mosh pits. These social situations often involve negotiation with other concert attendees, as he explains: "It's always weird being in a wheelchair trying to assert yourself in a mosh pit. People ask me if I want to go to the front near the stage." When he explains that he's waiting for the pit, they say, "'You're going to mosh? Are you sure? It can get pretty rough.' I say it can't get too rough; this is what I live for." While it takes some effort on his part to make the case for moshing in a wheelchair, the results have paid off in terms of developing a level of understanding with some TAB concertgoers. Drew explains that at one concert, a woman came up to him and asked if he wanted to go to the front. He said no, he was going to mosh. "During the next song she came over and just clocked me in the face. I was like, please marry me."

While this story could be read as Drew making himself the butt of the joke, since not many people may understand why someone would want to get punched in the face, it can also be read as mocking a society that considers him too "delicate" for certain environments. The narrative suggests a poor world-to-agent fit because of the social construction of disability that assumes people in wheelchairs should not be in mosh pits. Yet Drew positions himself as someone with agency who makes the case that he belongs in the mosh pit. In this instance, his spina bifida won't slow him down so much as other people who worry about him being in the pit. His description of mosh-pit culture reveals an ableist belief structure since he is questioned as to whether he belongs there, thinly veiling the assumption that he is frail. The comic element in the story occurs when he finds understanding with a TAB person who knows he wants to be treated like everyone else. Getting punched in the face becomes an absurd occasion for celebration, since in that otherwise violent act he is being embraced by another member of the metal community. Drew suggests that after he's acknowledged his disability, he wants to be treated like anyone else at the concert. He's there for the same reason—getting beat up while he beats up other people—yet his narrative reveals the frustration he experiences at the fact that disability is an overriding factor in how people interpret his body.

Drew often tells this story to TAB and disabled friends when trying to explain "the state of moshing . . . why I feel the need to get hit in the face at concerts . . . usually it's to describe what a mosh pit is and why it's necessary for my mental health." He also tells the story "to other metalheads who are usually able-bodied" when sharing mosh-pit stories, since "not many other disabled people go into mosh pits." He jokes about his disability with his TAB friends, so they will "know how to deal with it. But you have to bring it up enough so they know that you are a human being and you want to be treated as a human being." Drew realizes that other people won't be able to disregard his disability, so he must explain how to behave around him, the times when disability matters and the times when it doesn't, and how others don't have to treat him like a delicate object. While laughter at this joke could connote a shift in thinking about disability—guys who use wheelchairs can also be moshing metalheads—it is important to note that Drew chooses his audiences carefully. He includes individuals who he assumes will sympathize with his perspective, and those to whom he wants to explain himself, since not all his friends understand his love of mosh pits. While Drew's aim is to create a shift in the minds of listeners, either related to his enjoyment of violent environments or his disability, his careful cultivation of audience suggests his awareness of how easily a joke could become a laughing *at* as opposed to a laughing *with*. At the same time, telling these kinds of stories is a way for Drew to assert his personhood and independence and rid others of the assumptions they make about his body.

Nathan tells another story that reveals how people with disabilities are often more capable than may be perceived by TABs. He explains that he started advocating for himself when he was in junior high since he knew he had to speak up for his abilities. As a college student, he was taken aback when he went to his girlfriend's house for dinner and was not given a knife to cut his meat. When he asked her mother for a knife, she asked why he wanted one. He explained that he wanted to cut his meat, and she said, "What? You'll cut yourself!" Nathan explains, "I didn't know what to say, I sat there like, 'Seriously?' [He laughs.] I was twenty-one at the time, and I know how to cut my own meat. Some blind people don't, but I needed a knife to cut my food." This is a joke he has shared with disabled and TAB friends, and "usually the sighted people are in disbelief and the blind people are laughing about it," but everyone asks why he wasn't given his own knife.

In this comic tale Nathan is able to show listeners his perspective and allow them to read the situation as absurd. As Freud notes, this kind of humor allows the joke-teller to "exploit something ridiculous" that could not be revealed without "[bringing] in a joke to their help, and this guarantees them a reception with the hearer which they would never have found in a non-joking form, in spite of the truth they may contain" (1960, 122–23). Nathan positions himself as someone who can confidently negotiate the world and its sharp edges despite his lack of visual cues. TAB individuals who lack the same faith in people with disabilities become the butt of the joke, as his audience laughs at how easily he could be underestimated. Similar to his basketball story, without the "inscription" of the joke by a disabled teller, the story could be read in a different manner, with Nathan being considered the "absurd" butt since he wants to cut his meat but cannot see it. Again, while certain listeners might direct laughter at Nathan, he tends to curate his audiences and reserve the tale for people who will laugh with him. While their perceptions on disability might shift, this change may not be due to their surprise at his abilities, but with his girlfriend's mother's lack of understanding. Some audience members' laughter may connote a change in perspective after being sensitized to this ableist notion. As Reid, Stoughton, and Smith observe, one of the functions of crip humor is to focus on problems that arise not from the body, but from "disabling" and restrictive environments (2006, 639–40). Nathan admits that his narrative also points to the variability within disability communities since not all blind people have the same skill level and would have requested a knife. He acknowledges that disability can make it necessary for individuals to develop certain adaptations, but at the same time, his tale suggests that we cannot make assumptions about the abilities or limitations of any individual.

DECONSTRUCTING THE ABLE-BODIED/ DISABLED DICHOTOMY

Another function of crip humor is to twist the notion of "disability" through jokes that suggest how TAB individuals can be socially or physically "disabled" in certain environments. Thomas tells one such story. Because he was performing in comedy clubs to a hearing audience, he had to adapt his material and use humor to negotiate with TAB hecklers:

> About 75% of my routine was based on my hearing impairment. This was mainly because my accent comes from my hearing impairment, and also because I sometimes had to deal with hecklers I couldn't understand. There was always somebody who thought it would be

funny to shout out something crude knowing I wouldn't catch it, but I'd hear that something was said, and say, "Wow—that's an attention span to be proud of. Hey, you, wherever you are, I just told you, I'm deaf. Dumbass."

Through his use of a cutting remark, Thomas positions himself as socially able, while the TAB heckler becomes the butt of the joke since they have revealed a deficiency and suggested they are "disabled" because they didn't hear Thomas's comment regarding deafness. In this comic reversal, Thomas situates himself as more "able" than the heckler and reshapes an intolerant world into one in which he can emerge as the dominant figure, since the problem with understanding was not his fault. In this narrative, the disabled person is portrayed as the one who knows how to communicate, while the TAB person is lacking in those skills. Laughter at this joke could indicate a shift in audience members' thinking, as Thomas fluidly negotiates a potentially embarrassing moment and maintains control. Some audience members might laugh at the "poor guy" who can't hear what the heckler is saying, but Thomas demonstrates himself to be socially able by preparing himself for that occasion. In displaying this combination of forethought and wit, it is difficult not to laugh with Thomas as he bests his detractor and wins the audience to his side. He shows how his disability has helped him to develop cunning and creativity when combating ableism and allowed him to get the best of detractors. This is also a space in which Thomas can potentially find sympathy with audience members who have been paying attention to his routine. These listeners may side with him as socially able, as opposed to siding with the annoying heckler.

Eric tells a similar story about reframing his disability in terms of ability when joking with his family. He explains that since he was a skinny person and had no legs below the knee, he'd often get the middle seat when they traveled on airplanes. Eric says, "Even though I was an amputee I had abilities in that I never needed leg room. I would be comfortable no matter where I was." In this reversal he teased his TAB family members, making them the butt of the joke by showing how they were disabled on cramped airplanes while he was comfortable. His disability made him more adaptable to the smaller spaces, allowing him to redefine disability as increasing his versatility. Eric says that this is a story that he tells often, both to TAB and disabled friends, "because everyone has their frustrations with flights, and I don't have those same frustrations. It's humorous to everyone." In part, the meaning that Eric makes of his disability is that it can be a highly amusing occasion for gloating.

This story may also reflect a measure of glee at the opportunity to make fun of TAB passengers on an airplane, where people without legs have an advantage. Not only does the narrative make it clear that disability is determined by environment, but it does so through demonstrating that airplanes are a space in which Eric can literally "fit." His story reflects Shakespeare's sentiment that "reversal of expectation is always richly comedic, and there is no greater reversal than treating what is commonly represented as a tragedy as if it is a farce" (1999, 51). Laughter at this joke would seem to indicate a shift in thinking about disability, as listeners imagine how lovely it would be to have legroom rendered a moot point. Eric shows how he can turn ableist logic on its head, as his disability becomes a form of adaptability and legs are a cumbersome accessory when traveling.

DISABLED PEOPLE AS VICTIMS OF SOCIAL PERCEPTIONS

As Gilbert notes, comics who belong to marginalized groups often critique dominant society by portraying themselves as "victims" in their humor (2004, 137). This technique is different than a comic making themselves the butt of the joke since these jokes mock societal standards and reveal the concept of the "normal" to be a social construction, framing the comic as a victim of senseless standards (Gilbert 137). This type of humor might seem dark to those outside the in-group, yet as Amy suggests, often this method of joking is used to challenge dominant society's notions of disability. She is an amputee who has worn a prosthetic foot since childhood, and she says, "People think disability is such a tragedy, that your life will never be the same again. That's so ridiculous it's laughable. You bring in the humor to show people you are not an object of pity."

As an example, she explains that amputees are "very casual" about losing limbs and that they joke to confront common disability stigmas. One of Amy's favorite stories is about a practical joke she and her roommate played on Halloween. They opened their door a little bit and stuck one of her prosthetic feet outside "to see what people would do." TAB individuals who would be shocked at the sight are the butt of the joke since they cannot imagine anything more horrific than a bodyless foot, though the real object of their terror is the idea of a disabled footless body. Amy positions herself and her roommate as having the agency to be tricksters and play with the normative expectations of TABs. Her story mocks the perception of disabled people as helpless while revealing that they are often the victims of that misconception.

Similar to Eric's narrative, this joke challenges the definition of a "normal" body and suggests the potential for adaptation and a casual, comic attitude toward disability. Laughter at this story also implies a rethinking of disability on the part of listeners, indicating their appreciation for Amy's practical joke. This is not a story of happenstance but deliberate joking behavior, potentially sensitizing the audience to ways that individuals can creatively play with disability. Here Amy demonstrates how she defines disability as a space for questioning bodily norms, sometimes intentionally, through using the specter of disability to shock others. Amy explains that one of her favorite sayings about disability is "There are no normal people, just people who haven't found their disability yet." While people she tells this idea to may smile at first, she says, "Then there's this awkward silence." The TABs realize that they are not immune to becoming disabled, yet the point of this joke is that disability is part of being human. In this comment, Amy shows that while the prospect of disability can seem dramatic and frightening, in practice, it can be mundane and an occasion for comedy.

Joshua tells another story that reveals how disabled individuals are often the victims of social constructions. He's a wheelchair user with a master's degree who notes that sometimes his joking responses to questions are taken seriously by TABs. Often their reactions reveal stereotypes regarding people with disabilities. He explains that some TABs ask "questions like 'How do you take exams?' I say . . . they just give me the degree, I don't have to take exams. That one people believe because people don't have high expectations of people with disabilities . . . other times they say annoying things, like 'You're up and about, we think you're a hero for going to school.' I say, 'No, I'm trying to live my life.'" In this narrative, those who believe that Joshua was given a degree because he is disabled become the butt of the joke for failing to acknowledge his intelligence. Joshua portrays himself as a victim of the assumption that living with a disability takes great courage, an idea that falls into what Clare calls a "supercrip" stereotype. These stories "focus on disabled people 'overcoming' our disabilities. They reinforce the superiority of the nondisabled body and mind. They turn individual disabled people, who are simply living their lives, into symbols of inspiration" (1999, 2). In relating this narrative, Joshua counters the supercrip image by positioning himself as someone who had the agency to pursue an advanced college degree, making it clear that he was not merely handed his diploma. He recognizes that disabled people are more than capable of great achievements, yet at the same time some TABs will doubt he did the work to achieve this goal. Disability doesn't detract from his ability to succeed, but rather his ability to be given credit for his success. At the same time, he is in control of the narrative through positioning himself as a trickster and playing with the low expectations TABs have of disabled people. Joshua portrays himself as educated and hardworking, yet he also suggests that disabled people do not "fit" into the world because they are not recognized for their intelligence, and others assume they need special treatment.

Joshua explains that he tells this and similar stories to friends who use wheelchairs and friends who are TABs. He says, "Sometimes people would talk about the weirdest things that ever happened to them, and that would be me chiming in with my stories to top them off." This may be a form of joking that is not necessarily meant to shift opinions, but to solidify group cohesion with a round of we've-all-been-there chuckles. At the same time, those who are familiar with Joshua's intelligence may laugh in disbelief, indicating a sensitization toward ableist assumptions regarding disability. Not everyone in the audience may have realized he has to put up with this kind of tooth-gritting frustration at those who doubt his capabilities. Joshua also displays a keen sense of audience awareness during these storytelling events since he relates the tale to friends and acquaintances who he thinks will understand the absurdity of the question and his response. He recognizes that such in-group humor cannot be shared with everyone and adjusts his joking practice accordingly: "I try not to do it around people that have a lot of empathy or supervisors that really cannot laugh at the joke, because someone who supervises you, they're not allowed to laugh as it gets tricky that way."

Along these lines, Shakespeare comments that crip jokes can be easy to misread, observing that "context, interpretation, and meaning are important, because this sort of humour treads a dangerous line between challenging and reinforcing stereotype. . . . There is no simple answer as to which jokes are offensive, and which jokes are liberatory, because it depends on nuance and intention" (1999, 52). Joshua's response could even hit a sour note among some disabled individuals, who might miss the humor and interpret his comedy as implying disabled people expect special benefits.

SOCIAL CORRECTIVES AND DEFENSE MECHANISMS

Crip humor can also be a transgressive means to assert power by poking fun at TABs and intentionally making them uncomfortable or acting as a form of social corrective against inappropriate behavior around disabled people (MacPherson 2008, 1086; Reid, Stoughton, and Smith 2006, 635). Another story told by Joshua serves this function, revealing the cultural assumption that disabled people do not or cannot have a sex life (Siebers

2008, 138). Along these lines, Joshua explains that sometimes he is asked personal questions such as "How do you have sex?" which might imply that the asker assumes he cannot have sex or that he has sex in a manner that would be considered socially deviant.

Joshua explains that he doesn't shy away from the question but answers in a forthright and comic manner: "I'd say, 'I have the girl sit on a chair, then I back up and go forward as fast as I can.' One time I didn't say anything I just did this" [he moves his chair back and then forward again]. While his response may strike some as humorous and absurd, Joshua explains that he receives varied reactions, and that "some people do believe it." In this story, social perceptions about disability and sexuality become the butt of the joke as Joshua pokes fun at TABs who may believe that disabled people are sexually disempowered. He also mocks TABs who feel it is their "right" to ask people with disabilities such personal questions, which they would most likely not pose to individuals without visible disabilities. Somehow disability seems to mark people as subject to interrogation about their sex lives, yet Joshua shows how those assumptions can be used to make fun of TABs bold enough to pose such queries. He positions himself as a teasing trickster, joking about the TABs who assume disabled people are "innocent" and either wouldn't have sex or would never lie about such matters.

Through incorporating his wheelchair into the joking response, Joshua positions himself as someone with sexual agency who is not a passive recipient but fits the stereotypical masculine role as the instigator of sexual activity. But Joshua adds that even in joking, his responses often have another function: to open a dialogue about disability. He reflects, "Sometimes I use it for my benefit, as educational. . . . I'm not too shy to talk about myself." On occasion, he follows this joke with an explanation of his sexual activity, allowing humor to open a space for more serious discussions. This is a joke that could be met with laughter, either raucous or uneasy, at Joshua's forthright response and performance. While some people might blush and chuckle out of embarrassment, others might have their perspective shifted if they did not expect him to exhibit sexual behavior or if they assumed he would skirt the question. Yet as Joshua notes, laughter can be a way for the genuinely curious to become engaged in a longer discussion about disability and sexuality and change their understandings. In this case he also suggests how easily disability and sexuality can be misunderstood, so through making a joke, he finds occasions for a teaching moment after the pantomime.

This narrative might offend some disabled individuals if Joshua did not correct the misinterpretations of his listeners, yet he makes it clear that joking can be a segue to sensitization, and he feels a responsibility to explain himself to audience members who have misconceptions regarding disability.

Joshua finds another kind of instructional moment in the questions that children ask about his disability, explaining:

> I always get asked by kids, "What happened to you? Are you sick?" And I always reply, "Oh I just didn't listen to my mom and that's how I became this way." One time I said I was lazy and I just stayed inside all day and so that's how I got this way. And the parents get really surprised, they can't believe I just said that, because they think it's a self-deprecating joke, but I try to put a positive spin on it by teaching the kids something.

While the children's parents realize this is a kind of joking behavior, the kids aren't sure how to respond. Joshua explains, "They look at their mom and say, 'Mommy, is that right?' and then they point at me, and then the parents get really confused and flustered because they don't know what to do." Joshua positions himself as having control of the situation by answering this question in a way that counters the parents' expectation of his response. While adults may often tease children when answering their questions, parents do not expect such teasing to happen in response to the "serious" matter of disability. Situating himself as a joker with the agency to direct the situation as he sees fit, Joshua suggests he is telling children to mind their parents.

Yet the children's questions are provocative since they confront Joshua's disability head-on, something their parents would likely prefer to ignore. Ironically, kids may reflect the curiosity many people have about disabled individuals and pose questions their parents could also be contemplating but will not ask since such inquiries would be impolite. Joshua plays with the cultural imperative mentioned by Couser for disabled people to "explain" their bodies, teasing children and reassuring them they will be "safe" if they obey their parents and play outside. This story may elicit an uneasy laughter from parents who do not expect disability to be cast in this manner. Some may feel compelled to further educate their children about body variability and explain that there are reasons someone may need to use a wheelchair other than being "lazy." Thus, Joshua's story also suggests ways that he doesn't "fit" into the world since he knows his body is always being interrogated by those around him, whether or not they're asking the questions aloud.

Some disabled individuals may disapprove of this kind of joking around children since Joshua is playing into the stereotype that disabled people are somehow to blame for their disabilities. As Garland-Thomson notes, people with disabilities use different tactics when educating children about disability, and some consider it their duty to respond truthfully to children's questions and teach them about bodily difference (2009, 89). Yet others may argue that Joshua's response has the potential to begin a discussion between children and parents about disability that could continue beyond that encounter. Joshua realizes that disability isn't something many parents want to discuss with their kids, so he starts the dialogue for them, assuming it's better than ignoring issues surrounding body variability.

Amy tells another story related to "educating" TABs, yet it is one that reveals the potential of crip humor to be used as a defense mechanism against prying. She explains that some people think that if you have a disability, "they deserve to know more about you," so she is often asked how she lost her foot. When she feels that someone is being too dramatic about the matter, Amy tells them, "Well, I was swimming, and there was this shark. . . . Typically, this is a third-date story. I draw it out until I can't help laughing." She makes her date the butt of this joke for assuming that she lost her foot due to a tragic accident, positioning him as too willing to believe the drama of the situation. Amy emphasizes that TAB individuals who ask those questions want to confirm that they could prevent such a loss by being careful or proactive. She positions herself as a victim of the dominant cultural perception that she must have experienced an epic tragedy, yet she is in control of the situation through playing with the expectations of her TAB date. In this case, she defines disability not as tragic but banal, showing how disability itself can be used to counter the beliefs of TABs who demand a dramatic story to prove they can protect themselves from impairment. She explains, "The shark story is always for people who are able bodied, and normally for someone I'd want to gauge and test . . . [It's] prompted by someone being very concerned, and they say 'how did it happen?'" She uses the story not only as a social corrective, but also to convey her attitude about disability to her date: "I often share the shark story . . . because it's instructive. When you deal with [disability] all your life you learn to make light of it. You don't want to have a serious conversation all the time. It's also a screening mechanism because I need someone who will laugh. I need someone who as soon as he knows as I'm pulling his leg will laugh about it." Amy suggests that just as TABs may be nervous around people with disabilities because they fear their own fragility, people with disabilities can counter that reaction with humor that frames bodies as adaptable. Joking becomes a means to take the perceived drama out of disability.

This story also points to feelings of entitlement by TABs to ask questions about the bodies of disabled people. Disabled bodies do not "fit" into the world, since they are labeled as "different" and thereby open to study and investigation. In her story, Amy critiques the fact that disabled individuals have not been able to escape the status of "research subjects," even at bars or on dates. Amy says she also tells these stories as a means of making connections with other disabled people, explaining, "I will tell stories about my own experience as an ice breaker . . . Sometimes when someone is talking to me about their experience, they get emotional or angry, so I'll throw out a funny or sad story about a time I was treated badly, so they know they're not alone." As a form of in-group humor, her stories become a way to build community and create a feeling of understanding between individuals with similar experiences.

This story presents an occasion for laughter on two different levels. First is the laughter at Amy's date and the expectation that disability must be connected to a tragic accident, potentially indicating a change in audience members' thinking about disability. Second is the laughter of identification on the part of disabled people, who understand misconceptions about disability. These individuals may be familiar with the need to do an "acid test" with prospective dates and friends to gauge their sentiments regarding disability and their willingness to change those thoughts. This kind of laughter may also indicate a shift in the thinking of people with disabilities as they remember they are not alone in experiencing these daily frustrations. As Amy notes, many people with disabilities don't have those kinds of connections, and it's important for them to know they have communities to lean on if they so choose.

Drew tells a third story about using humor as a social corrective, explaining a time when he and a friend who is also a wheelchair user were at a concert and had to go up one floor to find their seats. Outside the elevator, several middle-aged persons were waiting to get on, and Drew's friend whispered in his ear, "I hate it when masses of abled-bodied people try use the elevator." Drew said aloud, "You hate when able bodied people try to use the elevator, James?" A few people left the line to use the stairs, but the remainder boarded the elevator with Drew and his friend, shoving them to the far side. Everyone else seemed to be going to the fourth or fifth floor while Drew and his friend had to go to the third, so he said, "It's going to be really awkward when we have to get off at the third floor and all of you have to get off the elevator." The two friends were able to exit the elevator on the correct floor, but Drew says the situation was uncomfortable. In this story, TAB individuals become the butt of the joke because they must be shamed into using the stairs, yet some are still determined to use the elevator. At the same time, Drew incorrectly assumes that by simply looking at someone's body, it is easy to discern whether or not they are able to use stairs.

Drew explains that at the time of our interview, "That was a recent story . . . [but] I would repeat that story . . . people just use the elevator because they don't feel like carrying their luggage up, but it can grind your gears . . . that would be a story for other disabled people, if people ask what annoys you." While Drew suggests he would restrict this story to audiences of disabled people who "get it," it isn't difficult to imagine the story being told to TAB audiences and eliciting uneasy laughter as individuals recall occasions when they didn't need the elevator but used one anyway or when they parked in a spot that was reserved for people with disabilities. Drew positions himself as having the agency to assert himself in this situation, yet Drew and his friend are not allowed to fit in the world, since TABs are pushing them to the margins and not giving proper consideration to their needs. Drew focuses on the irony that, while facilities may allow disabled individuals access to public venues, sometimes they cannot easily reach their destination due to TABs using amenities designed for disabled people. At the same time, the story may also point to the invisible nature of disability and how everyone who needs to use an elevator may not be sitting in a wheelchair.

BRIDGING THE HUMOR GAP?

As these narratives suggest, one of the primary difficulties in telling stories that incorporate humor and disability is that these comic moments can be interpreted in numerous ways depending on the teller, the audience members, and their thoughts on what it means to be disabled. Within disability communities, disability has variable and complex definitions, causes, and forms of embodiment, so individuals differ widely in their definitions of acceptable humor versus humor that crosses a line. This variety in attitudes toward crip humor was clear in the range of stories I gathered from my collaborators. Humor is always a personal matter, and perhaps crip humor is even more so.

This idea is highlighted in the careful control that joke-tellers maintain over their audiences, as they determine which kinds of jokes fit their purposes for which listeners and the meanings they want to give disability in that context. This intentionality affects reception since joking is a political and rhetorical tactic and the audience must be primed for comedy. While tellers often gauge their audiences in part on expected sympathies, there is often some educational facet to the joke telling since the teller wants to explain an aspect of living with disability and how their relationship to disability is different than the listener might expect. While certain jokes are deemed fit for a general audience, tellers are more cautious around people who might be sensitive or overly empathetic, in which case the disability might overwhelm potential laughter. For some people, disability can't mean anything other than tragedy. These joke-tellers realize that some listeners may not be able to laugh at the idea of having no feet to step on, failing to make a basket because you can't see the net, or not being able to hear someone clearly. If audience members focus more on the loss connoted by disability, not the adaptations made by the teller or how the jokes show that bodies are inherently malleable, any attempt to create a shift in listeners' opinions may be lost.

In their analysis of humor by disabled comedians, Reid, Stoughton, and Smith pose an important question about the effects of crip humor on the TAB community, stating, "For disabled audiences, disability comedy may play a role in creating an in-group that challenges dominant culture. On the other hand, in a mainstream setting, such humor could build tension and discomfort. The question remains whether these powerful and unsettling effects are momentary" (2006, 641). A similar question can be asked about the potential for individual disabled people to create social change and help others rethink disability by engaging with TABs and using humor to address disability in a creative manner.

These stories suggest that one way of broadening the meanings of disability can be recontextualizing it as a social construction and highlighting aspects of culture and the built environment that pose barriers and impediments to certain kinds of bodies. These barriers can include anything from forms of greeting that involve visual cues and physical touching, to an absence of clearly labeled accessible entrances to buildings, to the failure of businesses to provide text in large print or braille. It is this lack of accessibility that births much of the public fear of disability, since as Kleege notes, people are most afraid of losing their independence and autonomy (1999, 29–30). Western culture is so invested in individualistic I-can-do-it-myself attitudes that the thought of interdependence and needing to rely on others is terrifying. These stories serve an important function in working against the idea that people with disabilities are wholly dependent. Instead, they reshape the meaning of disability to show that interdependence is far from shameful, such as when friends help you pick up the pieces of your cane, when your mom drives you to school to get your legs, and when a kind lady punches you in the face at your request.

Related to this casual attitude toward disability, possibly the most difficult aspect to convey in writing this chapter is how these stories were told with obvious glee, making the research process a truly enjoyable experience. At the same time, many of my collaborators stated that they do not tell certain jokes to newly disabled people or to disabled people they have just met. Until they can gauge these individuals' feelings about their impairment, embodied status, and interdependence with others, it is easier to refrain from jokes that might come off as crude.

These joking practices are not ones that can be adopted by all people with disabilities or seen as humorous by some TABs. It is crucial to note that my collaborators all have congenital disabilities, while other people become disabled due to social inequities or living in an oppressive, racist, and/or violent society (Barker 2014, 105–6; Kafer and Kim 2017, 128; Schalk 2017, 141). The meaning of disability is always impacted by its origin, and in some cases the cause of disability may be such that it's difficult to ever interpret as comic. At the same time, blindness, deafness, being an amputee or a person with autism or a wheelchair user are all viable ways of living. To further the dominant cultural acceptance and embrace of all bodyminds, these disabilities can be a space for the comic. The absurd. Crip humor. Moments when the possibly tragic turns laughable because ultimately the joke is on us. Our bodies are more adaptable than we may first perceive, and the world is indeed filled with people who have just not found their disability yet.

ON CHILDHOOD

I chat with Joshua, whom I haven't seen in weeks, and we happen to meet at the coffee shop that is my usual haunt. Joshua explains that he hasn't been around campus much this winter because his office moved, and the weather was harsh. Bitter cold and ice slicks aren't fun for people who buzz around in electric wheelchairs.

Joshua tells me that his mother died at Thanksgiving, and it's been difficult to bear. The rest of his family lives overseas, so he hasn't been home, but he talks frequently with his siblings. He reflects that, since he's a disabled person who started out as a disabled kid, the problem with losing his mother is the memory of protection, feeling that he was different from his siblings and received special care as a result.

"I was looked after more," he says. "It's strange to have that be gone, even though I'm an adult and have been away from home for so long."

I understand the fate of kids who are given an extra dose of worry whether they want it or not, recipients of a love that is huge and smothering, a love that makes grown children remind their caretakers that, yes, they are forever beholden for that care, and they don't need it anymore.

To many parents and caretakers, this does not matter. Does the fact we came from their bodies, or that they knew us when we were very small, leave a mark of responsibility in their minds, a duty of concern for the child they think will have a more difficult time garnering respect in the world? The cord is never broken, that invisible line between caretakers and children that connects us across states, across continents, with concern and consternation and the knowledge of our shared frailty, especially as those who cared for us get older. Joshua says that he and his siblings are discussing their father and his poor health, how best to make sure he is cared for as he ages, continuing the tradition of long-distance love.

How many times a week does my mother call or text to ask how I'm doing? How often does my dad text a heart? The wellness conversation goes both ways since now I'm more aware of the scans and tests and preventative measures that pepper their lives. But I'm also still their dear diligent child, looking both ways eight times before I cross the street, moving monocular through the world.

When my mom had cataract surgery a few years ago, she went home with one eye covered by a patch and no depth perception. Later she said she thought of me on that car trip back from the hospital since she figured that was how I always perceived the world.

"Well, kind of," I said, touched at the mention but wondering how close she could come to my perspective. Maybe she intuited that fact, but because she's my mother, she has to do what she can to identify with me, with my body. Yet it's hard to explain my years of experience to anyone else, the complications of my sitpoint, since there are some stories I don't like to recall.

I was teased in elementary school for my weight, my glasses, my tendency to hold a book inches away from my face, and sometimes I was wary to tell new kids my name for fear they'd use it to taunt me. I don't remember how often that happened, but one time when I was around fourth grade, a boy asked for my name. Where were we? Who knows—I just remember it was during a meal. I was chewing and held up my hand so I could swallow, and then I said, "Why do you want to know?"

He thought this was hilarious, especially after my long and dramatic pause. I blushed hard. Maybe (probably) he was just curious, but experience had taught me to be wary and scared.

This tactic got me in trouble when I was at camp in fifth grade, in a group with kids from other elementary schools. The teacher leading our troop asked us to find out the name of at least one other person while we hiked through a grove of trees. When a boy asked my name, I just walked more quickly, and wouldn't tell him even after he called out after me.

"Hey," he said, "what's your name?"

I can't remember why I was quiet, what I feared he would say. But I remember fear.

At the end of the hike, the teacher asked him which names he had learned, and he said I'd refused to tell him mine. She rested one hand on her hip and glared at me.

"What is your problem?" she said, thinking I was standoffish and difficult. Another blush. I couldn't explain why I was scared. Shamed. Anxious. Sick of teasing. How could I voice years of feeling like an outcast in fifteen seconds?

Sometimes I think of this moment when I hear statistics about disabled kids being disciplined more often than TAB kids in the classroom. You can't tell your story of teasing or terror or trouble concentrating to an adult when you don't have the words to do it. You only know that the world is a place where you have a hard time fitting in, and people make fun of you for it.

Yet I realize I've had it easy in this regard.

My experiences of disability didn't harm my educational opportunities, which is far from the case for many children. As I noted previously, we can't discuss disability without incorporating race, class, and gender, among other identity factors. I was still a middle-class white girl in the classroom, a quiet one who sat as close as she could to the chalkboard and pressed her glasses to her face so she could see better. But this wasn't a problem that teachers read as disruption.

Audre Lorde writes of how her mother taught her to read and write when she was a young child, and she proudly knew how to pencil her name when she was four years old. Yet when Lorde went to a "sight-conservation kindergarten" with other Black children who were visually impaired, she discovered that "ability had nothing to do with expectation" (1982, 24). Her mother had taught Lorde that pencils were for writing, not the black crayon she was given, but it was difficult for Lorde to explain this to her teacher. She'd already been labeled a difficult student when the teacher asked Lorde to copy the letter "A" on her paper (24–27). When Lorde wrote her name instead, she was derided by her teacher and pronounced not "ready yet for kindergarten" due to her alleged disobedience (27). Lorde's parents moved her to a different school since her mother "knew very well I could follow directions" (27). How many people with disabilities are only allowed to meet the (tragically low) expectations that have been set for them and barred from achieving anything higher? But that's only one of many flavors of oppression.

Disability and education scholars Nirmala Erevelles and Andrea Minear tell the story of Cassie, a young Black girl who was the child of a poor single mother and had a learning disability. She was shunted from school to school as a problem child, was often teased, and was punished when she lashed out at other students. The many layers of her identity as Black, disabled, and poor made her vulnerable to dismissive and abusive treatment by teachers and administrators, who refused to consider her side of the story and simply wanted her out of their classroom. Erevelles and Minear argue that if she had been white and middle class, her disability would have been interpreted much differently, and she would have been more likely to receive help and empathy from the school system as opposed to having to fight for her right to an education (2017, 388–91).

Classrooms are often inflexible when it comes to teaching students with various kinds of visible and invisible disabilities (Price 2011, 58–59). According to a UCLA Civil Rights Project study published in 2015, kids with disabilities are often marked as disruptive and dashed out the door: "Among secondary-school students, 18 percent of kids with disabilities were suspended, versus 10 percent overall. Even more striking, a third of all K-12 children with emotional disabilities—such as anxiety or obsessive compulsive disorder—were suspended at least once" (Lewis 2015). Children with invisible disabilities can too easily be labeled as troublemakers. They may have ADD or anxiety, be on the autism spectrum or otherwise neurodivergent, but in the classroom they become the "kids who can't sit still, who challenge their teachers, or who struggle with social interactions . . . all of which can look like deliberate misbehavior or defiance and, in turn, lead to disciplinary action." When nobody knows how to quell what seems to be a child's fire, these students may "[be] tied up or strapped to a chair with materials such as bungee cords and duct tape" (Lewis 2015).

Overworked teachers might not know what to do with a child who seems out of control, especially when trying to teach a class of twenty-four students with varying needs. Yet some schools have started programs that assign counselors to children with disabilities when they are perceived as having a discipline issue, allowing the child to be better understood, maybe even heard. It isn't that these kids want to misbehave. Maybe they're distracted by the buzz of fluorescent lights or embarrassed because they require extra help with schoolwork (Lewis 2015). Empathy for these students isn't optional: it's a necessity if we want them to have access to an education, but it is difficult to garner additional resources for these children in a culture that still wishes to deride, deny, or dissolve disability.

Michalko writes that people with disabilities may be strongly discouraged from having children and passing on their disability to another generation. He relates an occasion when a genetic ophthalmologist explained to him "there was a chance, 'a two-out-of-four chance,' I remember his saying, that if I had children, they would suffer this condition as well. . . . His words were, 'You wouldn't want them suffering what you're suffering'" (2002, 41–42). While Michalko's parents didn't realize they could pass on retinal pigmentosa, he writes that now he would bear the responsibility and blame: "Blindness would not *just happen* to my children, I would *give it* to them" (42). Tinged by the warnings of his doctor, blindness became a preventable plague that Michalko could only pass on if he was audacious enough to have kids and allow them to "suffer."

Kafer comments on similar criticisms faced by a Deaf lesbian couple who wanted to have a Deaf child, but had to conduct their own search for a Deaf sperm donor since sperm banks "screen out" individuals who could pass deafness on to their children (2013, 76). Kafer notes that the couple was derided in the media for wanting to have a child who was Deaf, and "even some queer commentators found something troubling, and ultimately dystopic, about the idea," implying that prospective parents desiring disability was nothing but a twisted notion (77).

This is where I pause to consider the complications, how disability is often "so much more than merely sweet or merely hard" (Healey 2017, 102). When we're hanging out together, having coffee, shooting the breeze, Eric and Drew and I don't lament our embodiment. We tell childhood stories.

There's the time Eric was three and managed to turn his prosthetic foot all the way around while sitting in the grocery cart. His dad wondered why people were staring until he looked down and noticed his grinning cherub-cheeked toddler with toes pointing in opposite directions.

Then there was the time Drew had spinal surgery when he was eleven and woke up in a full body cast. Nobody had told him beforehand he'd be like that for a month, doped up on pain meds. He says there are some experiences it's best not to remember well.

I tell them how easy it was to ignore my mom when I was a driver-in-training, safely sequestering her in my empty space while she gripped the dashboard. We laugh, we giggle, we smile wryly, we tell more tales. Somehow, we always have new ones. As I get older, I've been adding to my cache as my parents spin their side of the story, adding layers to the narrative I thought I understood.

Excerpt from my mother's journal when I was just over three years old:

"Teresa told me today as we were reading library books that she could see only out of her left eye. She'd covered it (not right one) and said she couldn't see anything. Then she uncovered it and could see. I don't know how long she has had this figured out.

Excerpt from my mother's journal when I was four years and two days old:

"Teresa asked me this a.m. 'Why is one eye blind?'"

In the journal entry she doesn't explain how she answered the question.

"What did you tell me?" I ask her now, decades after the fact.

"I don't remember," she says. "I think I hemmed and hawed."

At my ophthalmologist appointment, my favorite tech, Renee, dilates my eyes and gives me her usual compliment.

"I'm sorry I always say this," she says, "but your right iris is so cool-looking, the way it's shaped like a star."

"My right eye might as well look interesting, since it's just hanging out," I say. This exchange has become our ritual, but today I tell her about an essay I read by the author of *The Color Purple*. What was her name? In the essay she explains how her eye was shot with a BB when she was a little kid. She was Black and living in the South, and due to systemic racism and lack of access to care, her parents couldn't get proper medical attention for her. Her eye became seriously infected, but she recovered and was left with a white scar. She was terribly self-conscious about that spot, hiding her face from the world until she had surgery to remove the blemish. Even after that, she felt strange about her eye and how it didn't match the other, but one day her young daughter studied her face carefully and said, "Mommy, there's a world in your eye" (Walker 1983, 361–70).

She has a world; I have a star. What was her name? Damn. Why can't I remember? Renee says she knows who I'm talking about, she likes the comparison, and the ophthalmologist will be in to see me after my eye has dilated. I sit. I wait. I watch the bright words on my phone grow blurry. Renee opens the door to the exam room.

"Alice Walker. I googled it," she says. This is yet another reason why I love Renee.

I call my dad after the appointment, joking that Renee always has to make sure that I can see light and dark and a little bit of movement with my right eye, but nothing much changes because it's still blind. Usually, I don't think about the hint of movement on my right because I'm focused on my vision in the left.

"Really?" he says when I mention Renee's waving hand.

"Well, yeah," I say. "I can't make out the number of fingers she's holding up, but she always wants to know if I can see movement with my right eye."

"Maybe if we'd covered your left eye and forced your right eye to see more when you were a baby, those cells would have developed," Dad says. "Maybe more of them stayed attached to your retina than we thought."

"Who knows?" I say, rolling my eye. The last thing I need is for my dad to start down a rabbit hole of parental regret. I doubt I would have wanted to wear an eye patch when I was eight months old so my right eye could have maybe possibly tracked along with the left. I'm accustomed to the fact that the right eye is independent and sees what it feels like seeing, even if it focuses on its own view of the world.

And why am I slightly—or more than slightly—appalled at my dad's simple suggestion? Is it the possibility that my right eye might have been less blind? The possibility that I could be different than I am now, an alternate version of myself who might not have been shaped the same way? But I don't want to consider theories of parallel universes. I'm the me of now, monocular and marvelous.

My pride exists in tension with the part of me that wants to go back in time and tell my younger self that it's going to be okay; things will work out; I'm not going to be teased forever. But I also know I'm still that quiet kid who's worried about rejection, doing things in a way that looks strange to other people, and who thinks having a blind eye is kinda cool.

We never leave layers of self behind, just keep adding and adding like rings on a tree or flavors on an Everlasting Gobstopper.

And I know my story isn't over.

Chapter 4

COMICALLY CRIPPING SEX IN
THE VIRTUAL PUBLIC

While searching for people who were willing to chat about the comedy of disability, I read numerous blogs written by disabled folks. I figured that if I could find elements of humor in their writing, they might be willing to talk about the ways they joked in everyday life. By this time, my thoughts had also turned to the search for disability sex jokes and the ways that people with disabilities (re)defined their sexuality with a dash of humor. I hadn't been able to find disabled folks who could remember sex jokes on command (then again, neither could I), so blogs seemed like a reasonable place to begin this quest. The format provided space for individuals to explore topics in a more extended narrative, going beyond the tweet, Facebook quip, or Instagram post to get down and dirty with details in an extended conversation with the reader.

I assumed sexuality would be a subject addressed with equal parts creativity and consternation since it has received less attention in the disability rights movement, despite the fact that disabled people's sexuality has long been disregarded and denied (Siebers 2008, 160).

Countering these dominant cultural messages, disabled people have been fighting back, and writing back. Through the perspective of disabled bloggers, we can understand the many ways in which disability can be sexy, and sexualized. Queer disability activist Andrew Gurza reflects on his sexual identity in two blogs, *Deliciously Disabled* and *Disability After Dark*. Gurza also explores disability, sexuality, and queer identity in his Twitter posts, in-person presentations, and podcast series. His web page describes him as "a Disability Awareness Consultant and Cripple Content Creator"[1] whose work "shines a light on the intersectionality of sex and disability, the fun found in sex and disability, and the vulnerability of sex and disability that we very rarely talk about."[2] Gurza's witty and sensual sensibility is displayed in one blog post titled "Deliciously Disabled Dalliances: How to Become a Fully

Functional Flirt!"[3] He notes that people he approaches for romantic banter are often taken aback, which he finds amusing: "I love the idea that I can use my words to make someone blush, smile and do a double take when they realize that, yes, this disabled guy sitting in front of them fancies them and is flirting." Painting himself as desirous and desiring, Gurza is matter-of-fact about asserting himself as a sexual being: "Let me be clear, I understand that I am the sexiest PwD out there, but I continuously feel as though I have to show this to others. . . . My thought process is: 'if I can show you that I'm sexy, everything else will follow.'"

On his blogs, Gurza is candid about his identity as a person with cerebral palsy who uses an electric wheelchair and has an attendant to assist him with daily tasks. He is equally frank about the pains and joys of disabled sexuality, sharing musings, fears, and frustrations on topics ranging from how to be a "bottom" when one is a wheelchair user who has problems with fluidity of movement,[4] to giving a blow job while risking the embarrassment of muscle spasms.[5] Gurza also uses this forum to lament about the lack of access he and other disabled people have to queer spaces, and his desire for a world in which his body can be considered sexy. His blogs alternate between serious and hilarious, juxtaposing moments of silliness with heartbreak, but there is no doubt about his goal to project a sexual disabled self and help others with disabilities do the same. Gurza and other bloggers serve an important function in online communities, as confident and honest voices writing about disability and sexuality as well as the everyday experiences of disabled people. Because so many people with disabilities do not have access to disability communities physically, these online environments have become key spaces for information, inspiration, and disability identity creation, sexual, political, and otherwise.

In this chapter I explore how people with disabilities such as Gurza are often denied validity and visibility as sexual beings and have problems accessing social spaces in a society that would rather ignore disability, disabled sexuality, and queerness. This is why disabled people have created online forums where their voices can be heard, places to express crip humor and find new ways to define disability and sexuality. In my tour of these virtual spaces, I read four blogs by people who incorporate disability, sexuality, and humor into their posts. All four are wheelchair users and post pictures in which their chairs are visible, if not prominent. I discuss not only the written content of their blogs, but also the ways these bloggers present themselves in photographs as confident and sexual and how their wheelchairs are incorporated as a vital part of their identity.

First, I examine how queer bloggers Jax Jacki Brown and Andrew Gurza address sexuality and LGBTQ pride in their posts. Both are unashamed of their bodies and identities, yet they have similar anxieties regarding how they are perceived by others. Their blogs are a nuanced exploration of physical and social access to sexuality, asking whether they will be able to enter a sex club and if other people will find their bodies sexy and sexual.

Taking an approach that is feminist and sometimes fashion-forward, bloggers Kimmie Jones and Magda Truchan argue that people with disabilities should have a place on the runways and in dominant culture. Their blogs embrace conventional ideas of white feminine beauty that some people may find constraining, yet they present self-portraits that portray the quirky girl next door and New York fashionista as unabashed wheelchair users.

These blogs situate disability identities as existing inside and outside of dominant cultural structures by addressing different facets of online disability communities. They are aware of the need to create spaces for disability pride, sexuality, humor, and creativity, and their writing argues for disability access to dominant and countercultural spaces, where people can shape their own definitions of disability and sexual identity. This is not an either-or question of where people with disabilities can find the best fit, but it is a fight for inclusion in all social environments.

SEX IN (E-)PUBLIC:
CREATING ACCESSIBLE NEIGHBORHOODS[6]

While more queer spaces have formed in physical neighborhoods in recent years, the fact remains that some people who want to access these communities may have problems entering buildings or even leaving the house. Gurza highlights this dilemma in his essay "Queer and Cripple in the 6ix," which he wrote for the book *Any Other Way: How Toronto Got Queer*. He includes an excerpt from this essay on his blog, describing his trip on an accessible bus to the queer district in Toronto.[7] On the journey he is "full of an indescribable sense of hope and excitement: soon I will be in the iconic rainbow district. Almost every time I go, I am imbued with a giddiness that perhaps this time things will be different." Gurza brims with anticipation when he sees the rainbow banners gracing stores and other businesses along the way. He cradles hope for a romantic encounter and "[the] chance that maybe I'll get lucky," yet he also feels "a mixture of excitement, fear, and trepidation" at what might happen next.

After he exits the van, Gurza's optimism dissolves when he encounters the usual sad story. While this neighborhood seems like it should be filled with like minds, there are no spaces that are hospitable to his mode of transport: "I pass all the bars, pubs, and kinky clubs with their back rooms, looking at them longingly. I know I can't get my wheelchair inside these sacred spaces where my community comes (pun intended)." Gurza is limited in his ability to be seen by other queer people as desirous and desiring since he and many others with disabilities are barred from being part of the social and sexual scene. Gurza ends the essay with an acknowledgment that since he cannot access certain spaces in the city, he must create his own space through his blog, tweets, and podcasts. He writes, "My work invites you into my village instead of my having to ask permission to enter yours." Through this online activism, Gurza endeavors to bring about the reshaping of physical and social spaces, envisioning a world in which seeing disabled people at a sex club would be greeted with a shrug and not a stare.[8] Members of disability communities have fought complete erasure from public spaces and conversations, yet oftentimes they are still prevented from making their presence known. This situation highlights the need for spaces where people with disabilities can congregate to shape sexual and political identities.

This desire is further documented by disability studies scholars such as Russell Shuttleworth, who interviewed twelve men with cerebral palsy about their sexual experiences. He found that the men "had in common a strong sense of encountering multiple, often intractable, barriers to being perceived as sexual beings and to accessing sexual experiences" (2012, 56). One of Shuttleworth's collaborators who would have liked to have a romantic relationship with a female friend explained that he felt he was being implicitly told, "You can come in to my house, but leave your dick outside!" (58).

Because of physical or other limitations, some disabled people can't experience what would be considered "normal" intercourse, yet Siebers argues that that shouldn't exclude them from being considered sexual beings (2008, 138). While disabled sexuality may ask us to redefine what it means to be sexual and have access to sexual activity and sexual spaces, this is a key step in expanding sexual rights to people with disabilities. The larger social repercussions of having a sexual self are clear. As theorists Lauren Berlant and Michael Warner note, "true personhood [is equated] with sex" (2010, 2609).[9] If disabled people are considered "unfit" sexual partners, they also may not be considered "true" human beings.

The opportunity to express disabled sexuality has improved in recent years due to the spread of the internet and the creation of virtual neighborhoods. In these spaces, people from a wide range of disability communities can reach out to others and find support in (re)defining and validating their identities. As queer disability activist and blogger Jes Sachse writes, "before 2001 i did not talk to anyone else with a disability, unless i was going to the hospital . . . before 2005 i had not spoken to anyone with my particular condition, which is a rare 1 in 150 million (approx 65 cases worldwide) . . . before 2007 i had not had sex. before 2008 i had not ever met another person who identified as queer and disabled."[10] Simply having a space to congregate and share stories, whether in real time or extended conversations over a period of days or weeks or months, has given many disabled people new ways to find community and like-minded individuals. While these online communities are not without problems, they also represent a vibrant space for identity formation as people connect through electronic prostheses.

CRIPPING[11] THE COMMUNITY: ELECTRONIC PROSTHESES, ACCESSIBLE SPACES, AND MEETING THE NEIGHBORS

Humans' need for machines to do everything from communicate to ensure mobility to maintain a steady heartbeat reflects how many people have come to rely on electronic prosthetics in daily life. As literary and cultural theorist Pramod Nayar suggests, "Bodies are more or less consistently connected/ embedded. . . . Bodies are bodies+machines where the body evolves in conjunction with assorted tools. All 'natural' and 'normal' bodies are always bodies+machines" (2014, 107). While access to these prostheses is still a problem in many parts of the world, it is clear how many people have had their lives physically and socially enriched by such technology and how easily individuals can feel "abled" or "disabled" depending on the type of machines they require to connect with others.

At the same time, the body does not fade away in the virtual neighborhood, especially for individuals who consider that aspect of physicality to be an important part of their identity. As literary scholar N. Katherine Hayles writes of entering online environments, "It is not a question of leaving the body behind but rather of extending embodied awareness in highly specific, local, and material ways that would be impossible without electronic prosthesis" (1999, 291). Embodiment can be a particularly important aspect to some online communities in which the basis of membership is a disabled identity. Such communities abound on social media, including ones for Deaf and visually impaired individuals, autistic people, people who use wheelchairs or have other mobility impairments, and those who have invisible disabilities, such as chronic fatigue syndrome, fibromyalgia, diabetes, and depression.[12] Some of these communities support chat rooms and message boards such as the ones I discussed in chapter 2, but Twitter feeds, Facebook groups,

Instagram, and personal blogs have all become spaces where individuals can share stories. These spaces are not without accessibility problems (Ellis and Kent 2013, 98–101),[13] but access to social networking and a variety of disability communities has not only provided a support system for people with disabilities, but it has also strengthened individuals' sense of having a political disability identity (Miller 2017, 517).

With the growth of such communities, crip humor has also flourished in online spaces, such as in photographs taken by Josh Sundquist, a cancer survivor and amputee, who posts pictures of Halloween costumes that are based on the fact he just has one leg. These include a pink flamingo standing on one leg, a gingerbread man with a leg eaten off, and the famous fishnet stocking-clad leg lamp from the movie *A Christmas Story*.[14] Crip humor is also used with relish in YouTube videos produced by the Mandeville Sisters, a pair of British teenagers, one of whom has one hand and one arm that ends just above where her wrist would be. In a video entitled "I Ate My Hand for Halloween," she demonstrates covering her arm with fake blood and applying liquid latex, which she later peels off to look like bloody skin. She explains that she decided to bite her hand off as a Halloween costume, since "all you need are a few inexpensive materials, and one hand." She later adds, "When people ask me would you like to have two hands, this is one of the reasons why I don't, because not many people can do this."[15] Through these online platforms, disabled people can find larger audiences to appreciate the playfulness of crip humor, demonstrating how disability has broadened rather than limited their interpretations of the body and its possibilities.

Other social media platforms, such as Twitter, have also become vibrant spaces for spreading crip humor and building community. For example, the Twitter account The Blind Onion (@blonion) tweets quips and jokes that are in-group humor for people who have visual impairments, such as "City planners recommend roundabouts to counter increases in blind population,"[16] "Sighted world not ready for competent blind people,"[17] and "Blind patient charges for soothing unprepared sighted therapist."[18]

While the advent of virtual neighborhoods has had positive impacts for members of disability and other marginalized communities, they aren't a perfect solution. Access to the internet is largely based on economic privilege and the ability to afford electronic devices, and many people with disabilities may not have resources that would permit them to go online. Also, while many websites are accessible to those with visual or hearing impairments, others are not. As Ellis and Kent note, if individuals can't use the internet, they end up feeling even more cut off from society and social networks than they were previously (2013, 95–96). Instead of making disability moot and shifting ableist ideologies, the internet has largely re-created those same problems and barriers in online spaces (Ellcessor 2016, 5; Ellis and Kent 2013, 97–98). As disability scholar Elizabeth Ellcessor argues, access to the internet must be considered not only in terms of whether individuals can pay for the service, but whether they can use it independently, or if they require assistance (2016, 8–9). While people with disabilities can be politically empowered by going online, they still may not have "opportunities for broader participation in culture and civic structures" (10).

Yet Ellcessor suggests that being an internet user who openly has a disability identity can be a "political action" in making their presence known online (2016, 81–82). At the same time, bloggers with disabilities may experience "frustration with inaccessibility of sites or services" and challenges in adding and sharing online content (164). For example, those with visual impairments may find "navigation of web pages as a barrier to access," and those with mobility impairments might fear they would seem "frivolous" if they asked the persons who help them with other tasks to also assist them in online spaces (165–66).

Another problem posed by online social networks is that there are few controls over who may enter, the kinds of dialogue they may add to the conversation, or the threat that may be posed by a voyeuristic presence. For example, some people fetishize disabled people and find them to be sexually attractive because they appear vulnerable. Kafer, who is an amputee, writes of her online correspondence with one of these individuals, a "devotee" who contacted her via email. Devotees are often able-bodied men who sometimes use the internet to connect with each other, track amputee women, and take pictures of them to post online. Kafer explains that while many amputees find this behavior to be highly objectionable and an invasion of privacy, devotees don't consider their actions to be stalking, but an expression of admiration and "desire" (2012, 332–33).

Yet Kafer also notes that while devotees' attitudes are problematic in the way they objectify amputees, there is an unexpected benefit to some amputee women: "For many women . . . it is difficult to learn to incorporate wheelchairs, prosthetics, scars, and stumps into their ideas of a 'sexy' experience. . . . Devotee websites might be the only places when an amputee can easily find images of women who look like her, images of women being 'sexy' while seated in a wheelchair, leaning on a cane, or donning a prosthetic" (2012, 343). In the end, while the development of virtual neighborhoods is beneficial in many ways to those in disability communities, we must not forget that it is likewise an ambivalent space.

DISABILITY BLOGS: THE SEXY, THE COMIC,
AND PICTURING DISABILITY

Blogs have advantages and disadvantages over other forms of social media when it comes to studying online communities. Chats on message boards, Facebook, Instagram, and Twitter allow individuals to have a more extensive back-and-forth conversation than on most blogs, yet comments tend to be short. Blogs allow individuals to post more lengthy reflections on self and personal philosophy, yet they can be difficult to maintain, and interactions with readers aren't as evident or obvious. As social media platforms such as Instagram and TikTok have become more popular, blogs seem to be less prevalent. Many individuals start blogs only to abandon them after a period of time, whether due to lack of readership, lack of writing time, lack of subjects they wish to write about, or other factors. Yet all modes of communication, digital and otherwise, are prone to shift, so it is still important to document this mode of expression and its contribution to disability culture. Most importantly, even if bloggers stop posting regularly, their thoughts often remain in the virtual neighborhood for others to read. The blog can thus persist indefinitely as a testament to the bloggers' ideas and presence.

The blogs I chose to study have overlapping and diverging functions, from educating readers about disability, to focusing on fashion and culture, to examining specific issues around disability and sexuality. Two of the bloggers are American, one is Canadian, one is British, and all are wheelchair users, though they take different approaches to their sexual identities. While Gurza and Brown openly identify as queer and discuss sexual practice and sexuality overtly, Jones and Truchant implicitly display sexuality through depicting the disabled body as beautiful and sexual, and disabled people as interested in sexuality.

Juxtaposing posts on these blogs gives us a window into various disability cultures and sitpoints, yet they all allude to the fight for the recognition of disability and disabled sexuality in social spaces. At the same time, all four bloggers are white, which raises questions regarding social privilege, who has the resources and time to devote to a blog, and who feels comfortable revealing disability identity and discussing these issues comically and at length. As I mentioned previously, if one is already a member of a minority community, it may be difficult to reveal disability identity and risk losing social power. It is important to recall that not all stigmas or experiences of disability are equal, and sometimes "coming out" as disabled can put one's safety and livelihood in jeopardy (Coleman-Brown 2017, 146).

In choosing blogs to analyze, I searched for ones that explored aspects of disability and sexuality with a humorous tone. These criteria narrowed my search since not all people with disabilities may feel comfortable posting sentiments regarding their sexuality or see their embodiment as a laughing matter. At the same time, audience members tend to pay more attention to serious material if it is sandwiched between the silly and irreverent. While joking may be playful, it is often a space to reveal insecurities and anxieties. In the case of the virtual neighborhood, some disabled bloggers use humor to explain how they have negotiated the often fraught space of sex and sexual encounters with lovers.

I also selected blogs that included photographs of the blogger, to explore how images complement the text and suggest ways of complicating the meaning of disability and sexuality. While not all disabilities are physically apparent, wheelchairs manifest that difference and force the realization of body variability, which is another important aspect of these blogs. Yet photographs are limited in the type of information they relay about a body since they can't express the three-dimensional embodiment of disability, such as the movements of someone with cerebral palsy or how a blind or hearing-impaired person negotiates the world. Garland-Thomson notes that photographs of disability are a long-running tradition but also problematic since having pictures "authorizes staring . . . with the actual disabled body absent, photography stylizes staring, exaggerating and fixing the conventions of display, and eliminating the possibility for interaction or spontaneity between viewer and viewed" (2002, 56, 58). At the same time, she argues that pictures have power in that they can "outstare the starer. . . . refusing to wilt under another's stare is a way to insist on one's dignity and worth," but this image is still only half of the exchange (2009, 85–86).

The meaning of photographs and of disability depends on how one interprets the pictures and the stories they attach to the person with the disability (Garland-Thomson 2002, 74–75). While the disabled body is in a sense "disembodied" and flattened on a screen, it is still connected to a person, a writer, who is telling a story through words and images and whose pictures may make a political point through their online presence. In posting photos online, bloggers must decide how to "perform" self and which sides of themselves they wish to show or hide. Presenting themselves seated in a wheelchair may pose a social risk, especially when one wants to focus on conveying sexuality. As Siebers notes, when individuals show that they are disabled, the disability can come to represent the whole of their identity in the mind of the viewer (2008, 109–10).[19] Along those lines, Perillo writes about feeling defined by her wheelchair after being diagnosed with multiple sclerosis, worried that people would see only her chair since it has a "black hole type gravitational power" (2009, 66). While Riva Lehrer is not a wheelchair user, she remarks similarly on the visual power of prosthetics and how some women with disabilities feel a compulsion to present themselves as sexual beings and counter disability stigmas of desexualization: "We know, whether our breasts or legs or hands or eyes or maybe just our voices are our 'best features.' Our hopes of desire are condensed into these segregated, illuminated parts" (2012, 240). In these situations when negotiating the gaze of others, individuals want to portray a "high status" so they are not "devalued" as people (Garland-Thomson 2009, 37). Part of that value can come through displaying one's body as sexual and sexually attractive. As Kafer suggests, such pictures can serve as important models for people with disabilities, yet she is troubled by the way devotees fetishize amputations, to the exclusion of all else about the woman in question (2012, 336, 343). Given her example, it is clear that photographs of disability can be a potentially liberating and constraining aspect of the virtual neighborhood.

In the end, it is important for people across the ability spectrum to have access to these blogs and the writings of people with disabilities who are reflecting on their politics, their sexuality, and their humor. These blogs are slice-of-life narratives in which people with disabilities can (re)define what it means to be disabled and express the many ways in which impairment doesn't affect their lives—but also the moments when, because of socially imposed or physical limitations, disability suddenly matters.

JAX JACKI BROWN:
FUKABILITY: DISABILITY AND SEXUALITY

On her blog, Jax Jacki Brown describes herself as "a disability & queer rights activist, public speaker, writer, spoken-word performer, disability sex educator and the co-producer of Quippings: Disability Unleashed, a fabulous disability performance troupe!" She blogged between 2012 and 2017, making four to sixteen posts every year. Her writing tends to focus on disability rights, advocacy, and sexuality, including posts about the abortion of disabled fetuses,[20] and entries titled "moving in non-normative ways"[21] and a "feminist critique of Guinness ad featuring wheelchair basketball."[22] She also posted links to articles she has written about disability and LGBTQA rights and links to YouTube videos of presentations she has given. Her blog is only one part of how she is making her voice heard in various disability communities, but it is a place where she can collect and display her writing, speaking, and other social actions.

Brown includes several pictures of herself on the blog. One that accompanies a post titled "I'm part of the Top 25 people to watch in 2015!" features

Brown sitting in her wheelchair wearing a black tank top, leggings with a black and purple zigzag pattern, and a gold necklace with a large gold pendant. Her short hair is dyed bright red, which is part of her signature style, along with her black Doc Marten boots with red laces that appear in all the photographs.[23] A second picture accompanies a post about a talk she gave in Melbourne regarding sexuality and disability rights. The photo features Brown onstage with another presenter, a woman dressed in a black shirt and pants who is standing. Brown sits in her wheelchair wearing a purple t-shirt and tan leggings as she looks out over the audience. Both women are in front of a screen with the title of her presentation projected in large aqua letters: "Intersecting and transgressive identities: Straddling the queer & disability communities, Or why people who are non-normative make the best lovers."[24]

A third photo accompanies a post titled "Queer Writing Unconference— my presentation on the importance of life writing and personal narrative for people with disability." In this picture, Brown sits onstage in her wheelchair, her hand raised and mouth slightly open like she is making a point. She wears a black T-shirt with white lettering that reads "PISS ON PITY" and black leggings.[25] A final picture that accompanies the blog post "On Radio talking Disability & sexuality, the social model and disability pride" focuses on the lower half of her body as she sits sideways in her wheelchair, clad in rainbow stockings and thigh-high black shorts, her legs resting over the wheels.[26]

The photographs and blog post titles highlight Brown's identity as queer, disabled, and someone who is unafraid to make her voice heard onstage. Often in these pictures she takes an active speaking role, and though the photographs are silent, the titles of her posts and presentations, as well as the words on her T-shirts, make her political points known. In none of the pictures is her wheelchair hidden, nor is it a focal point, but it is integrated into Brown's identity and means of mobility. These pictures present disability identity with evident pride, and a disabled person as a speaker and leader, not confined to the background. The implied message is that disabled people have ideas worth hearing; they do not need others to express their opinions for them or talk over their stories. In these photos disability is depicted as vibrant, creative, expressive, and authoritative, as opposed to passive and ashamed.

Brown's red hair and Doc Martens are other physical manifestations of her identity that allow viewers to "read" her body as counterculture and queer. Her playful and politically pointed choice of attire allows her to perform a side of herself that suggests she is not always a serious person, but that she wants to present various aspects of her intersectional identity and ally herself with certain communities and political and cultural modes of thought. Her love of colorful stockings adds to this portrait of Brown as having a sense of fun. While it is unclear from her blog how much Brown may be able to move her legs, in the photographs they simultaneously direct attention to and take focus away from her disability. While viewers may implicitly think that they should not be drawn toward Brown's legs, her stockings are very eye-catching. It's as if she's using the photos to say, "See, I'm disabled, and that's fine. Look at me, and get over it." She complicates the meaning of disability through showing how her disability matters, doesn't matter, and becomes an interesting aesthetic element, particularly in the photograph of her rainbow stockings and wheelchair, which symbolize a proud, queer disabled identity. Above all, the stockings construct Brown as the kind of person the viewer wants to look at rather than avoid. Her attire suggests that some disabled people want to be objects of a curious and admiring gaze, countering social norms that suggest TABs should avoid looking at people with disabilities (Kleege 1999, 39). Brown will not stay silent, either visually or aurally.

Brown's writing mirrors her visual presentation of self. Her posts focus on her identity as disabled queer activist, drawing attention to misconceptions about disability and sexuality. In a post titled "Do you have sex in your wheelchair?" she writes, "This is a story/poem that addresses the question that I get asked a lot particularly by drunk people 'do you have sex in my wheelchair?'" In explaining this query, Brown pokes fun at TABs who assume they are free to ask disabled people intrusive questions (similar to Joshua's story in the previous chapter). While her answer conveys a hint of the hostile joking impulse, the poetic response is sexually charged and comic and frames her wheelchair as an intimate object:

> I think of a lover, still fresh enough to sting,
> who was the first to include you in our kissing,
> in our cuddling, in our hot lead-up to sex.
> Times spent getting about the house with her on my lap,
> facing me wheeling us with her hands.
> No one before had thought this sexy, fun.
> It was something that she just did with
> laughter and passion leaving me feeling such a rush of
> love and intimacy with you, with her,
> with myself and this embodiment.[27]

Brown's verse suggests how her chair has become integrated into her intimate relationships and helped her gain a deeper appreciation for her body. This poem is also notable for the way it defines disability as an aspect of identity that can creatively expand rather than limit the possibilities of sexual experience. She treats her chair with affection, as a friend and the most intimate of partners, which may be a point of connection with other readers who are wheelchair users and feel the same way about their prosthetic devices. Yet she also suggests that incorporating her chair into her sex life creates problems, fearing that her sexual activities may leak into her public life. She is conscious of the idea that there should be a division between the two, but she has problems maintaining those boundaries:

> You become part of the afterglow of our fucking
> as parts of me and my lovers leak onto you,
> even as I try and keep you clean,
> to keep you out of it.
> Sex must not come with me as I wheel down the street
> to my parent's house, as I sit for dinner.

This second section of the poem revels in the comic image of sex following Brown down the road like an errant companion, a sensual self that cannot be contained. Many people may feel a similar tension about their sexual selves, acknowledging that sexuality is an important part of identity, but one that can only be revealed in certain spaces and contexts. At the same time, Brown knows that sex must accompany her because she is a sexual being, even if things that happened on her chair are not apparent to the casual observer. Brown's approach to integrating disability and sexuality, showing how her wheelchair has become a key part of her sex life, reflects Siebers's thoughts on constructing disabled sexuality as a creative act: "A crucial consideration for people with disabilities is not to judge their sexuality by comparison to normative sexuality but to think expansively and experimentally about what defines sexual experience for them" (2008, 151). Through "sexualizing" her chair, Brown demonstrates how disability can open up new possibilities for exploring and inventing sexual experiences with a partner, which may serve as inspiration for readers who are wheelchair users or have partners who are wheelchair users. While she relates how the integration of public and private sexuality is not without initial apprehension and tension, that is not a reason to let these spaces go unexplored. Brown also shows how lovers can be involved with creatively integrating disability into sexuality. Inventing new iterations of disabled sexuality can be a means to form even deeper bonds between two people as they experiment with various ways to enjoy each others' bodies. Far from hampering sexuality, disability presents an occasion for innovation and sexy play.

Yet Brown also writes about times when she has felt alienated from her body, such as in a post titled "Sex Toys for Fun-Loving Krips." She explains how she struggled to find comfort with her embodied self, a message that is vital for others in disability communities to hear, especially young people who may be negotiating their identity as sexual beings. Brown writes of her own path to validating her sexuality, stating, "Growing up with a disability I was taught to create a lot of distance between my actual bodily experience and my sense of self. It has taken me until recently, I am 28 now, to actually inhabit my body fully and what it is experiencing."[28] While making peace with her body has been a long process, Brown offers hope in explaining that she has found friends and lovers who helped her validate her sexuality. She writes, "I wish I have known of joys of sex toys long before now. I have only really invested in them in the last year; following an instance of bringing a lover home and having her go 'what you have NO sex toys?! You really need to get some! What kind of lesbian are you?' I am now the well equip kind :)."

Brown's post is comic in that it suggests the absurdity of anyone lacking sex toys, which are generally a taboo subject to discuss in public forums. She can also poke fun at herself due to this learning experience since she has now found the right equipment. The episode may have a tinge of familiarly for readers who've had a similar experience of being "educated" by lovers—lessons that include becoming accustomed to another person's sexual practices and preferences. Such instruction can shape an individual to be an even more inventive and considerate lover. Brown turns sex toys into another kind of prosthetic device, suggesting that both TAB and disabled individuals can benefit from an ample supply. In this post she also reaches out to disabled readers to let them know that she had to grow in confidence with her disability, and the journey took several years. She suggests that while she has a joyful and sexual disability identity now, that wasn't always the case, and she needed help to develop her sexual self. It isn't wrong for one's disability identity to be a creation that is bolstered by friends and community, not something one has to develop alone. This post serves as encouragement to others in her virtual neighborhood that they shouldn't shy away from sexual and identity explorations, alone or with others, because shaping one's idea of what it means to be disabled and sexual can (and perhaps should) be a group effort. Equally important is the way Brown portrays herself as a sexually active disabled person who is capable of loving, being loved, and taking a commanding role in her sex life.

A third way that Brown sexualizes her disability is in a post titled "I Must Not Find the Medical Profession Sexy," which includes a poem that humorously sexualizes the intimate experience of receiving medical care. She reframes what is a common yet invasive act as a bawdily amusing monologue:

> Doctor put your hands on me.
> Tell me all the things that make me abnormal.
> Make me different. Whisper them.
> Make my heart beat faster.
> Say what will happen if I don't let you touch me,
> cut me
> if I abandon this stumbling, shaking body,
> find wheels
> in search of my mind, of ideas.
> Tell me how my legs
> will bend
> and bend
> and bend
> until I curl about you.[29]

This post plays on the idea of the hospital fetish, which has sexual overtones because of the loss of control on the part of the patient, who must assume a submissive role. Yet in defamiliarizing a medical examination, Brown creates a comic power reversal, turning the medical into the sexual, since the patient is making demands of the doctor, rather than the other way around. The humor in this poem is further realized if one imagines the discomfort of medical professionals who suddenly find themselves removed from positions of authority. Even though the patient is asking to be cut and penetrated, she is also shaping the meaning of disability to be one that is sexually active, curling around the doctor and being the seducer while demanding seduction. Claiming sexuality in this case is claiming wholeness, while the abnormalities of the disabled body, such as bending legs, are framed as sexual attributes, not something that needs to be mended. Even the invasive act of cutting becomes sexually charged, a violation tied to medical procedures and yet an intimate act that involves a form of penetration. While in practical terms, a medical examination may never be "sexy," in revealing the connection between the intimate touch of medical care and defining oneself as a sexual being, Brown highlights the "fragile separation between the public and private spheres" in the sexual lives of disabled individuals (Siebers 2008, 136). While Siebers casts this lack of privacy in negative terms, noting how this invasion can lead to the sexual abuse of disabled people (146–47), Brown twists the idea to make the disabled patient the agent and actor. In presenting her sexuality with a sense of subversive play, Brown shows how the meaning of disability can be complicated yet again, to make disabled people vibrant sexual subjects who are actively making requests as opposed to being passive sexual objects. In this space, even the role of patient can be turned on its head as disabled people take control of caring for their sexual selves and bodies. In showing how disability can be a space of sexuality, play, and agency, Brown provides a means for readers with disabilities to re-see and recontextualize their bodies in the same way.

ANDREW GURZA: *DELICIOUSLY DISABLED* AND *DISABILITY AFTER DARK*

Gurza's blog *Deliciously Disabled* consists of ten posts made between March and May of 2015. His web page *Disability after Dark* includes an additional fifteen posts made between September 2016 and August 2017. Gurza writes thoughtfully and at length, presenting an appealing mix of seriousness and silliness, a fun and flirty self that asserts his queer identity while relating sexual successes and disappointments. Similar to Brown, Gurza makes a political point of blogging openly about his sex life and his right to have one.

Gurza also posts several pictures, including one that accompanies a post titled "Deliciously Disabled & Disrobed: When I am Naked, I am Free. What Nudity means to this PwD." In the photo, Gurza is naked and sitting in his electric wheelchair, which is directed away from the camera as he looks over his shoulder at the viewer. His bare left leg and left arm with a tattoo ringing his bicep are visible, along with a hint of his right arm and leg. Gurza's face is turned toward the camera and looking slightly upward. His dark hair and beard are close-cropped, and his expression is calm, yet his eyes are questioning, as if he wants to ask the viewer, *What do you think of my body? My sexuality? My nakedness in this wheelchair?*[30]

This image plays on sexual photos from magazines such as *Playgirl* and *Playboy*, which focus on scantily clad centerfolds, yet in making his wheelchair part of the focal point, Gurza integrates disability into the tease of revealing and concealing the body. Gurza's chair (and his disability) becomes eroticized because it is absorbing part of the gaze of the viewer, but it is also hiding sections of the body the viewer wants to see, playing with the notion of how wheelchairs can eclipse the body, but in sexually suggestive ways. Along the same lines as Brown, Gurza may inspire his readers with new possibilities for sexualizing their mobility devices, demonstrating how disability can eroticize bodies in conventional and innovative ways. While wheelchairs connote paralysis and passivity in dominant culture, in this picture Gurza plays an active role in the choice of whether to conceal or reveal his body. The blog post itself also confronts some of the practical aspects of disability and sexuality as Gurza explains the problems he has disrobing for intimate acts because he requires assistance. Needing help to express sexuality is a theme in his posts, as he explores ways his sexual identity breaks from the TAB "norm" and becomes a space for interdependence that complicates the meaning of disability, in the way that such cooperative efforts are both sexy and frustrating.

Similarly, Gurza's *Disability after Dark* home page features a background photo of Gurza and another man lying in bed, both bare-chested. Gurza's companion wears a black bracelet, his eyes closed and a slight smile on his face, while Gurza's lips are parted in a grin. His fingers are curled back, likely due to his cerebral palsy, while his companion's hand is in a fist, touching Gurza's open palm.[31] This scene is an intimate and joyful moment, and the first image to greet viewers on the web page. The photo encapsulates disability, sexuality, queerness, and the eroticism of skin against skin, displaying Gurza and his partner finding shared pleasure in togetherness. This is the only one of Gurza's photographs to depict him with a partner, yet by featuring this image at the top of the page, Gurza emphasizes how people with disabilities are "able" sexual partners.

Below this picture, links to other pages on the site are paired with photographs of Gurza. In one he wears a white shirt and gray and black checkered scarf, his eyes focused to his right as he sports an open-mouthed grin. The second photograph shows Gurza wearing sunglasses and a black leather chest harness, revealing letters tattooed on his right breast. The word "cripple" is visible, while another word is masked by the harness. Gurza appears cool, sexy, and suave, smiling faintly. In the third picture, he wears another chest harness, this one with blue accents. His gaze is pointed toward the viewer, a look that is serious and seductive.

In this trio of images, Gurza suggests various aspects of his sexual identity, ranging from playful to dashing, while the chest harness highlights his queer identity and love of leather gear. Similar to Brown, Gurza makes a new meaning for his disability in these pictures, suggesting one that is sexually active, assertive, and seductive, and in his case, openly queer. He discusses his affinity for harnesses further in the post "Harnessing My Sexuality as a Queer Cripple: Becoming My Super, Sexy Self." In this meditation on costuming, Gurza reflects on the pleasure of wearing a chest harness for the first time. After a friend assists him in donning the gear, Gurza sees himself encased in leather straps and chaps while sitting in his wheelchair and accesses a part of his queer identity that had previously seemed off limits to his body: "My chest was pushed up against the harness; it looked puffed out, strong and defined. My nipples stood erect at attention. My belly was snug underneath a leather strap." Witnessing his physical transformation elicits an emotional transformation. Gurza feels empowered in his queerness, enabled to visually enact a piece of identity that had been hidden: "I looked like I was in control of the situation, of who I was and what I wanted . . . for the first time in what felt like ages, I felt desirable and disabled, all at once."[32] In the picture that accompanies this post, Gurza is seated in his wheelchair, wearing the black leather harness, displaying the full upper half of his body and a seductive expression. Gurza's wheelchair is an integral part of this picture, his hands resting on the motorized controls, his head tilted coyly.

The post and photographs imply how relatively simple yet crucial it was for Gurza to have someone assist him in accessing this side of his queer identity. His writing suggests that the enactment of disabled sexuality does not have to be an elaborate production, but it may require help from thoughtful friends since the reality of disability (and embodiment in general) means that individuals may need assistance to bring their dreams to fruition. Similar to Brown, Gurza casts his sexuality as both an intimate and a cooperative act, and he has no shame in the fact that his enactment of queerness required a dash of interdependence.

At the same time, Gurza admits that there are occasions when he would like to have independent control of his sexuality, yet his disability precludes those efforts. In a post titled "Boys in Chairs: That Time I Couldn't Masturbate by Myself Anymore," Gurza writes of problems masturbating on his own due to a loss of dexterity because of his cerebral palsy. He writes that by "all accounts this is a pretty common occurrence for people who experience my level of disability; what the doctors refer to as 'severely disabled,' but what I will refer to as 'severely sexy.'"[33] He encapsulates the problem with a shot of humor that mocks medical terminology, while emphasizing his identity as a sexual being. The remark also fits him into a larger disability community that has similar dilemmas in terms of dexterity and is composed of "severely sexy" individuals.

Gurza jokes darkly when he confronts his limitations in dealing with this problem since it requires aid that he is hesitant to consider. While Gurza states that he is generally able to adjust to changes in his body, he wonders, "How the fuck does one adapt to this? . . . I've thought about asking my friends for help here, but this feels like a definite crossing of boundaries." It's a kind of interdependence that is difficult to fathom, "even for me, someone who prides themselves on being a saucy, seated individual and a provocateur with disabilities." Pondering the options, he wonders, "How would that conversation even start? 'Hey man, if you're not too busy today, do you think you might help me get off?'" Gurza's imagined comic conversation tries to couch the dilemma as a casual matter, alluding to the fact that this loss of control is emotionally painful, and he envies people who can pleasure themselves without a second thought. While Gurza can negotiate his current level of disability, this episode complicates the situation by suggesting that he does not desire further impairment. His blog post is an illustration of Kupper's rhizomatic model of disability, as she suggests that in spaces of disability "the extrinsic and intrinsic mix and merge, as they do in my own physical and psychical being when I am in pain . . . and take pride in my difference . . . and feel unable to speak of the nature of my discomfort, cannot find the words, but find comfort in the company of others whose pain might be different, but who somehow feel simpatico" (2013, 95). Proud and perturbed, Gurza's blog post shows how these tensions come into play in the balance between independence and interdependence. Disability can be a proud identity that is also complicated by daily frustrations. In this manner Gurza's blog provides a nuanced message to the "severely sexy" folks in his online neighborhood to know they are not alone and to seek solace in their shared situation.

His reflections echo Siebers's questions regarding ways in which people with disabilities can enact and express sexuality, including the extent to which friends and attendants should help people with disabilities engage in sexual practice. The transition to sexuality as a shared endeavor beyond one's partner(s) may not be easy, particularly in situations that may make individuals feel awkward due to the lack of privacy in what seems like should be the most intimate of moments (2008, 148–51). There are no easy solutions to these questions, only gray areas that ask individuals to consider and assess their level of comfort and flexibility when (re)defining the erotic self. Disability does not provide set definitions of how one should practice sexuality, and the emotional and physical barriers can be difficult to work around, but Gurza's blog shows disability to be a complex space of both frustration and creativity.

In another post, Gurza examines the role of intimate touch in the lives of disabled individuals, how the need for care can affect one's approach to sexuality, and how touch acquires different meanings over time. He writes, "In your life as a sexy but seated individual, who needs help with all the little things . . . you simply understand and accept that you require assistance, and that's all this is—nothing more."[34] With the lovely turn of phrase "sexy but seated," Gurza emphasizes the sexuality of wheelchair users and offers a verbal shrug about using a wheelchair for mobility. Needing assistance from others is a matter-of-fact situation. While touch is often an intimate act, he writes that when being cared for by an assistant, "there is no longer a sense of care in these actions—you are simply a job to be completed." Yet he reveals how this routinization of care has shaped his sexuality in a positive manner and enabled him to become a better lover. He intuits the intimate dynamics of physical contact with someone else since "I understand the importance of touch more than anyone, and the experience of disability has helped me to hone that. Think about the last time you hooked up with someone. Surely you touched them . . . but did you truly touch them? Did you understand what the touch meant rather than just focusing on the end goal?" Gurza suggests that through disability, he has come to a better understanding of the importance of touch, and of how sexuality encompasses a wide range of actions that have physical and emotional consequences. By defining touch in this manner, he accomplishes two of the objectives posed by Siebers in imagining disabled sexuality, to "[broaden] the definition of sexual behavior" (2008, 136) and "develop new ways to please [a partner] by creating erotic environments adjustable to differently abled bodies" (149). Gurza notes that disability has given him a better understanding not only of his own body, but also the bodies of others. He is sensitized to the level of care required by potential partners and "abled" to be a better lover. This is an important idea to add to conversations about sexuality in disability communities since it suggests another kind of erotic sensitivity, responsiveness, and agency that can be expressed by someone with a disability who is familiar not only with the needs of their body but understands the variable needs of all bodies. Gurza provides a means for his readers to reflect on their own strengths as lovers and consider how careful touch is a crucial aspect of eroticism and creative sexual practice.

Gurza further details his abilities as a lover in the post "Deliciously Disabled Dalliances: How to become a Fully Functional Flirt!," which I mentioned earlier in this chapter. The post features a picture of Gurza in a three-quarters view, a head-and-shoulder shot in which he wears a white tank top and eyes the camera seductively as he holds a chicken wing to his mouth.[35] The photograph is at once a parody of sexuality and an expression of Gurza as a sexual being. His eyebrows are raised in an overtly suggestive manner that seems to mock racy photos and present Gurza as sexual and comic, a theme that he draws out in the rest of the post.

He explains that while a "cheesy one liner" is "not particularly tasteful," it still conveys his interest to possible partners. His approach uses the same brand of pick-up lines that are often heard in bars, yet they have a particular kind of spin due to his disability. Gurza embraces the idea of integrating disability into sexual practice, emphasizing that, "if you use a mobility device like a wheelchair or a cane, you have all that you need to make disability flirty and flavourful." He suggests lines such as "Man, it's a super good thing I have my chair with me. You're so cute, I got weak in the knees and fainted." Perhaps this is a cringeworthy come-on, but Gurza's point is just that—to be as shameless a flirt as the next person at the bar, while integrating his wheelchair into his sexual identity. He writes that it is important to creatively incorporate prosthetics into one's sex life to add playfulness to the experience: "It's so rare that we have fun with these devices that are at our disposal. . . . They have become medicalized and sterilized, much like our bodies. . . . Let's break it down for just a sec, my chair is an extension of myself, so why wouldn't I use it to get mine? It's time to get delicious and devious with our devices." The idea of using the wheelchair as a means not only to get around but to "get mine" may raise a smile from the reader, but this joke also suggests a frustration that he is not getting his due recognition as a sexual being, perhaps because others do not interpret his wheelchair as a sexual enhancement. In this post, Gurza simultaneously reveals his bravado and confidence, but he hints to some insecurity as a "sexy but seated" individual. This is an important aspect of his blog since he not only is a voice for disability pride and political empowerment, but he also speaks to the barriers he has found on the dating scene. While he encourages others in his online community to use their prosthetics with flirtatious abandon, Gurza recognizes that disability can present obstacles, physical and otherwise, to intimacy. His blog is not simply a story of triumph but also one of exasperation. Gurza realizes the importance of revealing complications to his readers in terms of social and physical barriers to intimacy, another aspect of his blog that may help his audience connect with his experiences. His blog sings of the triumphs as well as the frustrations that give his writing a ring of authenticity and allow readers to identify with the high and low and in-between points of having a disability.

Gurza's complex experiences exploring his sexuality are also apparent in his post "Doing It Deliciously Disabled Style: That Time I Had Sex with Another Queer Cripple." Gurza writes about arranging a date with a wheelchair user, which meant considering the steps to their romantic encounter: "Would he be able to lift me into bed? Would I have to call someone to help us . . . ? In that moment, I understood what all the guys who I had hooked up with must have felt on some level . . . whether we want to admit it to ourselves or not, each of us has a schematic of how sex, including the preamble, should look."[36] While past fantasies had involved a lover who could pick him up, Gurza writes, "I had no clue how to process the possibilities." He realizes his previous sexual encounters had a script that he had not diverged from in the past, including notions of how sex was supposed to "work." It may be comic to think of sex as a performance, lending formality to this intimate act, yet Siebers suggests, "Co-thinking sex and disability reveals unacknowledged assumptions about the ability to have sex and how the ideology of ability determines the value of some sexual practices and ideas over others" (2008, 136). Even while his definitions of eroticism and sexual activity may differ from those of other people, Gurza admits that thinking outside the box was challenging. At the same time, he considers the situation full of "possibilities" as opposed to limitations, structuring the encounter as one to be greeted with creativity rather than cynicism.

He eventually found the process of navigating this encounter to be liberating: "For once, the stumbling felt natural, sexy. It wasn't precipitated by fear that if you touch me, you'll break me. It was rushed out of desire not deterrence." From his perspective, crip sex was even better with another crip who had a similar form of embodiment, so what felt like a "mistake" could be recast as part of the experience. Yet his partner did not sense that same potential, as Gurza writes of their heartbreaking conversation afterward: "He said that we couldn't see each other again because . . . I was 'too disabled' and 'too much work.' I was absolutely floored by what I was hearing. I couldn't believe that someone who most likely had experienced all the same stumbles as I had was being so very ableist." Gurza realizes people with disabilities can still discriminate against others with disabilities, engaging in horizontal hostilities. This particular lover may not have wanted to shift from his perceptions of what sex should look like with a TAB partner, suggesting that not all people with disabilities may be striving for innovation and flexibility in shaping the sexual self.

In this episode, Gurza's blog delves into the problem of how sexual chemistry can be complicated by disability on a practical level. While he wants to encourage his readers to feel sexually liberated, in any sexual experience, one person may feel like it was a great success, while their partner does not agree. Disability complicates the matter further, since we must ask if Gurza's partner refused a second date because he did not feel a certain chemistry with Gurza, because of the unsexy "work" required to have sexual relations, or a combination of the two. Gurza's partner may have also found himself physically exhausted at the end of the sex act, deterring him from continuing with the relationship. While people with disabilities sometimes need help from attendants to engage in sexual practice (Siebers 2008, 167–69;

Sienkiewicz-Mercer 1996, 221–22), not everyone with disabilities may feel comfortable introducing third parties into the act.

Because of the physicality bound up in sexuality, Gurza admits that disabled individuals may have desires that their partners may not be able to fulfill. His writing serves to emphasize that both environment and the expectations of others render a body able or disabled (Nayar 2014, 103). TABs and disabled individuals can both have "disabling" attitudes when they are unable or unwilling to think creatively about the possibilities for intimacy. This idea provides another key reflection point for Gurza's readers, an opportunity to mull over the ways they may inadvertently harbor ableist ideas. His blog reflects how a disabled individual's need for interdependence and cooperation can be a strength, but also a weakness when one has a partner with different views regarding bodies and eroticism.

In a final post titled "5 Reasons Why Going on a Date with that Disabled Dude Will Be Totally Worth It," Gurza writes of how he was contacted by a young queer disabled man who was happy to have found Gurza's blog but had internalized a great deal of negative stigma related to his disability. Despite positive role models, it was difficult for him to shake those feelings. This interaction led Gurza to google questions regarding disability and dating, after which he notes, "I found that the main question being posed was *Would you/could you date someone with a disability?*"[37] He critiques how the "question suggests that there is some sort of risk in dating a disabled person (ummmm, isn't there a risk in dating ANYONE?)," yet Gurza is willing to grant a little slack to TABs who might type such queries into a search engine. He states:

> While it is okay to be apprehensive (being around so much awesome all at once can be overwhelming), the question should in fact be the statement:
>   "You SHOULD Date someone with a Disability!"
>   Well, of course you should. We are no better or worse than other options (true fact though, I AM BETTER).

Gurza continues the post by articulating the reasons why people with disabilities are superior partners for an evening of intimacy. If individuals are "looking for something different" in their next romantic encounter, Gurza makes a strong case to delight in disability. He writes, "If different is what you want crips got you covered. What could be more different than your date rolling in the bar through the backdoor in their tricked out 300 lbs. chariot? Don't lie, as you watch them coming towards you commanding their chair with confidence—you can't help but getting a tingle in your nether regions." Gurza's writing employs the mock egotism that is often part of his humor, as his quips are simultaneously self-aggrandizing and self-effacing, suggesting both his confidence and lack thereof. In Gurza's posts, there is the texture of a wink, a smile, and a weary sigh, asking why he needs to prove this point on the desirability of disabled people again and again, until the blessed moment when TABs stop turning to the oracle of Google to ease their anxieties about such dating choices. As Gurza alludes to in other posts, "severely sexy" individuals are often treated as exotic creatures, at least in terms of their desire to be present in sex clubs and other spaces where individuals can freely flaunt their erotic selves.[38] His post also illustrates the overwhelming task that Gurza feels is before him, trying to be a positive voice in presenting disabled sexuality to TABs and people with disabilities who need to see pictures of guys in wheelchairs wearing leather harnesses. This is what disability can look like, feel like, be like, with a dash of interdependence and a couple kinky friends. But even with all of his quips, Gurza highlights the challenge in inspiring masses of seated individuals to find the sexy that he knows is in their soul of sensual souls.

In his online activism, Gurza contributes a thoughtful and seductive voice to the virtual neighborhood, expanding both the meanings of and conversations around disability and sexuality in innovative ways. He demonstrates himself to be creative and realistic, flirtatious and crestfallen, covering the spectrum of joy and disappointment in having an identity that is "deliciously disabled."

KIMMIE: THAT GIRL IN THE WHEELCHAIR

Kimmie describes herself as in her early thirties, and a resident of Nashville, Tennessee. She blogged from 2010 to 2017, writing 65 to 150 posts every year on a variety of topics. While she identifies as disabled, Kimmie explains that her blog encompasses much more than disability-related issues: "Trust, my chair is but a supporting character in my life. This blog is mostly about the loves of my life: Nashville, my mentally unstable mutts, my ginger boyfriend, my wild pack of friends, bargain shopping, reality TV that rots the brain, live Americana music, weird shit I find on the internet and really anything else that happens to strike my fancy." This introductory section features a close-up picture of Kimmie's face: a young woman with brown hair and glasses, wearing a striped scarf. Further down the page is another photo of her seated in her wheelchair on a wooden boardwalk, wearing a long violet dress and pointing to a Tyrannosaurus rex in the background. Her mouth is open in mock fear, and the picture is captioned "like dinosaurs for example."[39] Kimmie positions herself as a sort of anygirl, emphasizing the idea that disability is but one facet of her personality and interests. Her introduction makes it clear that disability can't be excluded from her life, but it's also not a focal point.

Another important aspect of Kimmie's blog is her sense of humor, highlighted in this introduction through the comic picture of her screaming and about to be "eaten." The playful photo reveals that she is a wheelchair user, yet the dinosaur is a much larger concern. This picture, like the blog itself, does not shy away from disability, but it is devoted to her interests, musings, and quirkiness.

Of the blogs I reviewed, Kimmie had the largest number of disabled readers who commented on her posts. Several responded positively to her introductory section, one person writing, "I can't believe I've found another girl in Nashville that doesn't mind being called 'crippled'! I often refer to myself as 'palsied' for identification purposes. So happy that Caity tweeted about you. We should talk ;-) Spashionista (Alicia)." This post makes it evident that Kimmie's blog is being promoted through other forms of social media, including Kimmie's link to her Facebook page, which also appears on the blog. Kimmie responded to everyone who posted comments, thanking them and building ties in her virtual neighborhood.

While Kimmie doesn't highlight sexuality, it is implicitly mentioned in posts suggesting that people with disabilities can be sexy and sexual. One of these focuses on Halloween costumes created by wheelchair users who integrate assistive devices into their attire. She notes, "Since childhood, I have realized that people in chairs have a HUGE advantage on this holiday, because [their costumes] can be completely impractical and impossible to walk in."[40] Not only does she define disability as having creative benefits— someone can roll around in a massive Halloween costume as opposed to walking—she highlights the innovative nature of disability cultures in the ways that individuals can integrate wheelchairs as a facet of costume design. The photos she posts include a boy dressed as Batman, his chair covered in cardboard and painted black to look like the Batmobile. Another is of a young boy dressed as a deep-sea diver, with a gray cage built around the top half of his wheelchair. A large shark (perhaps paper-mâché) is attached to the cage as if swimming around it. A third picture is a head-and-shoulders shot of a woman wearing a long blond wig and heavy eyeshadow and eyeliner. She gives the viewer a toothy smile, but her arms are at her sides, so only her shoulders are visible, and her wheelchair has been concealed by a cardboard box that is painted pink. In front of the woman is a plastic tray with various colors of eyeshadow, a cosmetics brush, and an open compact. Kimmie's caption reads, "I am only mad I didn't think of this costume. It's a Barbie styling head. My sister and I will forever call these 'Barbie Big heads.'"

This costume merits particular attention, since Barbie has been a symbol of white middle-class beauty and sexual norms for years, though the vanity tray box both integrates the wheelchair and hides it from view. While the disabled woman is portrayed as sexual, it is in a normative way that conceals the rest of her body, including the wheelchair that would risk drawing the gaze and potentially desexualizing her for the viewer. The costume is comic in that it is exaggerated both in size—the original Barbie styling heads were not large as life—and in the overt display of femininity and sexuality that Barbie herself represents. She has come to epitomize an unattainable and unrealistic standard of female sexuality, to the point of becoming a parody of herself.

This costume could be read in a number of ways, from one that conforms to sexual "norms" that fragment the bodies of women and suggest they must shape their bodies in certain ways to be considered beautiful, to a costume that mocks those beauty standards by focusing on how the chair and the rest of the woman's body is hidden yet in plain sight, and how the costume restricts her movement and is in certain ways disabling. The "story" this picture tells is largely dependent on the audience members in question and their relationship to issues of beauty and disability. While the Barbie Big Head will likely draw a smile from those who know about the toy it is referencing, the costume is troubling in the way it demonstrates how accustomed some people have become to isolating and preening sections of their bodies, particularly women's bodies, for the gaze of others. It is also telling in that, for this woman to be cast as sexual, her wheelchair must be hidden. Many of the other costumes also fall into this ambivalent space of making a practical and fun use of wheelchairs, while simultaneously concealing them. The presence of the wheelchair doesn't eclipse the individual's body, yet there is an impulse to hide the reality of its function. The costumes expand on and complicate the meaning of disability by suggesting how it can be an aspect of personality that is simultaneously concealed and revealed, implicitly celebrated and shamed, presenting an occasion for creativity while realizing the multiple ways of reading such artworks.

Another one of Kimmie's posts that explores issues of disability and sexuality focuses on a fashion show that included models who were wheelchair users. The show was advertised as "Nashville's first fully inclusive fashion show, Fashion is for Every Body." Kimmie participated in the event, and writes, "It was neat to see a 6 foot tall fashion week pro walk the same runway as someone who had never done this at all before . . . and who wasn't actually walking."[41] Being in a fashion show means that one's body is on display, and should be interpreted as sexual and attractive. While subjecting oneself to the gaze of an audience can objectify women and their sexuality, an inclusive fashion show can also be read as breaking down the barriers to the catwalk (or maybe just adding a ramp) and presenting wheelchair users as desirable.

Kimmie posted several photos that were taken of her during the fashion show. In one she wears a black dress with a red sash, a black and white kimono-type robe, white pantyhose, short black boots, and a wide gold necklace. Her arms are flung out and her head tipped back, eyes closed as she gives the audience an ecstatic smile. The long sleeves of the kimono partially hide the wheels of her electric wheelchair, though it is apparent that she is a "sexy and seated" individual. Kimmie includes two other pictures of her grinning self in different outfits: one is a navy T-shirt, worn gray jeans, and black boots with chains wrapped around the ankles, and the other features her in a black satiny top and matching pants, a red and white shawl draped over her shoulders and arms, and a gold chain necklace. As Clare notes, while mainstream feminists often decry women being considered as sexual objects, they focus on "the generic objectification of women, meaning middle- and upper-class, white, nondisabled, heterosexual women," and do not take into account "race, class, sexual orientation, gender, and disability," or the "pleasure" that may be found in being considered a sexual object (1999, 114). Kimmie sharing these pictures and her experience is one way to validate disabled women's attractiveness and sexuality. Perhaps as much as clothing, these women are modeling attitude, being confident and secure in their right to the runway.

Further down the page is a photo of Kimmie and a makeup artist applying lip liner to Kimmie's mouth. While the headrest of her wheelchair is visible, this picture is more intent on conveying the arduous process of preparing the body for display, a ritual that all the models must endure. The last photo is a picture of Kimmie wearing a violet dress with spaghetti straps, her face in full makeup, hair neatly coiffed. Beside Kimmie is her friend Alicia, the person who organized the show, wearing a black dress. This picture is centered on their heads and chests, but there is a hint of their wheelchairs—a wheel visible under her friend's arm, and Kimmie's headrest behind her shoulders.

While some would argue that these photographs focus on normative beauty that doesn't push the envelope beyond adding wheelchairs to the catwalk, there is value in integrating disabled women into this cultural display and validating their sexuality. The fact that this was the first all-ability fashion show in Nashville says much about how the bodies of people with disabilities are often left out of the picture, physically unable to access the runway due to the lack of ramps and metaphorically unable since they are not considered sexual, attractive, or "as a romantic object" (Mairs 2002, 162–63). The fashion show also returns us to Shuttleworth's idea that some disabled people don't want to push the envelope too far; they just wish to be considered sexual beings in the same conventional ways that TABs are considered sexual beings (2012, 66). As the range of photos on Kimmie's blog suggests, these women may not want to tear down all social structures, but they find appreciation in the dressing room and on the runway.

As Garland-Thomson writes, more disabled people are being included in fashion photography, though they have "bodies that at once depart from and conform to the high-fashion body" (2002, 67). She suggests that these photographs can have multiple meanings to the viewer and "produce a fresh, attention-grabbing brand of exotic radical chic that redefines disabled identity for the disabled consumer" (69). While the disabled body may in some sense be "exoticized" in these pictures, they also depict disabled bodies as sexual and attractive and give some people with disabilities the chance to see models who have a form of embodiment similar to their own. Further, as Garland-Thomson notes, staring can have many functions, and among them is "giving [the body] a story" to make it look less "strange" to the viewer (2009, 7). Yet this type of display highlights the debate within disability communities about what kinds of social structures should be challenged. McRuer criticizes Garland-Thomson's analysis of disabled people as subjects in photography, suggesting the photos merely integrate disabled people into a "progress narrative" and a capitalist system of "production and consumption" that should be abolished due to the economic inequities it creates (2006, 178). Similarly, the fashion show photographs could be critiqued as integrating people with disabilities into an overly prescriptive and restrictive set of white feminine sexual and beauty standards that still privilege certain kinds of bodies (Kafai 2018, 231–32, 234; Berne et al. 2018). Even while some people who use wheelchairs are included in the picture, how many are still denied access? Yet perhaps by the end of this fashion show, wheelchair users on the runway didn't strike any audience members as being out of place, but simply as models in their element rolling down the catwalk.

Kimmie also highlights a side of the fashion show that readers might not expect in the bond formed between TAB and disabled models: "I lost any shred of modesty after look one. Pretty soon we just all were full nudie booty smashed together like sardines . . . I am thrilled that all involved were some of the most fun individuals I have ever had the pleasure to be around . . .

therefore I didn't mind them seeing me in nada but my stick on boobs, whilst getting doused in additional hairspray." Kimmie makes this intimate space one of comedy and community in the crush of "nudie booty," where everyone is stripped of clothing and modesty. Her body becomes not so much a sexual object but simply an object that has to be dressed and preened, like the other bodies. Her comments reveal a level of comic artifice to the show, but one she appreciates since all the models' bodies are being likewise groomed. In this unceremonious treatment of skin, she reveals a level of comfort she found with her body and everyone else's as they endured the unglamorous process of being readied for the spotlight. This comment presents the fashion show as an ambivalent spectacle that simultaneously glorifies certain types of bodies, yet it places disabled and TAB bodies on a similar plane as blank canvases ready to be splashed with makeup and clothing. While disabled bodies are often subject to poking and prodding in medical contexts (as suggested in Brown's poem), in a fashion show everyone is subject to such scrutiny. Kimmie suggests that through this delightful ordeal, models of many forms found camaraderie. She relates the experience as enjoyable and liberating, something to be shared in the virtual community and hopefully inspire others to stage similar productions where bodies of all kinds can be sexually attractive and set for (or subject to) the catwalk.

In a third post, one that is perhaps the most explicit about sexuality and disability, Kimmie reviews a series of pioneer romance novels by an author who features disabled characters. The romances are marketed as "clean," but the fact that disability is so prominent in the title is too interesting for her to resist. She writes, "I first checked out Morgan's book *Crippled Mail Order Bride for the Unexpected Horse Whisperer* . . . I had to find out if his love of her was unexpected . . . or his ability to whisper horses unexpected."[42] While she finds humor in this lack of clarity, the author's choice to use disabled characters as love interests is intriguing. Kimmie admits that she was initially wary about the author's approach to disability: "I guess I probably should have been up in arms about the use of the word 'cripple,' but I use it lovingly quite often and I hoped that since this book took place during the 1800's that they were striving for authenticity in the vocabulary used . . . I was more nervous about how disability was going to [be] handled . . . That answer is—HEAVY HANDEDLY!" Kimmie makes her frustration comic through all-capitals emphasis, but in this statement, she also reveals her anxiety about how disability would be treated in the plot and subsequently regarded by readers.

The problem she finds with this book is that the characters' disabilities are foregrounded overtly and fall into the stereotype that disability is all of a character's being. As Garland-Thomson notes, often disabled characters in fiction are not three-dimensional figures since the fact they are disabled seems to override everything else about them (1996, 11). The author in question has committed a similar error, as Kimmie reflects that, "On every page, there was some eye roll inducing mention of her disability . . . It definitely deserves a mention, but it was tacked in SO AWKWARDLY . . . I couldn't handle reading the next 50 pages." While the disabled characters may be portrayed as sexual, the author's insistence that love will conquer all in spite of disability is so explicit as to render the book sadly comic. Why should it be amazing that disabled people are lovable and sexy? Romantic plot line aside, one would hope that the author would have some insight into disability and sexuality; however, this doesn't seem to be the case. In Kimmie's post, this tension between the way disabled people may recognize themselves as sexual beings versus the way TABs construct that sexuality is evident. To her mind it's obvious that disabled people are sexy and should be characters in romance novels. In the mind of the novelist, however, the "surprising" sexuality of the disabled characters must be driven home with a very large, clunky, indelicate hammer, or the (presumably) TAB audience won't believe that particular plot point.

Kimmie includes pictures of this author's book covers on her blog, and notably there is no image to reference disability. The women on the covers wear lush period dresses (perhaps to hide their crippled legs), and the men are silhouetted on horseback (with no indication of whether they may need to use a cane or have a visual or hearing impairment). Disability is effaced from the pictures of the protagonists, and the covers could easily be reproduced on any other cheesy Western romance. As Kimmie's post suggests to those in her virtual community (and perhaps aspiring crip romance novelists), we need cheesy romances involving characters with disabilities, but not this overbearing sort. Kimmie's blog makes a case for "normalizing" disability and disabled sexuality within dominant culture in a way that doesn't challenge as many sexual conventions as Brown or Gurza; thus, some activists and scholars might suggest she should push for additional changes that are sorely needed. At the same time, her blog is an example of the many forms that disability cultures may take and the range of voices within disability communities that demand their own kind of recognition.

MAGDALENA TRUCHAN: PRETTY CRIPPLE

On the "About" page of her blog, Magda describes prettycripple.com as "a humorous blog about fashion, food, music and pop culture, written by

Magdalena, a New Yorker, artist and irreverent mad hatter." Regarding content, she adds, "Here's what makes me roll: the art scene, music, artisanal food, great fashion, global politics and my love for animals. Graphic design is my profession and I've branched out exponentially. Fun-loving with an infectious laugh, I love great conversations with amazing depth." After this description she explains the nature of her disability, writing, "I get around in a wheelchair due to unfortunate circumstances in the 90's. Nothing stops me from living life to its fullest. Obstacles are simply challenges I overcome."[43]

Magda's introduction is similar to Kimmie's in conveying a wide range of interests, while explaining that disability is but one aspect of her personality. While the story posted here could be critiqued as a kind of overcoming narrative that elides the financial problems and social and physical barriers experienced by many people with disabilities, Magda displays an assured and self-confident personality that lets the reader know she is not afraid to speak her mind. This page is accompanied by one of the many photos in which Magda highlights her love of fashion and style. She wears a long-sleeved burgundy sweater, a plush gold scarf, and a black skirt pulled above her knees to reveal black fishnet stockings. She compliments the outfit with black boots and a velvet burgundy hat.

Magda has blogged since January of 2014, writing numerous posts that are often accompanied by photos in which she shows off her unique sense of style and fashion. She frequently includes political commentary, notes on local cultural events, and posts about her travels around New York. Her tone is always comic, involving quips and one-liners that highlight her liberal political opinions and independent personality. Similar to Kimmie's post about the inclusive fashion show, Magda's posts are implicitly sexual, allowing the reader to view (and perhaps stare) at Magda's body and wheelchair. She looks back at the viewer with a gaze that is direct and confident, suggesting *I know I look hot in this chair*.

In a post titled "A Midsummer Night's Dream—my #StyleCrush," Magda writes about being "featured in the lifestyle section of 'WearYourVoice.com,' a feminist media website. The website mission is to be a platform for women's voices, sharing personal stories which inspire and give hope, without judgment."[44] Her blog drew attention from the site's creators, which led to Magda being featured in the "StyleCrush" section that focuses on "women whose personal style is noteworthy." In the accompanying photograph, Magda wears a leopard-print hat and short-sleeved button-down top, and her pants have an abstract geometric pattern in muted olive, peach, and beige. Her short blond hair is coiffed and curled, and she wears dark red lipstick and heavy eyeliner. She holds a wine glass, her hand poised on her thigh with her elbow jutting out, giving viewers an appraising smile like she might be examining their wardrobe while they look at hers. She appears confident and a little sassy. The wheel of her chair is under her elbow, and as with many photographs of Magda on her blog, the viewer's eye is not drawn toward or away from it. Her chair is simply part of the classy and cosmopolitan composition, treated in the same way a photographer would use a patio or upholstered chair. Similar to the attitude she expresses on her "About" page, Magda shows how she has integrated her wheelchair seamlessly into her lifestyle, placing it in a context that is both fashionable and matter-of-fact.

In this post Magda speaks to her philosophy on life, explaining, "I am known for my directness, honesty and living life to the fullest, despite challenges. I often run into people who are victims, who harp on their victimhood and talk endlessly about themselves. I'm DONE with that. Everyone's life has challenges but better to tackle them quietly and move on." As a voice in this virtual community, Magda continually emphasizes how needing to use a wheelchair has not dulled her drive or interest in fashion. She refers to her disability indirectly, primarily focusing on how it hasn't impeded her from achieving her goals. Some of her statements could be interpreted as potentially derogatory toward people with disabilities, painting them as whiny victims. Magda frames disability as an individual problem that she has tackled on her own, without reference to social webs that have helped her succeed. Some might criticize this attitude, noting that Magda has white privilege, which means she is treated differently than people of color who are wheelchair users, and she may have had financial resources that others lack. Since disability is but one part of an individual's intersectional identity, we cannot overlook how these factors may have come into play in her career success and as a fashion blogger. Yet part of her stance may also be a reaction to a society that wants to focus on the wheelchair and not the person sitting in it, leading her to emphasize how she is much more than her disability, and she doesn't need anyone's pity.

Further down the page, there is another photo of Magda wearing a bright pink top with a wide collar under a black jacket with wide lapels, gray pants, silver boots, and a black hat accented with a wide pink ribbon. Her blond hair has been straightened, so it grazes her shoulders, her hand is curled over the seat of her wheelchair, and her legs are crossed, perhaps to better accentuate her silver boots. As in the previous photo, the chair is integrated into Magda's photo as a fact of life and a facet of her mobility. Even if the viewer wanted to focus on it, Magda's bright pink top is so arresting that the eye is drawn there first, then to her hat and boots. It is easy to imagine how Magda's pictures may benefit other women with disabilities in her online community, modeling disabled fashion and sexuality as Kafer suggests is sorely needed. At the same time, as with Kimmie's fashion show pictures, the images are ultimately pictures of white heteronormative feminine beauty which don't verge outside the dominant cultural box of fashion and sexuality.

Another blog post that is more erotically and comically charged is titled "NY Fashion Week leaves me scribbling." A photo of Magda is featured at the top of the page. Her hair is cut in a blond bob, and she wears sunglasses with dark pink frames and a short-sleeved shirt with navy blue lace edging the neckline and two u-shaped breasts drawn over the chest, approximately where her own breasts would be. The breasts are crude and comic representations, with nipples accentuated as circles the size of quarters. Magda's mouth is closed and smiling coyly, her chair barely visible behind her arm, but that is not where viewers are meant to focus their gaze. The caption reads, "What do you think of my rack? I may be a C cup, but baby, my world is EEE. Here's to my newest DIY scribble doodle print tshirt for NY Fashion Week."[45] Magda explains that the shirt was made by a friend of hers and inspired by a Fashion Week design. Below Magda's photo is a picture of a model wearing a similar shirt with her caption, "Just in case people forget where your boobs are, this tshirt is the perfect diagram. Purchase a TATAS TEE." The shirt mocks standards of femininity and sexuality, and the way that certain regions of women's bodies tend to be stared at more than others. Instead of allowing people to joke about women's breasts, women turn the joke around and imply *I know what you're probably looking at, so I'll just make them easier to see*. These breasts are also a parody of themselves, appearing as ones that might be drawn in a mocking cartoon or doodled by an adolescent kid.[46] The shirt represents a way for women to take back the right to represent their bodies, albeit in a comic manner, while shaming people for wandering eyes. At the same time, others may find this caricature of sexuality so overt as to be offensive as it still focuses on drawing eyes to women's breasts. Magda twists the meaning of the shirt further by sexualizing her body in a normative way and suggesting women who are wheelchair users can be stared at just as TAB women tend to be. Far from being desexualized, the blushing viewer has an imperative to look at her rack, whether they want to or not. In this way Magda complicates the meaning of disability by demanding that people stare at her as a sexual object and subject, as she looks back from the photo. Since wheelchairs and other prosthetic devices tend to desexualize disabled people in the minds of TABs who avert their gaze, the T-shirt is transgressive in the way that it draws the viewer back to Magda's sexuality and her wheelchair simultaneously.

Further mocking the sexual styles displayed at Fashion Week, Magda comments on another photo of a model wearing a "penis bikini top." She notes, "Just what I have always wanted—a penis bikini top. It was designed by Nan Li and Emilia Pfohl for VFiles. Photo by Masoto Onada. I emailed my mom this top and asked 'Mom, can you ask Santa to put this in my stocking this year? I have a new venture in the New York. I am starting a new porn site for dudes who dig women in wheelchairs.' She hasn't responded yet." Magda's joking with the genitalia-inspired styles of Fashion Week makes it clear that she is not sexually innocent, yet her remark about "dudes who dig women in wheelchairs" could be read as a jab at devotees who are sexually attracted to disabled women, or perhaps it is a jab at her mother, who may not want to think about her daughter being considered a sexual subject or object. Similar to Kafer's sentiments about devotees, Magda's comments may reflect that she doesn't mind men finding her sexy, but she also doesn't like the idea that they would do so only on the basis of her being a wheelchair-user. Her ironic twist on the penis bikini top simultaneously sexualizes herself as a person with a disability and makes the misdirected fashion statement out to be a farce.

Overall, Magda is unimpressed with Fashion Week, stating, "If the clothing from the majority of collections could speak, they would moan and kvetch. I felt sorry for them, the same kind of sorry which I feel for haggard suburban moms with greasy hair pulled back in ponytails, shoved under baseball caps, without a moment to schmear on lipstick." In this note, Magda suggests there is a problem when women have no time to look preened and put together. While her personal style and confidence help her define fashion to include the fashionable disabled body, there are standards of femininity and "looking good" that she does not try to tear down. On this level, her comments could be read as offensive to women who don't share her priorities or care that their ponytails are under ball caps. Then again, her audience may not be the makeup-less mom who juggles a wheelchair and two kids, but the fashionista on wheels who wants to strut her sexy self down the sidewalks of New York. Once again, her blog speaks to a subset of people in disability communities that desire to be included in cosmopolitan fashion culture. This perspective can be critiqued in the same way that disability studies itself has been criticized, as not considering crucial aspects of race, class, gender, and other intersectional identities, and constructing a definition of disability and sexuality that focuses on heterosexual white femininity (Bell 2007, 407–11; Brownsworth 1999, xix; Samuels, 1999, 198–200). At the same time, Madga seems to have a sense of a particular fashion-forward readership that both aligns with and departs from certain constructions of feminine beauty, and clearly all blogs will not connect with all people.

Magda's thoughts on fashion, as well as her political stance, are also apparent in her post "Wheelchair Barbie and I are having a fashion revolution on Earth Day." As with Kimmie's Barbie Big Head Halloween costume, disability is paired with a doll that symbolizes the unattainable (white middle-class heteronormative) ideal of feminine sexuality. At the top of this post is a photo of Magda wearing a black-and-white striped T-shirt with black lace sleeves, black hat with a bright floral design, and black pants. As if mocking overly cheerful vacation photos, Magda holds a Wheelchair Barbie up with one hand, her other hand waving while she gives the audience a wide grin. Wheelchair Barbie has one plastic arm raised in greeting, and she is dressed to the nines in a light blue vest, pink T-shirt, and darker pink capris and sun hat.[47] Their pictures are superimposed over a larger image of Magda sitting in her wheelchair in profile. She looks to be rolling up a green hill with Wheelchair Barbie poised on her lap.

Magda writes, "For Earth Day last year I made a floating vessel out of plastic green gingerale bottles for my wheelchair Barbies." This note is accompanied by a picture of two Wheelchair Barbies floating along in their innovative recycled watercraft. Disability has not barred them from taking to the waves. While this photograph only shows Wheelchair Barbie in sporty active wear, and we can't know what prom dresses and miniskirts may color her ensemble, Garland-Thomson has criticized the makers of Wheelchair Barbie for shaping her as more sporty than sexual. She notes that Barbie's friend Becky uses a wheelchair and gets to be an athlete and wear comfy clothes, but in this trade, she loses her sexuality (2017, 372). At the same time, we must ask why Wheelchair Barbie can't be considered sporty and sexual, as Magda may be suggesting since she includes the iconic doll in a blog that features T-shirts with crudely drawn breasts, penis bikini tops, and a woman with a sense of style that Barbies of all ability levels might envy. Perhaps Becky only comes with active wear, yet in the spirit of friendship and clothes-swapping, surely Barbie could lend her a sweater and leggings, or even that to-die-for silk blouse and miniskirt.

As Magda notes in the About page of her blog, she often uses her writing for political commentary, and the Earth Day message is no exception. Her note provides a fashion-conscious twist on being a responsible consumer: "Please be cognizant of the clothing you wear and where it is made. This can be a reality, since even in China wages are rising as a result of workers' protests. One day we will live in a world where workers are as important as the corporations who profit most." While her Wheelchair Barbies are integrated into the post to make the political message more playful, ethical consumerism is an issue that Magda feels is pressing. Similar to Kimmie, while her blog does not evade aspects of Magda's life that involve disability, her primary focus is making a point about key issues. She presents disability as her means of being in the world, a fact that is no more or less important than other facets of her life. The fact that she often doesn't mention her disability in her blog posts is a political statement in itself. By focusing on consumerism and environmentalism, Magda complicates the meaning of disability to suggest how it can be banal and mundane and that the reader's interest should be drawn to other matters. This is yet another reason why she is an important voice in the (fashion-conscious) disability community.

WRITING ON THE WALLS IN THE
VIRTUAL NEIGHBORHOOD

While the totality of one's bodymind cannot be captured through words and pictures, various forms of social media allow people with disabilities to have a voice in virtual neighborhoods and join larger conversations as they develop their political and sexual identities. Part of the larger question addressed by these bloggers as they make meaning of disability and sexuality in their writing is how much they want to work inside, outside, or explode dominant social structures regarding disability and sexuality. Some want to make the cultural pie larger to include folks with disabilities, some want to blow up the pie, and yet others say forget about pie, it's inherently limiting, we need to expand into a whole dessert buffet.

Culinary analogies aside, as with any form of activism, bloggers may wonder how far their voice is traveling across virtual and physical spaces. Along with shaping his sensual and sarcastic self through his blog, Gurza uses his writing to express frustration over whether his advocacy has been able to enact social change. In his post "Working as a Queer Cripple: My Feelings Around Presenting Sex, Disability and Queerness," Gurza tells of leading a multiday workshop with a community theater group regarding disability and sexuality. When asked by the director how he felt about doing these presentations, Gurza said he loved the work. When the director persisted in asking the same question (twice), Gurza writes that he "looked at the director square in the face, and with a glimmer of tears in my eyes, I said: 'I'm tired.'" He continues the post by relating frustrating moments in sexuality advocacy, moments when "instead of showing you Powerpoint presentations about how great sex, disability and queerness is, I want to scream out to the group and say, 'Does anyone find me sexy?! Would any of you fuck me? Honestly?!'"[48]

Gurza explains that he must constantly re-experience his own painful moments of sexuality and disability, highlighting the fact that he isn't just a cheerful poster child preaching for a world in which everyone has equal access to leather harnesses and sex clubs. Gurza ends his post by suggesting that "the next time someone with a disability presents about sex, disability, queerness, or any facet of their lived experience for you, know this: we're tired, we're angry, we're horny, and it took every ounce of strength for us not to leave the room. Maybe buy us a drink and flirt with us after . . . that'd be nice. And maybe instead of just taking notes, take down my number." Gurza situates himself in the community he is advocating for, not as its spokesperson but as a member with desires and disappointments and dreams, one who is willing to make his life a symbol on PowerPoint presentations to illustrate the pinpricks and punches of shared pain. Being disallowed from having a sexual self has taken an emotional toll. Yet by cataloging these ideas on his blog, he provides a testament for others to read while perusing the highways and byways and curving alleys of the virtual neighborhood, seeking a space of like sentiments. While many people think of political activism as confronting rules, regulations, and various aspects of the law, Gurza shows how it encompasses changing attitudes toward disability and sexuality, a shift that may come much more slowly, but has a daily impact on his life and the lives of other people with disabilities.

Not only do Gurza and other bloggers provide posts to ponder, but they can also serve as models for other people who find it easier to express themselves through written rather than spoken words. Clearly the blogosphere and other forms of social media have enabled disabled individuals who may have otherwise been silent to strengthen their voices and increase their volume, planting the seeds for long-term social change and creating room for people with disabilities in dominant and counter-cultural spaces.

At the end of Gurza's essay "Queer and Cripple in the 6ix," he writes, "I imagine what it would be like if I could enter these long-standing institutions, these palaces of possibility and playfulness. I picture each club with no stairs or tiny doors that I can't access, and envision myself rolling through the front door with a smile on my face and a good-looking guy on each armrest of my wheelchair. Those images fall away as I continue down the street."[49] His call for accessible queer spaces adds another voice to those asking for these imagined neighborhoods to blossom to reality, enacting the accessibility of online spaces in the physical ones.

ON METAPHOR

No one has ever, in a moment of frustration, yelled at me, "What, are you blind?"

Is it wrong to gleefully imagine such a scenario, and my comic pang of pleasure when replying "Yes"?

Disability scholar Tanya Titchkosky critiques the way that some people within social justice movements have employed disability-related metaphors that imply the lives of people with disabilities are somehow lesser than those of TABs (2017, 270). In describing colonialism and colonizers as "blind" and suggesting that some men are "deaf to gender distortions," Titchkosky asserts that activists seek to "diagnose" social justice problems so they can be cured (271–72). But these metaphors also marginalize people with disabilities by reinforcing the idea that disability stands for brokenness and an unacceptable state of embodiment. At the same time, Titchkosky acknowledges that metaphor can be helpful since it "is a form of social action; it gives meaning to people and events by expressing them in relation to each other through a comparison" (275–76). While such turns of phrase can be unwittingly discriminatory, Titchkosky argues metaphor has the potential to reshape modes of thought, be "a place where we nurture the capacity to let new understandings arise," and allow people to think creatively about body variability (277).

In a similar vein, Vidali critiques the work of linguists George Lakoff and Mark Johnson, who suggest that metaphors are figures of speech that "everyone" can identify with since metaphors often refer to bodies, yet Lakoff and Johnson refer to "'natural' bodies [and] exclude disabled bodies and experience" (2010, 36–37). She takes issue with their assumption that all people have the same types of bodies and move in the same way, stating, "I would suggest that instead of 'universal' bodily experience, the preponderance of ablebodied metaphors reflects a refusal to recognize and include disability, both as human experience and metaphoric phenomenon"

(41). Vidali argues we must find new ways of using metaphoric language that employs disability creatively, without repeating negative stigmas. She notes this approach would "engage the full range of disability; resist the desire to simply 'police' or remove disability metaphors; actively transgress disability metaphors by employing a diverse vocabulary; and artistically create and historically reinterpret metaphors of disability" (2010, 42). Through incorporating different ways of experiencing the world, these metaphors would reflect an appreciation for a wide range of bodyminds and means of developing knowledge.

Vidali writes that the idea of "knowing is seeing" is particularly problematic since it raises questions about how much anyone can "know" something based on visual perception, and limits how people gain knowledge through their bodies (2010, 46). She poses practical ways that individuals, specifically teachers, can apply new metaphoric language by "asking students to find the 'scents' of previous course ideas while reading a new article" or asking "colleagues [to] taste and digest a new subject, in order to encourage bodily ways of knowing and interacting that go beyond 'witnessing' texts. Changing the verb from see/highlight/envision to a new sensory experience not only recognizes, but creates, new ways of knowing" (47).

I've stopped counting the number of times people have asked whether I would have surgery on my blind eye if that would allow me to see. They're perplexed when I say I'd refuse to go under the knife. I wonder if they think something is wrong with me other than just my vision, but I could easily turn the question back on them: Why do you think two eyes are so goddamned necessary?

But even if I argue that my blind eye has granted me ways of knowing that aren't visual in nature, people still tend to look at me with their heads tilted when I give them my answer. I sigh, smile, shrug, and continue sniffing for my perfect metaphor.

Disability scholar Alyson Patsavas has created a photographic *Archive of Pain* as a response to annoying questions that people with chronic pain are often asked by TABs. Individuals are expected to explain what they might have done to cause their pain and thereby "take responsibility" for it. Patsavas argues, "At their worst, these questions—and the answers that they compel— fuel the brand of ableism that uses the presence of pain to justify the dismissal and devaluation of disabled life." Her *Archive of Pain* endeavors to "reframe the questions" and visually represent complex moments of embodiment with images that explore how sleeplessness and comfort, exhaustion and desire, might weave into the tapestry of pain:

> When Does It Hurt? Long Walk, Perfect Night: Slightly out of focus cobblestone walkway, covered in a light dusting of snow. Five out of focus lights disappear into the background. The foreground of the picture reveals speckles of snow. Two tire tracks on the cobblestone start in the foreground and disappear as they move toward the five (street) lights in the background of the photo. (Patsavas and Egermann)

These photographs reveal moments that are sweet and gritty and frustrating, sensations indescribable but through an image, layers of emotion coexisting in a space that does not have words, only the chill of an icy evening and the stark poetic quality of its description.

> How Does It Feel? Like Shit, in a Bag, Frozen Over: Close-up shot of an old tire, turned into a planter. The word DESTINATION is visible across the top of the tire. Inside is filled with water, frozen over. A dead branch from a plant sticks out of the ice in the top left-hand corner. Two bags hang over the tire, one in the top right of the picture, one in the bottom left. They are both partially frozen into the water. (Patsavas and Egermann)

The photographs evoke snapshots of my own memoires that cannot be labeled with a specific sentiment. I think of my partner squeezing my hand at the ophthalmologist's office, telling me I'm strong even when I don't feel like it. I think of the peculiar chemical odor of ophthalmologists' offices, the television in the corner trying to distract me with reruns of *Jeopardy!* while the room grows brighter, hazier, due to my dilation drops. I wonder what the world will look like in a year, if I will still see three moons.

Titchkosky notes that metaphors critiquing colonization and its lasting effects often involve images of disability and "include colonized people amputated from their homeland, from mainstream thought, and from history; people amputated from learning, tradition, and indigenous knowledge . . . self amputated from self" (2017, 277). Yet she argues it is likewise possible to use disability in figurative language to pose alternate means of embodiment, analyzing how Franz Fanon employs the metaphor of amputation while "refusing to accept this impairment condition as a sign of nothingness or death" (277–79). Along these same lines, Titchkosky suggests that we should not abandon disability metaphors, but explore "our capacity to imagine a different world" and "attempt to straddle disability by understanding it as a way of being that could incite a critical imagination" (280). In this way, reimagining the body through playing with the meaning of metaphor becomes a means of reinterpreting the world.

When I meet Eric in my usual coffee shop, he tells me that last weekend he went to a tournament in Pennsylvania with the wheelchair basketball team, and they saw an accident by the side of the road on their way back.

"I said we should stop and look for recruits for the team," he says. "The other guys started laughing, or they stared at me like they were shocked I'd just said that."

Good disability jokes are often edged with the macabre.

"The bus should have turned ambulance chaser and gone to the hospital to see if the person had all their limbs," I say.

"We could have offered a ready-made social group to help them through the rehabilitation process with a lot of dark humor," says Eric.

"Damn," I say, pretending to peer into a hospital room at an injured patient. "They've still got both arms and legs. Maybe they'll have a persistent limp. Would that be enough to qualify for the team?"

"Maybe the doctors could take off a little toe," says Eric.

"Asthma," I say, "really bad asthma." By now we're laughing perhaps a bit too hard, but Eric reminds me that his coach used to skim newspapers looking for accident victims.

"It's how he found more than one team member," Eric says with a shrug.

What to call that? Aptly amputated?

Eric cheerfully changes the subject to the long list of body parts he figures he could do without. Since he's an amputee with many disabled friends, this is the kind of thing he considers in his spare time.

"You can take my legs, that's fine," he says. "My hands are a bit harder, but I can do a lot with the stumps. Arms would be a bit trickier, but I could get along. I have a problem with my ears and my eyes. I have a lot of blind friends and I know it's not that bad, but still, I have a hard time making up my mind between hearing and sight."

How can I not love the way he shrugs at subtraction and says sure, no big deal, like bodies are made of Lego parts. If something snaps off you say "Those are the breaks," and get on with things. Admirably amputated. Insert your own metaphor here.

Within the bounds of literature, characters with disabilities have often taken on symbolic significance rather than being people in their own right. Snyder and Mitchell argue that such works "lean" on disabled characters to provide insight to the larger story. The disabled body becomes the primary means "of characterization for characters constructed as disabled," whose bodies convey a "message" about social structures that are in disarray (Snyder and Mitchell 2017, 206–7). At the end of such narratives, the disabled character often dies or is cast out of society due to bodily deviance, which also erases the social ill they were meant to symbolize (211). In this interpretation of literature, disabled characters aren't people but props an author uses to make a point.

Yet disability scholar Ato Quayson counters that a disabled character's identity in a text is not set, and can shift as the meaning of the disability shifts. While disability may play a role in how a character is perceived, that isn't the only factor in the reader's mind (Quayson 2017, 228). Quayson suggests that while reading about someone with a disability is not the same as seeing a disabled person in public, TAB readers may feel a similar discomfort when they encounter a body they assume isn't "whole" or "normal," whether they see that person on the sidewalk or through the lens of a story (222). Quayson contends that while disabled bodies in literature can represent social problems, they also represent social attitudes toward disability (222–23). Readers' attitudes toward disability may change as the disabled characters become more realized in the story (227), people for whom disability is but one aspect of a multifaceted identity.

Similar to Quayson, disability scholar Sami Schalk poses an alternate means of interpreting characters with disabilities. She argues that "disability can take on both concrete and metaphoric meanings in a text. This approach to disability metaphors seeks to understand how these representations of disability can symbolize something other than disability while still being about disability" (2017, 141). Complicating readings of disability gives added depth to the characters, as well as illuminating the social conditions, discrimination, and stigmas surrounding disability. In this way, Schalk suggests that examining disability in literature can be a fruitful space to explore "the historical and material connections between disability and other social systems of privilege and oppression such as race, gender, sexuality, class, the nation, and more. Such metaphors need not be either/or (i.e., this representation is either about race or about disability); in fact, they are often both/and, due specifically to the mutually constitutive nature of oppressions" (141). Examining disability in this manner, Schalk suggests, allows disability to represent itself and be used as a metaphor to represent "discrimination and exclusion" in a broken social system that creates conditions that are physically and emotionally disabling (141). Employing such an expansive mode of reading reveals disability is a lived reality, a valid form of embodiment, and a means to explore the systemic forms of social violence that further disable individuals. Metaphor doesn't have to strike only one chord. It can strum many.

Sometimes I write to get out of my body, and sometimes I write to be in it, searching for modes to explain how my body is daunting and delightful and often aches from my drive to get more done than I can physically accomplish.

Sometimes it's like knitting a scarf from many tiny yarn balls or piecing a quilt from odds and ends of fabric. It's beautiful and chaotic, unified and not, stitched tight and unraveling. It will never look the same way twice. It will never be finished. I just keep adding bits of this and that.

I know my story isn't over.

Chapter 5

"MY OTHER RIDE IS MY VIBRATOR":

Sex, Disability, and the Emancipatory Potential of Jokes

Despite two false starts, I wasn't going to abandon my quest for disability sex jokes, a space that seemed rife with confrontations and transgressions. I wanted to understand the ways comics with disabilities could prove themselves delightfully desirous, maligning the miles of myths that made disabled sex into a deviant spectacle. In the end, I turned to the virtual comedy stage through the magic of YouTube, watching performance after performance and seeking the sexual aside, the bluest of blue humor, quips by folks who use wheelchairs or canes or have a stutter. They spin stories and smile slyly to the audience who laughs in delight, or perhaps surprise, to hear the topic turn to sex. But what better spot than the comedy club to tell the titillating tale and try to turn the world upside-down to make it right-side up?

Ally Bruener begins her set by introducing herself to the audience as a "pretty normal twenty-two-year-old girl except I haven't had an abortion." She pauses while the audience laughs and then adds, "yet." The audience chuckles again, and Bruener goes on to reassure them, "Don't worry, it's scheduled for Monday" (Bruener 2011). This is political humor, edgy humor, a joke that plays with the dead baby trope and is further complicated because Bruener uses an electric wheelchair. While female comics portraying themselves as sexual subjects tend to walk a fine line between admiration and abjection from audiences (Foy 2015), female comics with disabilities heighten the tension since women with disabilities are often portrayed as desexualized in dominant culture. This space of discomfort and social anxiety makes it the perfect atmosphere for comedy.

People tend to joke about the subjects that make them most anxious (Dundes 1987, vii), so it's logical for humor to comment on relations among genders through sex jokes. As psychology and gender scholar Mary Crawford observes, "Humor is perhaps the most flexible and powerful of indirect modes, and sexually focused encounters perhaps the most complex of interpersonal situations. It is not surprising that people so often cope with sexual ambiguity, vulnerability, and danger by using humor" (2000, 180). Fear of disability is another space in which there is much cultural anxiety about the fragility of bodies (Barrick 1980; Dundes 1987, 15–18). These paired topics have led to a tradition of sex jokes about people with disabilities that depict them as passive sex objects, thwarted would-be lovers, or victims of sanctioned sexual violence.

Yet disabled comics have responded to these jokes with crip humor that can work against this negative frame. Their jokes may break down stereotypes about disability, find comedy in mainstream society's reaction to disability and sexuality, and make TABs the butt of the joke, arguing that people with disabilities are due full consideration of their sexuality, agency, and humanity.

At the same time, we must ask about their potential for long-term social impact. Gilbert discusses how comics follow the tradition of the "wise fool" (2004, 47) who is a cultural critic, but "a *reflector* rather than a *reformer*" (49), highlighting problems within a culture but not necessarily shifting norms. While comics with disabilities may reveal social constructions that lead to sexual oppression, the question remains as to whether that action can create cultural change.

In this chapter I complicate the readings of jokes that involve disability and sexuality, tangling with the ambivalent nature of joking practice and how it can simultaneously be a liberatory act, deconstruct stereotypes, and reinscribe them. First, I explore jokes (ostensibly) told by TABs about disabled people and sexuality, examining sex jokes found on four different websites. In my readings I focus on how the jokes reflect stereotypes about disabled people and sexuality. While many of the jokes were likely posted by TABs, some of them also appear on a website maintained by a man who identifies himself as a wheelchair user. We can't rule out that these jokes have circulated in both TAB and disability communities, though tellers may have different goals in repeating them, from making hostile jabs at people with disabilities, to mocking the idea behind the joke. As a whole, though, these jokes seem to be barbs meant to deride and dehumanize, condone sexual violence, portray people with disabilities as passive sex objects, and deride TABS who find disabled people sexually attractive.

In the next section, I analyze performances by male and female comics with disabilities who joke about sexuality and disability. I examine how these jokes might be responses to older jokes about sex and disability, ways the comics create spaces of identification with TAB audience members, and mechanisms used in the construction of the joke. I also analyze whether the comics critique dominant society by portraying themselves as "victims," mocking social standards (Gilbert 2004, 137). I investigate the question of who has access to the comedy stage, why certain topics are considered joking material while others are ignored, and I note differences in the social perception of male and female persons with disabilities and how these distinctions affect the jokes that comics with disabilities choose to tell.

As with all comedic performances, we can never be sure how a joke will be interpreted by disabled or TAB audience members. Aspects of the joke that may be funny to one person might be construed by another as no laughing matter, or people may laugh at the same joke for very different reasons. As Reid, Stoughton, and Smith note of this instability of interpretation, "Like all communication, comedy is dialogic—an ever-shifting construction of meaning between comedian and audience—and therefore, is neither wholly predictable nor describable in static terms" (2006, 632).

Along these lines, I argue that these sex jokes could be read in a number of ways, from mocking social perceptions of disability to presenting people with disabilities as "able" partners. At the same time, some of these jokes risk doing harm to people with certain kinds of disabilities, creating a form of disability hierarchy that suggests some disabilities are "worse" than others (Dolmage 2014, 46). Other jokes can be read as misogynistic, openly mocking women, or they may play with the idea of the overly libidinous disabled person, a trope that some disabled people would find distasteful while others might consider it to be a hilarious assertion of agency. I conclude my discussion by exploring jokes that have the potential to expand joking practice to queering sexuality, a topic has not been widely addressed by disabled comics.

My search reveals the comedy stage to be a turbulent and terrific space of ambiguity and absurdity, where the question we always return to is why everyone is laughing. The answer is never the same twice.

DISABILITY, SEXUALITY, AND STEREOTYPES: LAUGHING MATTERS?

There is a tradition of disabled people being cast as laughable and comic figures, or ones ripe for abuse (Dundes 1987, 15–18). As Shakespeare writes, "Within performances on stage or film, there is a particular relish of the disabled figure of fun, a shared enjoyment of the peculiar pleasure of laughing at the abnormal. Many classic cartoons—Elmer Fudd and Mr. Magoo, Dopey and the other six dwarfs—centre on physical difference or mental incapacity" (1999, 48). Folklorist Gershon Legman elaborates on possible reasons for making disabled individuals comic, since joking behavior often hides some kind of antagonism or conflict: "Jokes originate as hostile impulses of free-floating aggression in the tellers of the jokes, as a response to or an expression of social and sexual anxieties they are otherwise unable to absorb or express" (1968, 20). Because TABs either consciously or unconsciously worry over the tenuous nature of their own bodies, jokes about disabled people often depict them as beings who are less-than-human, and must be othered.

This fear of disability leads to disabled people being stereotyped as sexually undesirable, needy, and impotent in sex jokes. As Mairs writes, TABs are often "Made uncomfortable, even to the point of excruciation, by the thought of maimed bodies engaged in erotic fantasy or action . . . the repulsion lies buried so deeply in consciousness as to seem natural rather than constructed" (2002, 162). Along similar lines, scholar Judith Anne McKenzie notes that disabled people are often depicted as unable to understand sex, since there is a range of "persistent myths about disabled people. Most notably, they are deemed to be asexual and not part of the world of sexual interchange. In this light, disabled people are construed as innocents, who must be protected from sexual knowledge and discouraged from learning about their own sexuality" (2013, 374).[1]

On the opposite side of this sexual spectrum are individuals who fetishize disabled people and consider them to be sex objects. Some of these devotees also argue that no one else could find people with amputations to be sexually attractive. As Kafer notes of devotee logic, "The key difference between a devotee and a non-devotee is the value afforded an amputation: devotees bestow attractiveness and desirability upon it; non-devotees are disgusted by it. But both are assumed to cast the presence or absence of an amputation as the determining factor in a woman's sexual attractiveness" (2012, 336).

This objectification of the disabled body is one of the themes in jokes about sex and disability that I collected online. The jokes often negatively stereotype disabled people, casting them as the butt and condoning violence against them. Some of these jokes were posted on a web page designed by Penn W., a man who uses a wheelchair due to a spinal cord injury. While many of these jokes were likely invented by TAB individuals to make fun of disabled people, we must also consider that TAB and disabled tellers may lend different meanings to these jokes and have a variety of reasons why they find these jokes funny. Disabled tellers might repeat them due to internalizing negative stereotypes about disabled people, or they may locate other, more subversive meanings that work against dominant cultural stereotypes of disability. Generally, my readings of the jokes did not suggest they were destabilizing stereotypes, but that does not mean such interpretations aren't possible.

JOKES THAT CONDONE SEXUAL VIOLENCE
AGAINST DISABLED WOMEN

So I've got a new girlfriend. She invited me around to her place for dinner the other night. We were in the kitchen, just about to start making dinner when she asked me to turn on the veg. Apparently, fingering her tetraplegic daughter was not the right move . . . (W.)

This is a disability joke as well as a pedophilia joke since it involves taboo sexual contact with minors and suggests that predatory behavior is laughable as opposed to a traumatic sexual violation. The joke also promotes a stereotype of disabled people as passive vegetables who should be grateful for any sexual contact they receive, even if it is tantamount to rape. It further supports the idea of "disability drift" (Dolmage 2014, 46), implying that people who are physically disabled also have a mental impairment. The teller would likely not attempt such an act with his girlfriend since she would speak up and refuse, but not so her disabled daughter who is denied agency. The joke condones such actions, suggesting that even if disabled women aren't willing or happy to be turned on, they can't resist and express displeasure, so their desires don't matter. Disabled women are restricted from their right to sexual choice, denying them an important facet of personhood, and the ability to be a sexual subject and not a passive object.

What's more fun than raping a quadriplegic? Raping and killing a spastic! ("Disabled.")

What do you do after you rape a 12-year-old deaf and mute girl? Break her fingers so she can't tell her mother! ("Disabled")

Who is the cruelest man in the world? The guy who raped Helen Keller then cut off her hands so she couldn't scream for help. ("Helen Keller")

These graphic jokes are particularly brutal in their depiction of sexual and physical violence against disabled people, especially disabled women. Raping them is sanctioned since they can't fight back or call for help, rendering them easy victims. Killing disabled women is likewise permissible since they have a "deviant" form of sexuality and should not be allowed to procreate. Under such a premise, killing disabled people is eugenically sound since they could possibly have disabled children.[2] Disabled people are targets for hostility since they can't act or communicate in normative ways. Since they are deviant in terms of their embodiment, they are fair targets for mistreatment. These jokes are particularly chilling given the widespread incidents of sexual abuse of disabled people (Siebers 2008, 146).

Version 1: *One day a man is walking along the beach and sees a quadriplegic girl on the boardwalk, sitting in her wheelchair and crying. He decides to be a good samaritan and asks her what's wrong. She replies sadly, "I've never been hugged."*

So he hugs the girl, which seems to cheer her up and he continues on his way.

The next day he sees the girl again, still sitting on the boardwalk and crying, so he asks her what's wrong and she replies, "I've never been kissed."

So, he kisses the girl dutifully and goes on his way.

The following day, he passes her again, and once again, she's crying and he asks her what's wrong.

She replies, "I've never been screwed."

So, the man wheels her down the boardwalk, pushes her off the pier and says, "Now, you're screwed!" (W.)

Version 2: *There was a lady with no arms or legs sitting on the beach enjoying the sun and surf, when this man walks up and says, "Hey, lady have you ever been kissed before?"*

"No." the lady replied.

"Well," said the man, "Have you ever been licked before?"

"No." the lady said again.

"Hmmm," asked the man, "have you ever been fucked before?"

"No, I haven't. But I would like to!" said the lady.

"Well, bitch, you are now! The tide is coming in!" ("Disabled")

Both versions of these jokes stereotype female wheelchair users as needy, ignored, unlovable, and charity cases for affection. In the first joke the disabled woman is portrayed as sly and whiny in trying to gain affection from the TAB male. He is "dutiful" and a "good Samaritan," while she is cunning and slowly ups the ante until she pushes him "too far." Her suggestion that she could have intercourse with the "charitable" TAB man condones violence against her in the context of the joke. He is sanctioned in pushing her off the pier, since she is socially and physically deviant and doesn't deserve to have sex and risk the reproduction of disability.

While TABs may be kind toward disabled people, these jokes suggest there is a line that should not be crossed in terms of beneficence. Hugging or kissing may be an allowable kindness, but intercourse is not a possibility. When this taboo subject is brought up at the end of the joke, the punch line that follows hints to the drowning of disabled women who would dare imagine that their bodies could be sexually attractive.

These jokes also portray the (presumably) TAB men as the only persons with agency in this exchange, while the disabled women are passive recipients of charity who cannot act on their own. This refusal to allow disabled women to be sexual subjects does violence against them by abjecting their bodies, and shoving them out of the realm of people who can be considered desirable. While disabled people may wish for sexual contact, they are not fitting sex partners for TABs.

The first version of the joke was from Penn W's website, and since he also uses a wheelchair, it is interesting to contrast the portrayal of the whiny disabled woman to the portrayal of the disabled woman in the second joke, who is not whiny but minding her own business. The first version could be read as a caution to disabled people against seeming needy or calculating, given its inscription as being posted online by a disabled person. Don't take advantage of any pity you may garner because of your disability, the joke suggests, or you risk being screwed over.

The second version of the joke depicts a TAB man who is crueler than the man in the first joke, and a disabled women who is more innocent since he is mean to her without provocation. He seems to be offering the opportunity to have sex, teasing her with the prospect that she might be a fitting partner. While the disabled woman would like to be sexual, in the turn of the joke, he not only refuses her desire but does not help her. At the end of the joke, the implication is that she might drown, but since she is othered her demise is sanctioned. Further, the man asking the disabled woman about her romantic experiences suggests that he believes she hasn't had such encounters, and no one desires her. The joke promotes not only physical violence against people with disabilities, but also does cultural violence against them in implying they should be eliminated from the sexual sphere.

DISABLED PEOPLE OBJECTIFIED
AS PASSIVE SEX PARTNERS

There once was a lady who was tired of living alone. So she put an ad in the paper which outlined her requirements. She wanted a man who 1) would treat her nicely, 2) wouldn't run away from her, and 3) would be good in bed.

Then, one day, she heard the doorbell ring. She answered it, and there on the front porch was a man in a wheel chair who didn't have any arms or legs.

*I'm here about the ad you put in the paper. As you can see, I have no arms
so I can't beat you, and I have no legs so I can't run away from you."*
   "Yes, but are you good in bed?"
   "How do you think I rang the doorbell?" (W.)

This is another joke posted by Penn W., depicting the man in the wheelchair as
sexually available and well-endowed, even to a comic extreme since his penis
is his only functional "limb." Yet this joke also does a form of social violence
against him since his identity is essentialized to his function as a sexual object.
His dialogue suggests that he can only assert agency through using his penis
(and while he is very adept in that manner, one may also be curious how he
was able to wheel himself to the door). The disabled man cannot run from
or hit his potential partner, so he is cast as a relatively harmless but potent
and eager sex object, though he is also deprived of full personhood since
his identity is bound to his sexuality. At the same time, the joke could be
read as casting TAB men in an equally negative light, as individuals who
can do violence against women, overpower them, or run from them. The
disabled man becomes the "perfect" sex partner, because the woman can easily
dominate him. This joke depicts sex not as an intimate act, but a power play in
which the winner is the one in control. It is perhaps an unromantic notion, but
an expected one in jokes that juxtapose sexuality and overt or implied violence.

*What's the difference between fucking a girl with arms and fucking a girl
without arms?*
   *If your fucking a girl with no arms and your dick slips out, you have to put
it back yourself! ("Disabled")*

*What do you call a woman with no arms or legs who gives good head?
Partially disabled! ("Disabled")*

Similar to the disabled man in the previous joke, the disabled woman
in the first joke is depicted as having no agency to act on her own since
she is helpless to do anything but be a recipient during intercourse. She
is depersonalized except for her function as a sexual object, and even in
that act she has no ability to start, stop, or otherwise control the encounter.
While this context doesn't specifically mention rape, it is easy to see how
the joke could seem to sanction such conduct due to her supposed inability
to be a sexual subject. The social violence against the woman in the second
joke is also apparent since she can only function as a sex toy to please TAB
individuals. In these jokes, people with disabilities become little more

than sexual playthings with no will of their own and no ability to refuse intercourse, making them easy targets for sexual violence.

MUTES AND STUTTERS AS COMIC FIGURES

As Legman writes, individuals with speech-related disabilities have long been cast as the butt of jokes, mocking their intelligence and movements: "Mutes, stutters, and spastics are considered in jokes to be close kin to idiots, and the pretend agonies of stammering, and cruel imitation of the spastic's clutching gait, engaged in by the tellers of stories of this type, are not pleasant to watch" (1968, 160). Such jokes and physical performances again deprive people with disabilities of their personhood, suggesting they are somehow lesser than TAB individuals and can be targets of mockery. One example of such a joke is the following:

> A deaf-mute is witness in a rape case. "How did the girl go into the barn?" the attorney writes on the blackboard. The mute walks his fore- and middle-fingers trippingly across the table. The man goes in as the fore- and ring-fingers with the middle finger sticking straight out between. The girl then comes out as fingers held wide apart and stumbling, and the man as he went in but with the middle finger now drooping. The girl is pronounced raped . . . (Legman 1968, 160)

In another version there is an alternate ending: "Then the deaf-mute, gurgling and pointing excitedly to himself, made two fingers walk with the middle finger sticking up, rigid" (Legman 1968, 160–61). Legman notes that even someone who cannot speak in words and who is assumed to have a mental disability can understand sex, which is part of the reason why this joke is considered "funny" (160). The man in this joke is described as "gurgling," making him seem infantile, since he cannot distinguish himself as an adult through language use. Additionally, in this second version of the joke, his sexuality is depicted as deviant and cruel since he is excited due to a rape.[3] It is clear that he knows what has taken place, but the joke also suggests he can only be a voyeur who is aroused by the sex acts of others, he cannot be a viable sexual partner. This joke also harms his personhood and subjectivity since it suggests he was excited by the act and did not think to help the victim, implying he is controlled by his sexual passions and not his thoughts about the well-being of others. The social violence against people with disabilities is apparent in the way they are suggested to be juvenile in their behavior, deviant in their sexuality, and lacking in humanity because of their disregard for others, even people who are injured.

THE LIBIDINOUS PERSON WITH DWARFISM

A [person with dwarfism] went into a whorehouse. None of the girls really wanted to serve him, so finally they drew lots and Misty was unlucky and went up to the room with him. A minute later there was a loud scream. The madam and all of the girls charged up the stairs and into the room. Misty lay on the bed in a dead faint. Standing next to the bed was the [person with dwarfism], totally nude, with a three foot cock hanging down touching the floor.

The girls were dumbfounded by the sight. Finally one of them regained her composure and said, "Sir would you mind if we felt it? We have never seen anything like that before."

The [person with dwarfism] sighed, "Okay honey, but only touching, no sucking. I used to be six feet tall!" ("Disabled")[4]

The TAB women in this joke are unwilling to have intercourse with someone who has a different body type, despite the fact they are being offered money. The implication is that men whose bodies do not meet a normative standard cannot be able sex partners and are unfit for intercourse with "normal" women at any price. Similar to the woman-on-the-beach joke, this joke suggests that sex with disabled people should be considered taboo. Even in the turn of the joke, the TAB women are not sexually aroused so much as they have found another reason to treat the person with dwarfism as a curiosity. This makes him more closely akin to a sideshow display, as opposed to a person. Like the man in the wheelchair who is able to ring the doorbell, the person with dwarfism is stereotyped as being overly sexual to the point where his member is his most discernible trait. He is also made the butt of the joke since his sexual enthusiasm (a psychological deviancy) has led to his dwarfism (a physical deviancy), implying another kind of "disability drift" that makes him unfit for intercourse.

The horny [person with dwarfism] found that the best way to score with women was to be totally direct about it. So he went up to this tall, beautiful, blonde woman and said, "Hey honey, what would you say to a little fuck?"

She looked down on him and said, "Hello little fuck!" ("Disabled")

The disabled person is cast as sexually enthusiastic, yet refused by TAB women as a sexual partner. While he is confident in his abilities, his prospective paramour makes it clear that he should not imply the possibility of intercourse, and to do so is absurd. In calling him a "fuck," she turns his sexual suggestion around to make him the butt of the joke, conveying her physical superiority and that he should not be taken seriously as a sexual being. Even though he might have the right equipment and libido, his stature "disables" him from being her partner. As with several of the disabled people in the previous jokes, his characterization is limited to his function as a horny stereotype.

Two dwarfs decide to treat themselves to a night out at a brothel. When they arrive at the brothel they are given a woman each and they both go into separate bedrooms.

The first dwarf is disappointed, however, as he cannot get an erection. His depression is made worse by the fact that he hears "One, Two, Three. . . . Hup!" coming from his friends room. In the morning, the second dwarf asks the first, "How did it go?"

The first whispered back, "It was so embarrassing. I couldn't get a hard on!"

The second dwarf shook his head, "You think that's embarrassing," he asked, "I couldn't even get on the fucking bed!" ("Disabled")

The two people with dwarfism are depicted as sexually enthusiastic, but they end up frustrated and cannot consummate the act because they lack sexual potency, or the size and ability to access their partners. Both are "disabled" from having sex with TABs due to a physical quality—either their bodies are not a good "fit" for the TAB world, and thus they should not look for space in it, or they are sexually impotent and do not "belong" in a place where sexuality is the main currency. In both cases violence is done against them because they are barred from accessing certain spaces, and they become the butt of the joke since they are cast as physically and therefore sexually deficient.

TABS WHO HAVE SEX WITH DISABLED
PEOPLE ARE DESPERATE

This guy is working in the middle of Alaska for 6 moths and finally gets a couple of days vacation in the big city. He goes down to the local brothel, but there is only one girl left and she had a bad dose of scabies and one eye.

The guy was really desperate for a fuck and he had to put his cock into something, so the girl offered to take out her glass eye and let him fuck her socket.

After having the best shag of his life, the guy promised that he would be back again the next time he was on vacation.

The girl said, "Sure mister. I'll keep an eye out for you!" ("Disabled")

In this joke the disabled girl is portrayed as kind, desperate, and willing to please. No one will consider her as a sexual partner since she has body lice and is physically disabled, rendering her unfit and unclean for intercourse. The only kind of sex possible with her is deviant and not socially sanctioned for a myriad of reasons, but in this case the desperate TAB man doesn't care. While this sex is suggested to be quite good, it is also taboo, presenting an image in the listener's mind of disabled sexuality as obscene and laughable. Both individuals are the butt of the joke, since the TAB man is so sex-starved as to attempt this strange act with a disabled woman, while he would not have done so under other circumstances. In turn the disabled woman has become disabled because of having normative sex, resulting in body lice that renders her "unclean," and the glass eye suggests she doesn't fit normative beauty standards. The joke punishes her for doing sex work, while it does not punish the clientele who rendered her disabled. Since her sexuality is cast as undesirable, she is eager to please if only for economic reasons. Notably, she and her partner only engage in sex that will not allow for procreation, since other parts of her body are considered unfit for sexual contact. While this sex is apparently satisfying, it also carries no risk of replicating disability in offspring, rendering her to be a "safe" yet odd sex partner. The joke is also ambivalent in that it suggests her disability makes her a better sex partner, and if she replaced the glass eye that made her appear normal, those abilities would be diminished. While alternate forms of sexuality may be satisfying, the joke also implies they are worthy of mockery.

DISABLED PEOPLE SHOULD ONLY HAVE SEX WITH OTHER DISABLED PEOPLE

How did Helen Keller meet her husband? On a blind date! ("Helen Keller")

How do cripples make love? They rub their crutches together. (W.)

Define true love. Hellen Keller and Stevie Wonder playing tennis. ("Helen Keller")

These jokes suggest that disabled people should only find lovers and sex partners among other disabled people, since sexual contact with TABs is improper and taboo. Notably the joke that discusses intercourse does not involve contact that could create a child, but focuses on connections between prosthetic devices.

These jokes also rely on cultural knowledge of Helen Keller, a woman who learned to communicate with TAB individuals though she was blind and deaf. While Keller proved herself to be a brilliant person, jokes about her focus on her otherness.[5] In these jokes the bodies and sexuality of disabled people are portrayed as strange, suggesting sexual relationships should be with "their own kind." There is also a coldness in the sexuality suggested by the crutches joke since it does not depict bodies touching but extensions of the body, implying disabled bodies cannot or should not experience intimate contact. In this way people with disabilities are suggested not only to look different, but to have different sensations than TABs. If one reads this joke against the grain, it could suggest that disabled people may have innovative forms of sexuality that incorporate prosthetic devices and encourage intimate play; however, in this context, the joke seems to be more limiting than liberatory in its scope.[6]

CRIP HUMOR: WHO'S ONSTAGE?

In contrast to jokes that support stereotypes regarding disability and sexuality, disabled comics' sex jokes acknowledge these stereotypes, yet subvert them to suggest they are social constructions of disability and not realities. But even when jokes are inscribed by disabled comics, there is still negotiation between the comic and audience about why these jokes are funny (Shakespeare 1999, 52). Jokes told by disabled comics can also reflect a hostile impulse against dominant society, turning the tables to make it the butt of the joke. Since this comedy is from a disability perspective, it can critique the TAB world and reveal how disabled people are not allowed to "fit" into their surroundings, either physically or as validated sexual subjects. Similar to comic narratives told by people with disabilities in chapter 3, this type of joking can suggest that disability itself is not always a problem, but rather individuals become disabled when they are in an environment in which it is difficult for them to function.

This kind of crip humor can also be a space to mediate relations between disabled and TAB individuals and allow disabled comedians find spaces of identification with their audiences. Yet while disabled individuals telling stories to a few friends may have an easier time judging how their audience will "receive" a joke, comedy club audiences are much larger and incorporate a wider range of attitudes regarding disability. As Reid, Stoughton, and Smith write of the social dynamic that may exist within such venues, "Mainstream comedians' demeaning jokes [regarding disability] enable them to separate from difficult feelings by perpetuating an Us-Them mindset. Contrastingly, disabled comedians present an insider, although not essentialized, perspective, blurring the boundaries of the historical Us-Them dichotomy" (2006, 630). Yet while this goal may be the intent of comics with disabilities, it is difficult to gauge how any audience may react to a collective disabled/TAB "us."

As Thomas suggested in chapter 3 when discussing his comedy routines, it can also be difficult to translate a disability-based perspective to outsiders who aren't familiar with the range of disability communities and forms of embodiment. To perform for TAB and disabled audiences, disabled comics must frame their jokes in a way that can be understood by either group, even if different audiences will find humor in various aspects of the joke. Beth Haller and Sue Ralph note that the fact disability jokes are delivered by disabled persons is key: "For nondisabled audiences to properly 'read' the humor, they must understand that disabled people created it. If this is not understood, the humor is seen as cruel, rather than funny" (2003). The audience assumes that the disabled teller is sympathetic toward individuals with disabilities and therefore sanctioned to tell the joke. It is thus allowable for them to laugh with, rather than at, the comedian, though it is again difficult to discern why any particular audience member is laughing. Without a disabled teller as a source for jokes about disability, it is easier for the joke to be read as supporting instead of breaking down stereotypes about disability. As scholar K. A. Wisniewski suggests, jokes themselves are shifting entities since "language is a temporal process and meaning will never stay quite the same from one context to the next. Reading the undoing of reason—and the joke is already soaked in ambiguity—becomes more difficult" (2009, 11). Ultimately, we cannot pinpoint the nature of laughter, which makes comedy one of the most powerful and yet unstable of rhetorical weapons.

While comics have the ability to unleash cultural critiques and point to flaws within a society, they can never be sure whether their joke is having the intended impact. Brian Gogan notes that the "meaning" of laughter is elusive: "While shared codes might spark laughter, laughter evades language. Laughter cannot be read or written as parodic, subversive, alleged, racist-sounding, too hard, or anything else for that matter, because laughter does not signify in any shared fashion" (2009, 77). There can also be many ways to read a joke that go against the grain and generate interesting counter-readings that are still quite humorous, even though those meanings may be recognized by few audience members.

Perhaps the instability of laughter is one of the reasons why sensitive topics may be avoided by some performers in comedy clubs due to the hazards of misinterpretation. When studying joke-makers and their material, we must consider the people and topics that are absent from the stage. It is important to note that the disabled comics whose performances I analyzed are white, and while race is not an overt subject in their routines, it cannot be ignored as a determinant in terms of who has access to the stage and how their bodies are regarded.[7]

The performance of disability is interpreted differently depending on one's intersectional identity, which includes gender and race among many other factors. Racism in American culture has led to disabled Black bodies often being read by white people as threatening, supported by a centuries-long misconception of a link between disability, blackness, and mental illness.[8] People of color who recognize how often disability has led to abuse and violence may be unable to joke about the subject due to its social weight and connection to oppression (Erevelles and Minear 2017, 383; Schalk 2017, 141). Similarly, for queer people who acknowledge the link that medical practitioners made between queerness and pathology for decades, and the sexual abuse that many queer people endured at the hands of doctors, disability may be far from a laughing matter (Brownsworth 1999, xix). In these instances, we must acknowledge that not all people with disabilities have the same level of social power, which complicates disability disclosure, creative expression, and performance (Shuttleworth and Meekosha 2017, 184; Coleman-Brown 2017, 146). Other individuals may have a difficult time performing their disability status if they lack a supportive disability community or have internalized disability stigmas. For many people with invisible disabilities, it may be simpler to hide their status, avoiding the potential risk to their safety and personhood (D'aoust 1999, 115–17; Clare 2017, 28).

Because of the inherent risk to assuming the stage as a person with a disability, perhaps it is not surprising that my search for YouTube performances by disabled comics yielded many white males and few queer people or people of color. White men have a greater level of privilege given their skin color and gender, which makes it easier for them to joke about sexuality and disability with less social risk. Such comics may also garner acceptance from club owners who may be more amenable to signing on the white guy in the wheelchair who'll make sex jokes in a similar vein to his walkie counterparts. It is also worth noting that aside from Greg Wallach, all the comics whose performances I analyzed were heterosexual, another form of socially privileged identity.

Additionally, the comics in my analysis tend to focus on physical disabilities, as opposed to invisible disabilities such as depression, anxiety, chronic fatigue syndrome, and diabetes. People with invisible disabilities often face heightened scrutiny in dominant culture since they don't "look" disabled and are pressured to "prove" or explain their disability status (Samuels 2017, 347–49; Siebers 2008, 100–2). These individuals may also worry about revealing disability only to face stigma at work, or be told it's "all in their head" and they should just "think positive" (Siebers 2008, 101, Solomon 2001, 29–30).

For these and other reasons, it may be more difficult for comics to joke about invisible disabilities such as depression, though many comics report a history of depression both personally and in their families (Cavett 2014; Elder 2016, 60). Conversations around comedy and depression were launched in the entertainment industry following the suicide death of Robin Williams, since this disability is as difficult to treat as it is for those without it to comprehend (Cavett 2014; Corliss 2014).[9] Comic Brian Copeland, who has performed a one-man show confronting his battle with depression, calls it "'the scarlet D, our last stigmatized disease,'" and has used his performances to open dialogues about depression with people who have been affected by the condition in their families (Elder 2016, 60). This ongoing discussion points to another function of jokes aside from cultural critique, as a means to confront complicated social issues after the laughter has faded.

While it is difficult to discern all of the variables that affect a disabled comic's access to the comedy stage, we must at minimum consider whether someone is willing to claim a disability identity, able to find disability a joking matter, and whether they are deemed worthy of a public venue by club owners, who believe the comic will be accepted by the audience as opposed to pitied or given patronizing grins. In reading these joking performances, it is equally important to recall how many brilliantly comic lines may find their audiences in tight circles as opposed to the stage.

SEXUALITY AND DISABLED MALE COMICS

While both female and male comics with disabilities joke about sexuality, there are differences among the types of jokes they tell, and the stereotypes about masculinity, femininity, and disability they may try to uphold or subvert. For men, there may be a social imperative to support stereotypical images of masculinity since disability tends to feminize individuals as being helpless and objects of the gaze. Men with disabilities may feel like they need to "perform gender" if they wish to be recognized as independent and autonomous (Manderson and Peake 2005, 231–32). Joking about sex and sexuality by male comics with disabilities may also suggest a certain anxiety about having their sexuality denied in dominant culture, meaning that they must project an overly masculine persona to compensate. Yet this idea is not true of all male comics with disabilities who incorporate a wide variety of personas into their routines.

DISABLED PEOPLE AS SEXUAL, NOT SEX OBJECTS

Greg Wallach is a storytelling comic who walks with crutches. His joking style is calm and understated, and he maintains a broad smile during performances. Wallach uses a minimum of hand gestures, commanding the audience's attention with his voice inflection and cadence. He is a comic of smooth sarcasm and subtle jokes that come with a wink and a nudge.

One narrative he tells is about being asked by a friend, "Greg, is the reason you're gay that you are crippled, and you can't get lucky with women? So, you know, you had no other choice but to sleep with men for sex?" Wallach explains that yes, he would rather have sex with women, but since they have uniformly rejected him, he must have sex with gay men. He draws on gay male stereotypes such as "the parades, the clothes, the expensive party drugs. Not to mention the apartment in Chelsea" and then presents his "solution" to the problem of disabled people having to "become gay":

> That's why I started my own foundation. It's called "Fuck the Disabled." [Audience laughter.] So if you're a woman age eighteen to thirty-five and you think that you'd like to fuck the disabled, call us, 555-DISABLED. Are you attracted to subservient men? Well, crippled guys can barely stand up. [Audience laughter.] Have you had a fantasy involving a [person with dwarfism], or several [people with dwarfism]? [Audience laughter.] Call us, we can help. And you know what they say about mentally [disabled][10] men. Small intellect, big, well you know what I'm talking about. [Smiles as audience laughs.] So call us, 555-DISABLED. Fuck the Disabled, to keep the disabled from turning gay. (Wallach 2009)

In this story Wallach employs multiple meanings of the word "fuck," so "fuck the disabled" can be defined as "have sex with the disabled," and/or "treat the disabled unfairly." The duality alludes to how dominant society privileges able-bodiedness while ignoring, abusing, or denying disabled people their rights as individuals, thus metaphorically "fucking" them. This joke also responds to the woman-on-the-beach joke, since she is cast as the butt because she is fucked (disregarded) when she wants to be fucked (have intercourse). She is also "fucked" (psychologically abused) because she is toyed with by the TAB man who seems to promise intimacy, while he is instead all too happy to ensure her demise by drowning.

Wallach makes a society that would metaphorically "fuck" disabled people the target of his humor, suggesting that disabled people are either socially disregarded and dismissed, or pandered to as a charitable cause by people who purport to "help" them. His routine parodies organizations that allegedly work on behalf of disabled people, such as the Muscular Dystrophy Association Jerry Lee Lewis telethon that raised money for children with muscular dystrophy, and effectively "fucked" the disabled by portraying them as helpless victims who could not care for themselves.[11] Wallach mocks the idea that disabled people need assistance in all spheres of life (including the sexual sphere) from well-meaning TABs. He effectively turns the tables, shifting the frame so disabled people who have received patronizing attention in the past are now patronizing TABs who would treat them in such a derogatory manner, as he reflects their simpering smile.

Wallach also demonstrates how his friend's question is absurd, subverting the stereotype of the sexually rejected disabled man. He sarcastically suggests that he and other disabled people are so desperate for sex that they must turn to "equally desperate" gay men, challenging the idea that gay people and people with disabilities have an "inferior" form of sexuality. Wallach inflates the premise of "charity sex" until it is so exaggerated that it becomes comic and shows the stereotypes of both gay and disabled men to be a farce. In this manner, he adroitly argues that disabled people don't need this kind of "social aid" since they can make intimate connections without the help of a telethon, and are far more sexually savvy than his friend would assume.

The absurdity of his joke is meant to suggest that he is not gay because he is sexually desperate, but because that is part of his identity. As Gilbert writes, this kind of "self-deprecatory material [allows] a comic [to ridicule] the society that creates ideals for appearance and behavior as well as individuals who subscribe to those standards. The subtle social critique inherent in this material serves an important function . . . to voice [a group's] discontent with cultural norms and expectations" (2004, 141). His joke is a rejection of compulsory able-bodiedness and compulsory heteronormativity, ideologies that McRuer suggests are often paired (2006, 1). Wallach mocks the idea that gay men and people with disabilities engage in forms of sexual practice that no one would "want" if they could be straight, able-bodied, and engage in "normal" sexual practice. There is no inkling on the part of Wallach's friend that gay people and people with disabilities might be perfectly happy with their sex lives, thank you very much, making her the butt of the joke.

At the same time, there is no clear cue from Wallach on how to read this sarcastic and absurdist humor as it twists the idea of a telethon into something so overblown that it becomes comic. While some people may understand that calling a number to help disabled people for an interesting charitable cause is indeed a farce to make fun of well-meaning TABs, others may assume that disabled people are in fact that sexually desperate. At the same time, simply because Wallach is rejecting the idea of a Sex-Aid telethon, that doesn't mean that all disabled people have an easy time accessing their sexuality and finding sexual partners. His joke constructs disabled sexuality to be more complex than TABs would assume. Though it is short on specifics, it pinpoints the idea that TABs are wildly presumptive (and wrong) in their beliefs about the sex lives of people with disabilities. Yet as Gogan suggests of this type of parody, audience members may "detect no obvious intent," unlike satire, which is obviously condemning some action. Parody is instead "invisibly marked," which can make it a "complicit or subversive" tactic (Gogan 2009, 74–75).

Along similar lines, Gilbert points to how such humor may not always have its intended effect since that depends on how the audience interprets the joke. She writes, "When comics play the victim—whether of an individual or of society—they do what professional fools have always done—become 'fool makers.' Indeed, being wise enough to play the fool suggests the ability to make others the butt or target of humor in a variety of ways not always immediately apparent" (2004, 160–61). If the audience does not hear Wallach's voice as thick with sarcasm but instead longing for a "normal" sex life, the humor and cultural criticism will be lost, and the joke risks reinscribing rather than breaking stereotypes of sexuality.

Another layer of social commentary in this joke is the way it argues that disabled people are sexual beings who need intimate contact, working against the idea of disabled people as desexualized and not viable sexual partners. As Shuttleworth notes in his study on the sexual experiences of men with cerebral palsy, the participants "had in common a strong sense of encountering multiple, often intractable, barriers to being perceived as sexual beings and to accessing sexual experiences" (2012, 56). While Wallach portrays disabled people as sexual beings, he also responds to the jokes about sexualized persons with dwarfism, subservient disabled men in wheelchairs, and well-endowed disabled men who have a mental disability, all of whom become "recipients" of sexual charity. It is difficult to say whether repeating these stereotypes will break or reinforce them among audience members, yet those who understand Wallach's humor is performed with cutting sarcastic intent will realize the derision he adds to those depictions.

Wallach also mocks individuals who sexually fetishize disabled people due to perceiving them as easily controlled, and/or overly sexual. His comedy references jokes that turn disabled people into needy sex objects, pointing to the absurdity of TABs sexually "aiding" disabled individuals, but also suggesting how some people would find that to be a logical course of action since they interpret disabled people to be sexually attractive due to their perceived helplessness.[12] Again, his comedy is meant to give full personhood and status as sexual subjects to people with disabilities who can be both desirous and desiring and assert agency, but since he does so by ironically suggesting the opposite, this point may be lost on some audience members.

The butt of this joke is fourfold—it mocks a society that regularly "fucks" the disabled by ignoring, abusing, and denying them services, or treating them in a patronizing fashion that suggests they are helpless; those who assume being disabled or gay involves a "lesser" form of sexual expression that people don't "really" want to have; those who stereotype disabled people as sexually uninterested or seeking "charity" sex; and those who fetishize disabled people as little more than passive sex objects. Yet at the end of Wallach's routine, we are left with the question of whether one stereotype (of a sexless or sexually needy disabled person) or another stereotype (of disabled people as fetish objects) will linger in the minds of the audience or if the joke will destabilize both perceptions of disability and shift the attitudes of audience members to begin to understand both the sexuality and agency of disabled people and the frustration at how these traits are so often ignored or assumed to be lacking.

DISS "ABILITY"

In another of Wallach's routines, "About to Eat Cake," he relates a comic narrative about attending a service in an evangelical church with a friend. After they sit in a front pew, Wallach is approached by a woman who asks if he is "comfortable in that body." He starts to explain that the room is a bit warm, but realizes she is asking if he is comfortable with his disability. Before he can come up with an (awkward) response to say that he is fine with his embodied self, the woman hauls him to the front of the church. Wallach explains how the minster "grabs my head, and he says . . . 'I want you to get

the devil out of your body, I want you to throw down those canes and walk.'"
The minister "smacks" Wallach on the head, but Wallach does not fall down
as per the script. He explains:

> So he gets down on his knees in front of me and starts rubbing my
> legs and says, [Holds hands apart, palms facing each other, moves
> them up and down.] "I want you to get the devil out of your body, I
> want you to get the devil out of your legs, I want you to throw down
> those canes and walk." And he's rubbing his legs and, oh my God,
> guess what happened. [Audience starts laughing.] I got an erection,
> [Audience laughs more loudly.] which even for me is totally out of
> control. [He shakes his head a little.] And I'm thinking I am certainly
> going to hell now. [He nods slightly to the audience, audience laughs.]
> And he's rubbing my legs and saying, "I want you to get the devil out
> of your body, I want you to get the devil out of your legs." [He folds
> hands in front of his chest.] And I'm thinking "Sir, that's not where
> the devil is right now." [Audience laughs.] (Wallach 2008)

In this story Wallach makes the minister the "butt" of the joke through his
exaggerated actions and his belief system that calls for "exorcising" Wallach's
legs, suggesting his disability is of the devil and can therefore be cured. Yet
Wallach also makes himself the butt of the joke, explaining his erection at
a highly inappropriate time. The joke depicts him as a sexual being with
reactions he can't always control, "normalizing" his sexuality even while
making himself laughable. Yet as the object of the joke, he can still find a
space of identification with audience members since many people try and
fail to maintain similar sexual control of their bodies. As a butt Wallach still
has rhetorical power, as Gilbert notes, "Even when the audience identifies
with the comic taking a literal or figurative pratfall, the identification is with
the 'object' status of the comic—the butt of the joke" (2004, 155).

Wallach's story also works against standards of heteronormative sexuality,
since it is comic because he's a gay man and has this reaction to an unknowing
and possibly straight man rubbing his legs. The question we must ask is
why the audience may find this moment funny. Members could laugh with
Wallach because they find his predicament and inability to control his
urges to be identifiable, recalling times when their bodies have likewise
responded instinctually. They could also laugh with him at the minister,
whose intentions likely did not involve sexual healing. On the other hand,
they may laugh at Wallach because they see his sexual reaction as shameful
and deride him for it, since a straight guy might not find himself in the same

circumstance (but who knows). Yet one of the reasons why Wallach can tell this joke is because this erection is a reaction he expects from his body, even if he also finds the occasion to be funny and unexpected. For him the joke may be that while he's attracted to men, he doesn't want to be attracted to this guy in particular, especially in the middle of a church service. Right reaction, wrong circumstance, and therein lies the humor. A straight man who had the same thing occur might not be able to tell this story if he thought the bodily response was deviant, suggesting arousal would cause him such anxiety as to prevent him from turning the occasion into a joke.

Ironically, Wallach breaks the stereotype of the passive disabled person by asserting agency and playing a practical joke after his erection. He has been denied agency by being taken to the front of the church, and realizes the only way he can gain control is by doing what everyone in the congregation wants to happen but does not expect. Wallach explains he can walk a few steps without his canes, so he puts them down, stands up, and walks. He says, "The congregation is freaking out, and the minster looked at me like 'Oh my God, I actually did it.'" (2008). Wallach is temporarily empowered by going along with the rhetoric of the church performance and the "routine" of being healed. He would not have drawn such attention if he had decided not to "perform" ability and pass for a few moments, masking how little strength he has in his legs. The church audience becomes the butt of the joke for being tricked into thinking he has physically changed. More importantly, those who believe this kind of healing matters to Wallach are the butt, since he is concerned about the temperature in the room as opposed to his ability to walk without crutches, revealing yet another way that the joke is on them.

While Wallach's audience may have sided with the minister and congregation at the beginning of the story, at least in terms of what they considered to be a "healthy" body, Wallach upends that perception through this narrative. He complicates the idea of disability in explaining how he feels "whole" in his body and not in need of healing, despite the preconceptions of the church goers, and he displays (quite readily) that he is a sexual person. Wallach is only "disabled" and put in an awkward position when people take away his agency in an attempt to "reshape" him to fit their concept of wholeness, again twisting the meaning of disability to show how it can be a condition that is imposed by others. While the sexual aspect of this story is only part of the joke, Wallach creates a space in which he can subvert notions of disability and sexuality, showing how disabled people are often impaired more by the perceptions of society and being denied the opportunity to act, rather than their embodied state. His body does not need to be "healed," just understood and appreciated for what it is physically and sexually. In this way he demonstrates disability is another means of being in the world that is only disrupted when someone tries to impose an arbitrary set of standards, and/ or what unwittingly becomes an erotic massage.

RETHINKING THE LIBIDINOUS PERSON WITH DWARFISM

Brad Williams, a comic with dwarfism, plays on the stereotype of the libidinous person with dwarfism in his routine. He is an animated performer, one who paces the stage and makes use of props, sometimes chuckling with the audience as they laugh at his one-liners. While the jokes I found online about people with dwarfism often focused on hypersexualization, in part of his routine, Williams twists this stereotype to create a space of identification with the audience so they share his kind of sexuality:

> Two weeks ago I had sex with a three hundred and ten pound chick. Don't hate, motherfuckers, I got laid that night. Sheee-eeet. [Salutes audience with one hand, audience laughs.] But it was weird though, you got to understand something. I had sex with her for the same reason she had sex with me. For the story. [Audience laughs, he laughs.] That's it. [He laughs again.] Because we've all been there. We've all had that lay where, as it's going on, we're just like "Holy shit." [Turns his body sideways to the audience, thrusting his hips. Looks forward, looks back at the audience.] "Jesus." [Said as a hiss.] What the fuck am I doing? [Looks at the audience and then straight ahead. Audience laughs as Williams continues thrusting.] Oh well, it's going to be funny later. (Williams 2014)

Williams plays into the stereotype by being sexually enthusiastic and demonstrating his sex drive through performance. Yet the joke also exhibits a level of hostility against people with dwarfism, integrating himself into a narrative about sex that one has for "the story." Williams implies that past partners may have had sex with him because they wanted a good tale, and they were regarding him in a similar "What the fuck am I doing?" manner. Williams thus commits the same violence against himself as people who have told jokes about people with dwarfism being unattractive sex partners. The joke can also be read as one about fat-shaming, as it ridicules his partner as undesirable, and someone who he would only have sex with for the story. He constructs people with varying body types to not necessarily be desirable partners, but ones that make for an amusing anecdote. In this way he expands the notion and function of sexuality to not just be about pleasure and procreation, but narration.

Williams suggests that he, like everyone else in the audience, has had sex solely because they want a tale to tell about an absurd sexual partner. In this way, he implicates all of his listeners as potentially being the subject or the absurd object of such stories, "normalizing" an aspect of the experience and making it less shameful since it is a shared experience. Williams's overt sexuality may be identifiable to audience members who have possessed a similarly active libido. In this way he remakes the libidinous person with dwarfism stereotype so that it moves closer to a "stud" stereotype, a common persona used by male comics (Gilbert 2004, 134).[13] This depiction also contributes to his performance of male heterosexuality, or hypersexuality, to detract from the "feminization" of disabled people in dominant culture.

Williams further alters the stereotype of men with dwarfism since he is not looking for sex from a prostitute, as were the people with dwarfism in previously mentioned jokes. While those men had to pay for sex, Williams suggests his currency is in the form of a narrative that he and his partner will tell later. They are reaping the same benefit from the experience, in addition to whatever erotic pleasure they may derive. Williams is also not denied sex or depicted as unable to perform, but has intercourse with an equally libidinous woman. This is an important facet of his routine since in other jokes, the men with dwarfism were sexually interested and yet unable to perform due to some facet of disability. While he depicts the act as comic on both sides, he also shows people with disabilities as being sexually able.

The second part of Williams's story makes himself and his partner even more absurd, but in a way that may be offensive to some audience members because of its misogynistic tone:

So I get on top but then [laughs] she was so big that my arms weren't long enough to touch the ground [Stands with profile to the audience and leans over.] as I was on top of this woman, so I didn't look sexy. I was like one of those fucking ducks that are on your front lawn and its wings just spin in the wind or some shit. [Swings arm around in a circle.] Oh, shit. [Runs over to a high chair and pulls it over to the mic.] You guys have no idea. This is what I looked like trying to fuck that bitch. [Lies down with his stomach on the chair, flails his arms and legs as if swimming. Audience cheers.] Exhale so I can get down! [Audience laughs, he gets off chair.] But she was a trooper, she ain't care! She looked at me and she was like, "I don't care little man, I want to come." [Waves hands quickly up and down in front of his body, slows down, then speeds up again. Audience laughs.] She started using my head like a stick shift on a Maserati, just brr brr brr brr brr. [Buzzing lips together.] She had the nerve to yell at me, "Go faster!" Bitch, I'm not in control! [Audience laughs.] But we know all know when that happens, we all know when we have those weird lays, it's when we're too fucking drunk, that's when it happens. (Williams 2014)

Part of this joke can be read in a similar fashion to other jokes about libidinous people with dwarfism who are "disabled" from the sex act because of their size. While Williams can have sex, he presents himself as lacking control since he and his partner are not compatible in terms of stature. He also depicts himself as being used as a sex toy, similar to the joke about the doorbell-ringing man in the wheelchair, which fits the stereotype of disabled people as sexual objects or playthings. He is simply a vehicle for someone else's pleasure, though earlier in the joke he also made it clear that this was a reciprocal act, since he "got laid."

This is one instance in which Williams suggests he does not "fit" with the rest of the world. While not prevented from having intercourse, Williams describes himself as not looking "sexy" and as more anxious than aroused during the act. This joke may represent some internalized ableism on his part since he is unable to see himself as attractive at that moment. He risks reinscribing stereotypes in that he has been deprived of sexual agency, though he simultaneously breaks the stereotype in that he is disabled during as opposed to prior to the sex act. At the same time, his partner questions his ability to perform since she is yelling at him to "go faster," while he protests he isn't able to do so. In the larger context of the joke, this lack of control seems to be a price he pays for a good story.

On the other hand, Williams presents himself as having sexual agency since he wanted to bring this woman back to his apartment for intercourse, and he suggests he is an active sexual subject who is both desiring and desired. At the end of the routine he also subverts disability stereotypes by appealing to the idea that "we've all been there," a gesture meant to find identification with the audience and normalize an otherwise absurd situation since everyone has "weird lays" when under the influence of alcohol. Ultimately the encounter is ambivalent in its play with the shifting nature of who's in control and showing how sexuality may include an odd kind of strategizing.

Yet audience members could also read this routine as misogynistic and offensive to women since he calls his partner a "bitch," makes fun of her size, and portrays her as being a domineering person. While men may be overly libidinous and take over the sex act, as was often the case in the sex jokes I found online, woe to women who wish to do the same (such as in the woman-on-the-beach joke). This insulting depiction may turn a comic image into a cruel one and prevent some audience members from enjoying the rest of the joke. At the same time, Williams seems to moderate those derisive jabs since he is also the butt of the joke and mocks his own size, suggesting he looks like a "duck . . . on your front lawn" because his arms are flailing. In his joke disabled sexuality is depicted as complex, possessing agency and subjecthood, as well as control and lack thereof. By creating a performance that is both sexy and silly, Williams finds moments at which he can mock his own behavior but also implicate the entire audience by suggesting how easily sex can become a farce for disabled people and TABs alike. Whether this unity through absurdity can redeem the joke for audience members turned off by the misogyny is the larger question.

RECASTING DISABILITY AS BENEFIT

While Brad Williams suggests ways in which his stature may be disabling in the sex act, disabled comics can also re-present their disabilities in a sexual frame, suggesting ways their embodiment can be advantageous. Jackson McBryer is a comic who uses a wheelchair for mobility and has cerebral palsy. He wears a leather jacket and sunglasses in his performance, a costume that establishes him as a "stud" with a "bad boy" persona.

McBryer explains that because of his disability, he is able to use certain forms of "alternative medicine," including ones in the sexual realm: "You know, I was drinking and after one or two beers I started to walk better. So I asked my doctor about it. He was like, 'Well Jackson, you have cerebral palsy and anything that releases your muscles will help you walk better, like one or two beers, an orgasm, or a joint.' I was like, 'Really doc? I could get medicinal . . . blow jobs?'" [Audience laughs.] (Equity Institute 2013).

McBryer constructs his disability not as deviant and desexualized, but as something that would be desirable to other men who'd appreciate a similar "prescription." He's quite eager to highlight the sexual aspects of disability gain, and potential benefits one can draw due to disability (Barker 2014). McBryer constructs himself not only as a sexual being, but also as someone who has the agency to subvert societal norms in a way that may be admirable and enviable to his audience. Social conventions become the butt of the joke since things that are usually considered to be forbidden fruit change to a prescription for improved functionality. McBryer is able to invert standards that would construct his disability as problematic and through that inversion cast disability as something that will benefit him sexually.

In this joke McBryer risks reinscribing the stereotype of the overly libidinous disabled male since the first thing his mind drifts to is how he could profit from this new "treatment regimen." Some could argue that McBryer's joking may foreground his sexuality and portray him as someone who will readily accept any sexual partner or invitation. In the exaggerated language of sexual joking, it may be too easy to repeat that stereotype, which can do a great deal of harm since it may suggest that disabled people will welcome any sexual contact. McBryer's variation on the "stud" persona might reference as many stereotypes as it breaks, so we must ask if that would be helpful or harmful in shifting the perception of people with disabilities as having sexual agency.

But McBryer's joke implies that his goal isn't to break all social perceptions and barriers regarding disability. Instead, he wants to work toward an integration of people with disabilities into dominant sexual culture. If disabled people were included in stereotypical images of sexuality, he suggests, it might not be that bad. In an interview, McBryer explains that part of the goal of his comedy is to recast disabled men in a sexual light: "Until I see Stephen Hawking or some other famous crippled guy on the cover of some trashy romance novel, I'm still going to be forced to tell beautiful crafted dick jokes, because no one else is doing it" (Equity Institute 2013). Yet having men with disabilities appear on the covers of romance novels also repeats male heterosexual norms and implies that mold should not be broken. While a wider acceptance of non-normative sex practices would benefit people with all body types and abilities, McBryer doesn't seem intent on departing from that script (much like the men with cerebral palsy in Shuttleworth's study). As McBryer suggests in his above comment, he doesn't object to the libidinous stereotype as much as he does the stereotype of disabled people as unfit sexual partners for TABs. Since the disabled-guy-as-sex-subject stereotype shares characteristics with the stud persona, it may be less of a concern for white male disabled comics who don't have a problem supporting that standard of male heteronormativity.

THE RIGHT APPROACH

Michael O'Connell is a comic who uses a wheelchair and adopts a smooth cosmopolitan persona in his routines. He wears jeans and a black shirt and newsboy cap, maintaining a calm tone and deadpan delivery. He doesn't laugh at his own jokes, but his cool and collected demeanor allows him to use humor as social corrective for well-meaning TABs. In one of his sketches, O'Connell explains that on occasion people he doesn't know push his wheelchair without permission. He says this is a serious breach of etiquette and subsequently offers the following advice:

> I'm just going to give you a couple of tips so you can avoid this problem with your four-wheeled friends out there. I don't know if you're ready for this, but I want you to imagine the handles on the back of a wheelchair as breasts. [Audience laughs.] Just stay with me. [Audience laughs.] Wheelchairs have a similar set of rules. Rule number one, if you don't know the person they are attached to, [Audience laughs.] you probably shouldn't be touching them in the first place. [Audience laughs.] Rule number two, take the time to let it happen naturally. Now just slow down, cowboy. [Audience laughs.] There's a rhythm to this thing, get to know the person first, establish a connection. At some point you'll both know when the time is right. [Audience laughs.] And number three, and this is a good rule when you're going to manhandle anyone, would you just buy me a drink first? [Audience laughs, smattering of applause.] (O'Connell 2012)

O'Connell breaks the stereotype of the sexually disengaged disabled person by overtly sexualizing wheelchairs and wheelchair users. While the comparison of wheelchair handles to breasts at first seems explicit and absurd, O'Connell clarifies why touching or pushing a wheelchair without permission is a gross imposition on a wheelchair user's rights. These individuals often regard their wheelchairs as an extension of themselves since it enables their movement, thus it is an intimate device that could be violated the same way as one's personal space and body. Overly helpful TABs become the butt of the joke since it is evident that those who move wheelchairs without permission are denying agency to wheelchair users in dictating where and how they will move. The illustration clarifies how some people with disabilities endure this gross imposition every day and suggests how this form of "help" could easily be interpreted as an assault.

O'Connell's joke can be read as responding to the vegetable daughter and doorbell jokes, ones that cast wheelchair-users as passive and unintelligent or mere sex objects. His routine argues against the stereotype of disabled people as helpless, recognizes their agency in romantic relationships, and reminds TABs of disabled persons' rights, since it isn't polite to touch anyone without permission. He further sexualizes wheelchair users as desired and desirable since in the joke they are the object of the TAB's affection and pursuit. They are not desperate, nor are they easily won, explaining why the TAB must have the proper "approach."

At the same time, O'Connell suggests that the handles on a wheelchair are similar to breasts as opposed to male sexual organs. In this way he feminizes himself and other wheelchair users, although the metaphor may be apt because the handles of a wheelchair are positioned at a height and width that would more closely approximate breasts, and they would be similarly easy for TABs to (inappropriately) access. The analogy may also be fitting since individuals who are depicted as feminized are often perfectly self-sufficient, they are simply not perceived as such and thus given unnecessary aid.

The TAB who pushes the wheelchair is masculinized with the phrase "Slow down there, Cowboy" and the mention of buying the wheelchair user a drink. Since the joke-teller is male, audience members may imagine either a male or female TAB "pusher" assuming this dominant role. This joke could be read as working against male heteronormativity since O'Connell doesn't seem disturbed by assuming the feminized role (as long as his TAB "helper" asks beforehand). While some may consider him as falling into the stereotype of the "passive" disabled male sex object, he breaks the mold by taking control of the situation and explaining the rules of this encounter. Audience members might also insinuate that O'Connell wouldn't mind being pushed by a person of any gender, as long as they buy him a drink. This interpretation allows for a queer reading of the joke that opens up the masculinized and feminized roles to persons of any gender, while involving give and take from both parties.

O'Connell's sexualization of wheelchair users also positions them as potential romantic partners since the process of getting to know someone before making a move is a familiar form of dating etiquette. This routine further responds to jokes that suggest disabled people should only be romantically paired with other disabled people or that TABs who want to have romantic relationships with disabled people are somehow deviant since it situates their interactions in the frame of conventional courtship. O'Connell's jokes illustrate that getting to know a disabled person is no different than getting to know anyone else. Along similar lines, Shakespeare writes, "Because of the widespread segregation of disabled people, many non-disabled people may not have come into contact with disabled people, and may be ignorant of what is expected" (1999, 49). O'Connell explains one of those expectations in a comic manner, demystifying "intimate contact" with disabled people by showing how it can be successful if one masters the right "approach."

Similar to other marginalized comics, O'Connell is able to "open up a space for 'safe' discussions of taboo topics" (Gilbert 2004, 175) and explore relationships (sexual and otherwise) between disabled people and TABs. Even while the wheelchair user assumes a more feminized role, the encounter is still based on consent, and the agency of both persons is respected.

In another routine, O'Connell comments further on the patronizing or domineering attitudes some TABs may have toward individuals with disabilities. In particular, he discusses problems he's had at stores and other businesses, when people assume he is mentally as well as physically disabled. He explains:

> Employees of businesses can be helpful, but they tend to talk to me like I'm [an intellectually disabled] third grader. [Raises voice at the end of sentence, audience laughs.] It's like this other day. [He takes the mike off the stand and leans forward, speaking in a high, earnest voice.] Is there anything else I can do to help you? [Audience laughs.] Are you sure? [He shakes his head slightly, audience laughs more loudly.] You shouldn't be embarrassed to ask for help. [Shakes his head again, audience laughs.] We all need help sometimes, don't we? [Audience laughs, he lowers his voice back to his normal register and looks up as if taking to someone taller than he is.] It's like, "Lady, can you just finish the damn lap dance already?" [Audience laughs and applauds.] (O'Connell 2010)

In this joke the lap dancer, and anyone else who speaks to disabled people in a patronizing manner, becomes the comically absurd butt, while disabled people are the eye-rolling victims. Even before the twist at the end which makes the sexual nature of the situation apparent, the audience laughs at the exaggerated language of the person addressing O'Connell with a cadence similar to a preschool teacher. As Freud notes of this device, by making one's target "comic, we achieve in the roundabout way the enjoyment of overcoming them," while the audience notes their approval and agreement by chuckling (1960, 122). Just as O'Connell would not like to be addressed in such a way, neither would those watching his performance. He breaks the stereotype of the passive "vegetable" in the wheelchair and articulates how not to speak with disabled people. Further, in the turn at the end of the joke, O'Connell portrays himself as a person with a "normal" straight male sexual appetite. The beginning of the joke has already depicted him as running errands to different businesses, a "normal" daily task, so in the story he is also not defined solely by his sexuality, counter to the wheelchair-using man in the doorbell joke.

As with some of Williams's jokes, O'Connell's routine reinforces certain standards of male heteronormativity since it depicts him at a strip joint paying for a lap dance. Unlike his previous joke, this activity emphasizes his masculinity in conventional ways, as if needing to reassure the audience that he has (nonthreatening) straight guy desires. The fact he is paying for sexual contact is similar to the jokes about libidinous people with dwarfism, but going to a strip club may also be read by audience members as a "typical" heteronormative male activity. He is integrating himself into the sexual economy as a paying customer, so in many ways the joke reinforces heteronormative standards for sexuality and sexual activity.

Yet his joke also risks doing violence to people with intellectual disabilities since he uses a derogatory slur when explaining how the stripper speaks to him. Not only do many people in disability communities and the general public strongly reject the use of "the 'r' word" (Lyle and Simplican 2015),[14] this comment also does harm to people with intellectual disabilities by suggesting that they deserve to be spoken to in a demeaning manner. The joke can be read as supporting a disability hierarchy, as well as doing horizontal violence within disability communities.

In the second part of his joke, O'Connell highlights some of the problems unique to wheelchair users at strip joints. Again he challenges stereotypes around disability, yet risks doing harm to others:

> Actually, lap dances and wheelchairs don't mix very well. Like, you guys who get lap dances can figure it out. You know that chair that you get your lap dance in? Yeah, you don't have to take that chair home with you. [Audience laughs and groans. He takes a tissue out of his jacket, wipes off the arm rests on his wheelchair, puts the tissue back in his jacket.] You go to the office the next day with your armrest smelling like stripper. [Audience laughs.] There's a reason nobody makes an air freshener called "Stripping." [Audience laughs more loudly, a few groans.] The other reason is it just kind of ruins the experience of having a beautiful exotic woman writhing on your lap, when that woman is crying and telling you how brave you are. [Scrunches his features and pretends to get choked up on the last three words as audience laughs and a few people clap.] When I go to a strip club I actually get to touch the dancers because they all need a hug afterwards. [Audience laughs.] (O'Connell 2010)

The strippers, and by extension anyone who shares their sentiments about his "bravery" or the bravery of other people who use wheelchairs, become the butt of the joke since they assume his disabled status makes him worthy of pity. Apparently, they find it "inspiring" that he left the house. O'Connell corrects anyone in the audience who may have harbored similar sentiments, making the notion of pity absurd though depicting a stripper crying on his lap in what should otherwise be an erotic moment. She cannot find him to be a sexual object as much as an object of pity, even though the context of their encounter is intimate. O'Connell makes her comic through her excessive behavior, pointing to the fact that TABs are often not able to see past his wheelchair to the rest of his body (even when someone is sitting in his lap).[15]

Yet O'Connell does violence against the stripper by suggesting that she taints him with an "ugly" smell that he takes to the office the next day. The jab implies that she does not practice good hygiene or bathe adequately and is thus "unclean." This sentiment repeats the derisive attitude toward "dirty" sex workers while being uncritical of their clientele, much like the joke about the disabled prostitute with the glass eye. This joke could be read as O'Connell positioning himself above her socially since he is going to a "respectable" office job at which he needs to smell clean, while she continues to "rent" the use of her body in a profession where hygiene is not a priority.[16] There is also an insinuation that he must take the fact that he went to a strip club to work with him, and is thereby prevented from hiding it from his coworkers, as TAB men would be. His sexuality must follow him to work as opposed to being left at home (or in the strip club) in a manner that is considered "inappropriate" office behavior. This comment echoes Brown's poem in chapter 4 regarding wheelchairs and sex, reflecting on ways people often cannot leave the sexual self behind as a separate and compartmentalized part of one's identity.

While he displays a level of distaste for the strippers in terms of their personal habits, O'Connell also suggests his disability has unexpected benefits since he is sanctioned to hug crying strippers. This aspect of the joke brings into question whether the strippers stereotype him as being more sexually "innocent" than TAB men, thus allowing him to give them hugs. The contact permits him to assume a masculine role as comforter, although that duty is more paternal than that of a paramour. It isn't clear if the strippers need reassurance from O'Connell that he's perfectly fine, if they are emotionally overcome by seeing a wheelchair user, or if they want to hug him in congratulations for his "bravery." In any instance, O'Connell suggests that their need for comfort is another excessive action, but he seems willing to accept privileges that TAB customers would not receive.[17] In O'Connell's routines as well as McBryer's, while people with disabilities are shown to have a sexual self that is often ignored by TAB individuals, the jokes do not go so far as to question heteronormative practices. Disability is deftly shown to have certain advantages, yet these two comics do not invest much time in expanding the notion of sexuality. Similar to Kimmie and Magda, whose blogs do not push far beyond the bounds of heteronormative white femininity, their routines suggest how disability comedy, communities, and goals can run the political gambit from conservative quips to calls for complete cultural reform.

LAUGHING YOURSELF SEXY

If disabled men face serious stigmas when considering their sexuality, disabled women are doubly marginalized as women and disabled individuals. As Nomy Lamm explains of her experiences being an amputee who performed as a stripper, "it's uncommon—in any community, be it gay, straight, queer, whatever—to see disabled women portrayed as sexy . . . the environment is not supportive or inclusive enough to make a disabled woman want to expose herself in that way" (1999, 152–53). Often disabled women are excluded from "true womanhood," barring them not only from sexuality but from having a gender, since it is assumed that they will not be able to attract men (Garland-Thomson 2017, 371). Mairs notes the ways in which these societal perceptions harshly devalue disabled women, stating, "If you view women as commodities (and being social products, none of us can altogether escape such an unconscious assumption), then a disabled woman must inevitably be damaged goods" (2002, 159).

Additionally, TABs may be stigmatized if they dare consider disabled people to be sexy. As Garland-Thomson notes, "When the female spectacle is a disabled one . . . male heterosexual desire is no longer imagined as normative, but rather it becomes pathologized as deviant. Devoteeism, the term for heterosexual desire that issues from staring at the disabled female body, is almost universally considered to be pathological" (2005, 34). Thus, not only is the female disabled body culturally barred from being considered a sexual body, but those who think disabled people are sexy are considered psychologically disabled. Complicating matters further, disabled women may internalize these stereotypes and develop a negative self-image that does not permit them to see themselves as desirable, leading them to consciously or subconsciously imagine their bodies as "inherently unattractive" (Kafer 2012, 332; Vaughn 2015, 30).[18]

As the jokes I found on websites suggest, just as often as disabled women are desexualized in humor, they are victimized and raped because they are cast as not having the agency to be sexual subjects. Some of the jokes further imply that disabled women should be barred from reproducing, such as the woman-on-the-beach joke whose punishment for asserting a sexual self is death. While disabled men are sometimes cast as overly libidinous or sex objects, disabled women are more frequently depicted as needy, helpless, whiny, victims of sex crimes, and unfit partners who should be grateful for any sexual contact they receive.[19] Similar to disabled men performing hypermasculinity, some disabled women feel they must perform "excessive femininity" to be recognized as having a gender (Garland-Thomson 2017, 372; Lehrer 2012, 242).

Disabled female comics are positioned in a seemingly paradoxical social space, since while disabled women are frequently considered as sexually inadequate in dominant society, female stand-up comics are viewed as presenting themselves as sexually available. As scholar Jennifer Foy writes, "It is a cultural commonplace that, for women, joking converges with promiscuity . . . This social disorder manifests most immediately in the female comic's relationship with her audience when she makes sexual jokes" (2015, 703). Disabled female comics joking about sexuality directly confront the tension between being cast as libidinous and the desexualization or victimization of disabled women. Through humor these comics can potentially elicit laughter, present disability and disabled individuals as sexy, and assert sexual agency. At the same time, similar to male disabled comics and TAB female comics, the disabled female comic may present herself as overly promiscuous. Again, whether that persona is considered liberating, falls into the stereotype of the sexually desperate disabled person, or lands in some other space depends on the interpretation of audience members.

THE SEXY STUTTER

Nina G. is a comic who stutters and uses her disability as material for her comedy. Onstage she moves freely, making frequent hand gestures to the audience as if she wants to draw them into the conversation. Her manner is both assertive and personable, in contrast to jokes found online about stutters that make them seem socially inept and desexualized. Nina G. re-frames her stutter as a positive sexual attribute, saying:

When I go out it will be at a bar or something, and a guy will ask me what my name is. And that usually goes something like, [Grabs mic with both hands, scrunches her nose like she is concentrating.] Nnnnnnnnnn . . . [Takes a breath.] nnnnn-Nina. [Lets go of mic with one hand.] Which I thinks is kinda sexy, right? Yeah, I think I'm kind of a SILF. [Audience laughs.] Yeah, a SILF. A stutterer I'd like to fuck. [Audience laughs louder.] (Nina G. 2012)

Nina G. redefines her stutter to suggest that it is not an impairment, but instead is "kinda sexy," and could be construed as a form of disability gain. She also plays on the commonly known acronym "MILF" to coin "SILF," making sexy stutterers into a classification of people all their own, and suggesting that they are sexual subjects and objects of sexual desire. Some may say this joke plays into heteronormative constructions of femininity and feminine beauty, judging women based on their sexual attractiveness and availability for intercourse. At the same time, it is a joke that integrates speech patterns into one's sexual attractiveness, redefining and complicating the qualities that people may find sexy in another person. The joke was based on Nina G's observations on how the sexuality of disabled women was not regarded in the same way as the sexuality of disabled men. As she explains of the origin of the term SILF:

I was at a stuttering conference . . . we were talking about gender issues, and there was a woman—beautiful woman—who's my friend had said, "When a guy stutters it's kinda cute and vulnerable. But nobody thinks that it's sexy when a girl stutters." And from that I was like, wow, that's such a hurtful thing that I have friends who think that they are less attractive and sexual because of their speech. But that goes for a lot of different kinds of disabilities. So that SILF joke really came from that place of trying to rebrand ourselves and rethink about ourselves as sexual and attractive, even though society hasn't always said we were. (Nina G. 2015)

She is acutely aware that disabled men and disabled women may be perceived differently when it comes to the sexual sphere, and she understands that humor can be one of the most effective ways to redefine the significance of stuttering. Within her routine, the audience could read the comment about the sexiness of stuttering as honest, ironic, or somewhere between the two. Without the additional commentary and background from her interview, the joke could be interpreted as Nina G. making herself the butt and mocking her speech patterns, instead of working to define her own kind of sexy. Her comment presents possibilities for complicating the meaning of disability, suggesting that people with disabilities have the potential to shape how their sexuality is perceived by others, "rebranding" the stutter and perhaps other aspects of disability in the public imagination.

Yet while Nina G. argues that stuttering is sexy, in the routine she presents her stutter as so exaggerated that other people with similar speech-related disabilities may consider it more painful than comic to watch. Since people who stutter have long been considered objects of ridicule, we must ask why TAB audience members would laugh at her gesture. As scholar Jeffrey Johnson notes, "the most notable fictional comic stutterer is undoubtedly the Warner Brothers cartoon character Porky Pig . . . one of Porky's main purposes is to be funny when he speaks and to be an easy auditory gag for those who find stuttering humorous" (2008, 246). Audience members may laugh at Nina G.'s accentuated stutter as supporting the comic stereotype, but will they also laugh with her at the idea of the sexy SILF as positively re-presenting disability and breaking the stereotype? Would any audience members be so offended by the comic representation of stuttering, and how it may do social harm to people who stutter, that they would find nothing redeeming in the joke? While Nina G. wants to characterize herself as a SILF, her exaggerated gestures may simultaneously enhance and detract from that goal.

BARS, NOT BEACHES: ASSERTING AGENCY AGAINST SOCIAL ISOLATION

Disabled female comics' sexual humor can also be read as responding to the woman-on-the-beach joke since their routines place them in social situations as opposed to isolation. This setting allows them to be part of the public sphere and portray themselves interacting with others and engaging in innuendo and intimate banter. As Foy writes of this kind of sexual comedy, "When a tendentious joke is successful, that success is predicated as much on the figuring of the female wit as sexually permissive as it is on the content of the joke itself" (2015, 706). In short, female comics portray themselves as having their minds as deeply entrenched in the gutter as their male counterparts, though their wittiness means they can be read as sharp instead of needy and discerning instead of desperate. One example of this sexual comedy is when Nina G. jokes about how she goes to bars to check out men and be checked out by men. Part of the function of her joke is similar to O'Connell's, educating TABs about how to act (and not act) around people with disabilities:

And then in the midst of my N-n-n-n, what the guy will do is this. [Points her index finger, holds her hand out, and twirls her finger while moving her arm from left to right. Audience laughs.] Yeah, this. Because this fucking helps me! [Lowers eyebrows in angry expression, twirls finger.] This is good. [Continues twirling finger while audience laughs.] This is telling me to spit it out, those are all very helpful things. [Audience laughs.] I'd be like, is that what a girl does when you take out your dick? [Twirls her finger again to audience laughter, applause, cheers.] You know, where's the rest of it, Devin? [Grins. Audience applauds, laughs, cheers, whistles.] (Nina G. 2012) [20]

Nina G. makes the TAB man at the bar into a comic figure through the use of exaggeration, demonstrating how his prolonged finger-twirling is excessive and unnecessary (Freud 1960, 235). He appears absurd since his gesture is doing nothing to help her disability, yet he assumes he will "enable" her voice. By turning the joke around to focus on the size of the TAB man's penis, Nina G. suggests that men who make this gesture are less "masculine" than those who refrain from doing so. This joke inverts the positions of subject and butt from the woman-on-the-beach joke since the socially and sexually "disabled" TAB man is the butt, along with anyone else who would patronize a person with a disability. Nina G. reverses the power imbalance between herself and TAB man, who believes himself to be her linguistic superior. She is intelligent, while he is comic, and sexually desirable, while he is not. This joke also reinforces stereotypical images of masculinity as connected to men who are well-endowed, suggesting that men who are less so are less masculine. Yet Nina G. references this stereotype because she knows it is a form of joking shorthand that will resonate with her audience and have a shaming effect on her target, who would be embarrassed to have the size of his member questioned.

She also subverts jokes that suggest disabled people should only partner with other disabled people, positioning herself as someone who is sexually available and attractive to men. By referring to the TAB man's penis, she implies that intercourse between them would have been a possibility, had she not rejected him due to his patronizing gesture. Her routine can further be read as a response to jokes that portray stutters or others with a speech disability as unable to participate in intimate acts or interact socially. She is not a voyeur confined to the sidelines, but someone who can accept or reject partners as she sees fit. As a SILF, she paints herself as a sexual subject as well as an object of desire, with equal agency on the dating scene.

Yet as with many of the jokes told by comics with disabilities, the end effect of her routine is to uphold certain stereotypes, such as ones related to masculinity, and subvert others. While disabled comics can challenge some stereotypes, it is yet another task to turn everything upside-down and still make a cultural critique the audience will understand. Comics with disabilities situate themselves inside and outside dominant culture, picking and choosing which subjects they feel are in their best interest to lampoon, while keeping other structures intact. This isn't to say those other social conventions aren't worthy of questioning, but this tactic is arguably a strategic move to help comics maintain control and the attention of their audiences.

Comic Ally Bruener, who uses a wheelchair for mobility, is similar to Nina G. in that she jokes about her sex life and presents herself as a sexually available disabled woman. Like McBryer, Bruener may be read as playing up her sexual desire to an extreme. However, that exaggeration may be done for comic effect, as well as to counter the stereotype of people with disabilities as desexualized.

Bruener's routine can be read as working against the woman-on-the-beach joke that suggests disabled women are unfit sexual partners. She explains, "I'm a pretty normal twenty-two-year-old girl except I haven't had an abortion. [Pause while audience laughs.] Yet. [Pause while audience laughs.] Don't worry, it's scheduled for Monday. [Audience laughs.]" (Bruener 2011).

Bruener "mainstreams" her sexuality by suggesting that she, like other twenty-two-year-old girls, has desires that could result in unintended pregnancies. The pauses in her monologue are key to the humor since with every aside she changes the meaning of her joke and is continually repositioning herself and playing with audience expectations. In her first sentence, she makes other twenty-two-year-old girls the butt of the joke, suggesting that all of them are so promiscuous that they need to have an abortion. She initially excludes herself from this category, seeming to set herself apart from the copulating masses, but she turns the joke with the word "Yet." In a single utterance, she introduces the possibility that she may have an abortion at some point, implying that she is as sexually active as other twenty-two-year-old girls. In the third sentence, when she reveals that she has scheduled an abortion, she situates herself with the "normal" twenty-two-year-old girls as the butt of the joke. This is ultimately a transgressive act that upends stereotypes of disabled women as lonely and sexually inexperienced. The slow reveal of that fact in the joke is comic, as audience members realize how they may have misread Bruener and other people with disabilities. She delights in stripping away assumptions and gaining the rhetorical upper hand in reshaping perceptions.

The glee in Bruener's voice may strike some audience members as in poor taste, however, since she is joking about a weighty and politically charged topic and suggesting that many young women get abortions as a matter of course. Someone who has had an abortion, or knows someone who was physically or emotionally traumatized by having an abortion, may find the joke extremely off-putting. Further, there is a history of women with disabilities being cast as unfit mothers who cannot care for children and should not have them because they risk passing on disability. Women with disabilities have been forced to have abortions or be sterilized for this reason, meaning the punch line could have a much darker resonance for some audience members.[21] Yet Bruener tells this joke in a manner that suggests this abortion is her choice, and disabled women can have the same agency and control over their bodies as TAB women.

When joking about particularly controversial topics, we must consider Gilbert's admonishment that "these are the jokes, folks!" (2004, 140), meaning they exist to make a comic point and should not be taken too seriously. Yet different audience members will classify some kinds of subject matter as strictly off limits for joking. This is the risk that any comic takes in making politically charged jokes since they may lose some people as they bring others along.

Later in her routine, Bruener further deconstructs the notion of the isolated disabled woman when she discusses being pursued by a young man:

> I was at a bar the other night with my friends, and my roommate . . . said "Ally, that guy's checking you out." He was staring at me all the time . . . [A] little bit later I looked down and he's touching my leg. He's stroking my leg. Since when is that proper for a flirtation? If you're going to flirt with a crippled girl, touch her somewhere she has feeling. [Audience laughs.] And then he puts a line on me, he says, "Just so you know, if I were a dinosaur, I'd be the pleasurosaurus." [Audience laughs.] Oh, he didn't stop there, because apparently, prior to his extinction, the pleasurosaurus was a whorebivore. [Audience laughs.] And I thought to myself, a whorebivore. What do they eat? [Pauses while audience laughs.] I found out later that night. [Pauses while audience laughs.] That's right fellas, crippled girls put out. [Audience laughs and hoots.] I'd like to get a bumper sticker for the back of my chair, for the equally accurate, "My other ride is my vibrator." [Audience laughs and claps.] (Bruener 2011)

Bruner's joke can be read as responding to and inverting the beach joke, since she shifts the roles of pursuer and pursued. She is sexually desirable since a guy is "checking her out," not taunting or teasing like the TAB man in the beach joke. Her routine suggests that disabled people can be found attractive by TABs, opposing the notion that such encounters will only result in hostilities or victimization. Bruener also portrays herself as a savvy and sexually experienced disabled woman, while the TAB man is less so. Her admirer becomes the comic butt since he initiates physical contact prematurely, and does not know how to flirt with "crippled girls" since he should "touch her where she has feeling." This comment suggests Bruener has superior knowledge of sexual comportment. Similar to O'Connell, her remarks have an instructive function on how to interact with girls in wheelchairs—while flirting is fine and even expected, make sure your timing is appropriate and your positioning is correct, so your efforts will not be in vain. In this way she depicts people with disabilities to be discerning intimate partners, but just as in O'Connell's jokes, she implies that prospective lovers must have the right approach so they don't come off as more silly than seductive.

Some people in the audience may find her comment troubling since it suggests she is giving the young man permission to invade her personal space. While at first she seems upset that he is touching her, the joke turns on the fact that she doesn't mind the touch, but he is touching her in the wrong place. In this twist she could be read as a sexually promiscuous disabled person, or as assuming the bawd persona that some female comics adopt to project themselves as desirable and desirous (Gilbert 2004, 100).

Through the punning terms "pleasurasaus" and "whorebivore," Bruener plays on cheesy pick-up lines that may be familiar to her audience as part of dating rituals, yet she positions herself as the meal of the "whorebivore" and says "crippled girls put out." This rhetorical move sexualizes Bruener and other women who use wheelchairs, and it sexualizes her wheelchair, which she compares to her vibrator as her "other ride." Yet one could argue that she comes close to mimicking the promiscuity of the sexually available man in the wheelchair or the libidinous person with dwarfism, both of whom support stereotypes of male heteronormativity by emphasizing penis size and sexual appetite. In particular, the phrase "Crippled girls put out" could make women who use wheelchairs seem too enthusiastic or easy, to the point of hooking up with anyone who starts rubbing their leg in the right place. At the same time, she is situating wheelchair users among young people who go to bars and engage in casual sex culture. Bruener fits herself into a world her audience members are likely familiar with, one of one-night stands, bad pick-up lines, and people who are looking for a good lay. We must also consider that these jokes are part of Bruener's longer comedy set, in which she contextualizes her sexuality as only one part of her identity.

Bruener also twists the stereotype of the sexually promiscuous disabled person by showing that she has the agency to accept or reject her TAB partner and to critique his sexual prowess. Her performance casts her identity as far more complex than the disabled man in the wheelchair who can only have sex and ring doorbells or the libidinous people with dwarfism who approach TABs but are never approached themselves. While Bruener sexualizes and genders herself, she does not make that facet of her personality the center of her identity, and she situates herself within a dominant cultural scene in which this kind of behavior is expected and accepted. As Lehrer notes, people with disabilities must always perform gender or risk being denied gender (2012, 242), so comics with disabilities must balance a careful line when subverting versus upholding norms. The inherent conflict in many of these jokes reflects larger political debates within diverse disability communities, which have various agendas, goals, and positions within dominant culture that they find most desirable.[22]

MORE DISABILITY BENEFITS

In the same vein as McBryer, comic Francesca Martinez positions herself as a person whose disability has unexpected benefits. A comic with cerebral palsy, she performs while sitting on a stool to steady herself. In her routine, she explains that she is not a parent because she loves sleep more than kids. Martinez says that her disability is an advantage when it comes to avoiding procreation: "Luckily, though I have found a brilliant form of contraception, I have. It's when I put a condom on my boyfriend because, the amount my hands shake, it's all over before it begins" [Laughter and audience applause.] (Martinez 2012).

Martinez makes it clear that she is interested in sex and has a boyfriend and regular sexual contact. She becomes the butt of the joke when explaining how her disability has created a few "technical difficulties" when helping him with a condom, but the "problem" is equally advantageous since she doesn't want children. By laughing at the situation, Martinez not only prevents others from making the same joke, but she reveals a hidden benefit.

Martinez's joke could be read as suggesting that her disability disallows her from engaging in vaginal intercourse, so she might not be able to have children even if she wanted to. Putting on a condom overstimulates her boyfriend before intercourse, meaning that while she is quite good at some sex acts, others may be problematic. This facet of her sex life may prove frustrating, so the joke might hint to moments when she wishes for a different form of embodiment, though Martinez seems nonchalant about the situation. The joke also risks suggesting that people with cerebral palsy are sexually inept and unable to perform in the same way as TABs.

Yet this perspective privileges one kind of sex act, vaginal intercourse with a condom, over a multiplicity of others, and does not consider the ways that Martinez's boyfriend finds pleasure in the way her hands tremble. While she suggests she is disabled in one kind of intimate contact, Martinez subverts the stereotype of the sexually passive disabled woman by presenting herself as a sexual being involved in an intimate relationship. A larger contention with Martinez's performance, as will be discussed in the next section of this chapter, is that it defines sexuality and intimate contact narrowly, evading how disabled people often approach their sexuality creatively, especially in the realm of erotic touch.

Another important facet of her routine is how Martinez subtly questions the notion that disabled women can't be mothers. She makes it clear that she could be a mother, but she doesn't want to assume the role. Her disability does not affect her decision about parenthood, which is a key point since TAB and disabled women are often viewed in a much different light when it comes to being mothers.[23]

Mairs argues there is a strong stigma in the medical community against disabled women having children, and questions how much assistance would be given to a TAB woman versus a woman with cerebral palsy if both were trying to conceive: "Would the nurse practitioners and doctors . . . be just as eager to rush [to the] aid [of a disabled woman]? I have my doubts. Her infertility might even be viewed as a blessing . . . [H]ealth professionals might try to reason with her. How can you change an infant's diaper with so little control of your hands?" (2002, 160). Yet in joking about motherhood, Martinez makes it clear that she is capable of parenting, but similar to many TAB women, she has chosen not to. She suggests that for her, and by extension other disabled women, the choice of whether to be a parent does not lie solely in her embodiment, but whether she wants to accept the job.

HAND JOBS: SEXUALIZING HELEN KELLER IN DISABILITY SEX HUMOR

While disabled comics adeptly use humor to present themselves and disability as sexy, many disability rights advocates would argue they have only touched the tip of the iceberg in expanding our notions of sexuality and disability. The questions comics raise related to disability, sexuality, and sexual rights for disabled people generally privilege heteronormative sexuality and intercourse, not considering the full range of sexual preferences, behaviors, and how to define a "sex act," so it includes a "multiplicity of erotic desires and practices, both within and outside the parameters of heteronormative sexuality" (McRuer 2017, 107).

Of the sex and disability jokes I examined, the ones that came closest to exploring alternate forms of sexuality and erotic touch were Helen Keller jokes. As disability scholar Kim Nielsen notes, "These jokes depend on cultural attitudes that define people with disabilities as asexual . . . and then force the listener to confront the possibility of a sexualized Helen Keller. She is famous for transcending, overcoming, leaving her body and all its limitations behind. Helen Keller sex jokes force recognition of the bodies, the physicality, and the sexuality of people with disabilities" (2004, 131). These jokes have the potential to be emancipatory for disabled people because they position a disabled woman not only as sexual, but as engaged in sensual activities that fall outside the norm of sexual behavior:

Q: Why does Helen Keller masturbate with one hand?

A: So she can moan with the other. (Nielsen 2004, 131)

What's Helen Keller's idea of oral sex? A Manicure. (Rixon 1998).

These jokes work against the perception of disabled people as innocent and sexually inexperienced, presenting "stereotypes about blindness and deafness" and then subverting those stereotypes with "pornographic humor to lampoon Keller's virginal and saintly character" (Nielsen 2004, 131). Yet I suggest that instead of "lampooning" Helen Keller, the jokes can be read as lampooning her carefully crafted image as "virginal" and "saintly" since she was a far more multifaceted individual than she is generally portrayed in popular culture.

These jokes can also be read as opening possibilities for alternate forms of sexuality based on intimacy and erotic touch, an important site of sexuality that is sometimes discounted in TAB communities. As Siebers writes, "people with paralysis, who have lost feeling in traditional erogenous zones, have found ways to eroticize other parts of the body," outside of what are generally "limited erogenous zones" (2008, 149). Disability has the potential to change and expand interpretations of sexuality beyond penetration, and as such, the Helen Keller jokes can be read as suggesting ways to reimagine erotic spaces on the body.

While these jokes may have liberatory potential, it is easy to understand how listeners may assume that Helen Keller is merely the butt of such humor since her sexuality is based "only" in touch. As Haller and Ralph note, "Helen Keller jokes and sick jokes about quadriplegics were created by nondisabled people for other nondisabled people. Without disabled people involved in the creation of humor, these jokes can be read as insulting and patronizing" (2003). Further, even when disabled people create humor, the jokes may lose their liberatory potential when divorced from disability communities and a disability sitpoint. As with any other text, the meaning is not dependent so much on content but on how the reader or listener interprets the joke. Each is like a tiny firecracker tossed into the world to see who it could surprise, what it might upset, what shivers it could send through a culture, but will any of those moments have a lasting effect?

We must return to Shakespeare's assertion that there is no definite way to read a joke and that they may all have confining and liberatory potential depending on the teller and how the joke is received by various listeners (1999, 52). Perhaps if disabled people continue to tell Helen Keller–type sex jokes and inscribe them as coming from a disability perspective, alternative forms of sexuality may be taken more seriously outside the joking sphere and considered a viable form of sexual expression. This idea of expanding the notions of sexuality and sexual practice is a topic I will discuss further in the next chapter.

CRIPPING COMEDY

While disabled comics are becoming more prominent in comedy clubs with some gaining national attention, the resulting effects on the cultural perception of disability are less clear. As Reid, Stoughton, and Smith suggest, "For disabled audiences, disability comedy may play a role in creating an in-group that challenges majority culture. On the other hand, in a mainstream setting, such humor could build tension and discomfort. The question remains whether these powerful and unsettling effects are momentary" (2006, 641). While Gilbert agrees that jokes may only invert social norms in the space of the comedy club, performances by comics from marginalized groups can have an important social function since "humor creates a transitional rhetoric. By bridging the interstices between events and interactions in our social fabric, humor serves as a transition from one cultural moment to the next" (2004, 176). Comedy allows an audience to see things not as they are but as they could be since marginalized comics "depict for us how social relations could be transformed if their viewpoint were to prevail" (178). Comedy is a place to plant the seeds of change.

Kafer notes not only the need for such change, but the direction this change should take, writing, "I want to imagine a sexuality that is rich and robust not in spite of impairment, and not fetishistically because of impairment, but in relationship to it. How have disabled people crafted sexual identities and practices that take our impairments into account, not in order to overcome them, but to capitalize on them?" (2012, 346). While Helen Keller jokes capitalize on the idea of erotic touch, will TAB audience members interpret them as such? Does that matter if the jokes circulate within disability communities to promote sex positivity and a variety of forms of sexual expression as both viable and healthy?

Perhaps this space will be the next one for disabled comics to interrogate as they continue to push for cultural transformation in the perception of disability and sexuality, constantly treading on transgressive borders, never certain when a joke will be a hit and when it will be a miss, and why the audience is laughing. But comedy is not a science; it is a space of exploration and imagination. Its power and uncertainty lie in its play subverting stereotypes and presenting alternate realities, hoping that even after the words have been spoken and the audience has gone home for the evening, the instabilities will linger in the not-yet-real world that is the realm of social change and possibility.

ON SEXUALITY

Disability is a space to explore the erotic potential of bodies beyond the narrow bounds of sexuality imagined by compulsory able-bodiedness and heterosexuality. Clare writes of the sensual possibilities found in his cerebral palsy when addressing a loved one who is likewise disabled: "I've had lovers tell me how good my shaky touch feels, tremors likened to extra caresses or driving over a gravel road, their words an antidote to shame. But until now, I had never felt the pleasure they describe. Your twitches spread across my skin—tingle, echo, dance" (2017, 19). Disability becomes a potential space of creativity, allowing individuals to find new textures to intimacy, to relax and be inventive, though the specters of conformity will always peer over one's shoulder. Those insistent whispers to return to the cultural box are difficult to banish.

Drew and his new girlfriend Alexis meet me in the coffee shop on a Sunday afternoon. They've been dating for a week after meeting online and are happy to tell me about their sex life. They're in the honeymoon phase, adorable and anxious, and hold hands on top of the table. They thumb wrestle. His thumb is twice as long as hers.

When Alexis goes to the bathroom, Drew says it's important to make sure she's happy with their sex life. When Drew goes to the bathroom, Alexis says he's overly concerned with their sex life. Drew and I have talked about his need to overcompensate for his disability through being sexually above average. He figures people assume he can't have sex because he uses a wheelchair, so he has to prove them wrong. Did I mention he's a shameless flirt?

Alexis doesn't talk as much as Drew does, but she's being introduced to her new boyfriend's friend, which is a space of social calculation. What percentage of the conversation should be dedicated to social issues versus sex versus the number of times Drew has to go pee because of his tiny bladder? Alexis is a goth girl, with the expected dark eye makeup and purple hair and nose ring. She is the sort of person I can imagine dating a guy who uses a wheelchair and likes mosh pits, a guy who has read enough Judith Butler to know that gender (among many other things) is a construction, a performance, but since he uses a wheelchair, he feels compelled to perform his guyness, as do many other male parathletes (Manderson and Peake 2005, 231–32). I have told Drew that he's ninety-five percent testosterone and contradictions. He says it's an accurate assessment.

Mairs writes of how her multiple sclerosis and her husband's impotence have caused both of them to appreciate different forms of intimacy, noting George, her husband, "may stroke my neck when he brings me a cup of coffee. And since my wheelchair places me just at the height of his penis . . . I may nuzzle it in return. We carry on a constant, often hardly conscious, corporeal conversation regardless of our other pursuits and preoccupations" (1996, 54). Mairs notes that sensuality can be found in slowness, an altered pacing that reflects Kafer's idea of crip time (2013, 25–26), and the way people with disabilities may not be able to do things as quickly as other folks. Yet Mairs suggests there are benefits to the changed tempo of their life: "Without my disability to throw us together thus habitually, our bodies might spend their days racing separately from one activity to another, coming across each other only in time to tumble into sleep" (1996, 54). Sensuality can thrive in the appreciation of ourselves and our partners, a bond formed when intimacy is allowed to be space of experimentation and innovation, when individuals grant themselves long moments to linger.

How many facets of life truly have no rules, yet we feel bound to set them anyway?

I didn't include a photo when I posted my personal ad online, and I wonder if that would have made a difference in my disastrous date's decorum, alerting him to the scandal of my "lazy eye." Would other potential dates have noticed that my eyes weren't looking in the same direction, and would they have cared? When I choose pictures to post online, I've noticed they're ones in which both my eyes seem to be looking in the same direction, the right eye agreeing to go along with the agenda. For once.

Yes, I admire my eye's wandering spirit, and I claim not to care when it meanders away to ponder privately, but since I don't feel like explaining its character in paragraph upon paragraph, my profile pictures tend not to reveal its rebel spark.

Drew: I always tell people [about the wheelchair] before [I meet them for a date], so it's not a surprise. That can be a huge shock to people.

Does it matter? To some people it does. It really shouldn't matter . . . but I've told you stories where I was talking to girls on Tinder and explained I can't really feel my right leg, and I use a chair sometimes, and then next day you don't hear anything from them, and then you realize they're—

Alexis: —not worth it anyway.

My friends with chronic fatigue syndrome explain their screening questions for prospective romantic partners: Will you listen when I say I don't have the energy to stay up and watch a movie, to hang out with your friends, to go to that party? Will you take me at my word when I say I'm in pain, even if you can't see the pins in my legs, even if my body seems animated but all I can manage is the last push toward the couch?

Drew: With meeting people online, I tried to post pictures that showed evidence of my disability.

Alexis: You fucking didn't.

Drew: I have the picture with me and Eric. That's my wheel right there.

Alexis: In that lighting it looks like an arm of a chair. And you can't tell in that picture. You also can't tell in that picture.

Me: How did you choose the pictures?

Alexis: That's one that I don't look like I'm disabled.

Drew: You've got to ease people into that. Okay, fine, fuck it. I have friends that use pictures in their chairs and they have a lot of self-confidence with that, but I think things should be at a different angle when it's online.

Alexis: I would like to know more than a couple hours before we meet up.

Drew: But you came anyway. I would have been stuck with all the pizza if you didn't come, but I ordered the pizza that night. I would have watched Netflix anyway.

Drew once told me that at the end-of-the-season wheelchair basketball dinner and awards ceremony, there was a deejay and an open dance floor, but none of the guys ventured out to make use of the music. That surprised me.

"I always thought wheelchair basketball was great because of your choreography," I said. "You have to understand how other people are going to move, and maneuver to the right place on the court. It's like you guys are dancing out there."

"But dancing is for girls," he reminded me. I'd forgotten the bane of the wheelchair basketball player: to project hypermasculinity at all times in case anyone's watching (Manderson and Peake 2005, 231–32). It's best to assume that someone is always watching.

"Few people are more ableist than parathletes," Eric says. "The ranking system in wheelchair basketball is all about what you can and can't do and how much you can move your core."

I lament the world of lasting contradictions, how there always seem to be hierarchies, even among marginalized groups. Will we ever escape the tyranny of numbers?

In his essay "On Seeing a Sex Surrogate," Mark O'Brien writes about how his paralysis from polio limited his access to an erotic self. He was raised in a loving and devoutly religious family where no one acknowledged sexuality, so "the attitude I absorbed was not so much that *polite* people never thought about sex, but that *no one* did . . . convincing me that people should emulate the wholesome asexuality of Barbie and Ken, that we should behave as though we had no 'down there's' down there" (O'Brien 1990). This upbringing so constricts his sense of sexuality that when he employs a sex surrogate to help him gain comfort with his body, O'Brien is taken aback at the lack of divine punishment: "Whenever I had been naked before—always in front of nurses, doctors, and attendants—I'd pretend I wasn't naked. Now that I was in bed with another naked person, I didn't need to pretend: I was undressed, she was undressed, and it seemed normal. How startling! I had half-expected God—or my parents—to keep this moment from happening." Notably, O'Brien has always been a medical as opposed to a sexual subject, but in this moment of intimacy and emergence, he starts to find erotic joy in his body, acknowledging that he deserves access to his sexuality.

While he's eager for vaginal intercourse, O'Brien is surprised to find it isn't as exciting as expected. Much more emotionally resonant is the period afterward, when his sex surrogate employs other forms of intimate touch: "She put her hands down on the bed by my shoulders and kissed my chest . . . it seemed like a gift from her heart. My chest is unmuscular, pale, and hairless, the precise opposite of what a sexy man's chest is supposed to be. It has always felt like a very vulnerable part of me. Now it was being kissed by a caring, understanding woman and I almost wept." It is this moment of simple affection, one that validates O'Brien's personhood, that feels the most loving, the most sexual, that vibrates him to his core. So often sexuality can be found in moments when it isn't anticipated, the tiny gestures, the touch that surprises and delights.

My disability studies professor explained that the class wouldn't do a "disability simulation" exercise in which TAB students rolled around campus in wheelchairs or blindfolded and with a cane to understand the "disability experience." No one can grasp what it means to live with a disability after spending an hour or a day or a week as a wheelchair user, or through an equal amount of time wearing earplugs or a blindfold. These "simulations" are more likely to suggest to TAB individuals that having a disability means constant suffering, and the exercise grossly oversimplifies the variability of disability (Kafer 2013, 4; Nario-Redmond, Gospodinov, and Cobb 2017).

Instead of trying to re-create disability, my professor divided the class into groups and had students plan a date with a disabled person. How would we get from our dorms or apartments or houses to the theater or restaurant? Would we rely on paratransit with its unreliable pick-up and drop-off times? Would we pick up our date at the door if we had a car? Which restaurant would we choose, and was there a step or two or three to access the entrance (Elman)?

The assignment entailed a cruise downtown, measuring doors, scouring for accessible entrances, parking spaces, curb cuts, and areas for wheelchair seating. We asked about closed captioning in the theater, if there were large-print or braille menus, and checked for accessible nongendered bathrooms with bars along the walls to help people steady themselves. We considered what to do after dinner and the movie, if we could watch the sunset from the top of a parking garage (it had an elevator), whether our dorms and apartments had stairs if we wanted to hang out after dinner, have something to drink, chat a bit more, do . . . stuff.

The quest required class members not to pretend we were disabled but to consider access realities, structural barriers, the prevalence of steps, and think of disabled people as highly date-worthy individuals. It was an assignment designed not to draw sympathy but allegiance, one that reminded students of the shifting-drifting nature of embodiment and how disabled people are desirable and delightful. Of course, you'd want to take one of us disabled folks to dinner and hang out afterward. In the words of Gurza, "While it is okay to be apprehensive (being around so much awesome all at once can be overwhelming), the question [of whether to date someone with a disability] should in fact be the statement: 'You SHOULD Date someone with a Disability!' "

My partner says they walk on everyone's left side now, whether they are with me or friends or coworkers. I have trained them to sit or stroll there so I can see them, but I didn't realize the considerate conditioning would work so well.

> Drew: She says that if I meet her parents, the first time I have to stay in my wheelchair.
>
> Alexis: So they don't think that his dick works.

They grin at each other, and we hug good-bye. Drew texts me later that evening, still joyful and anxious in the honeymoon buzz of the first week of a relationship.

> Drew: I am so happy . . . I feel so alive. She gets me.
>
> Me: You were both glowing like fireflies.

They are still falling, lost in that oxytocin buzz, but it's what we all want, for someone to understand who we are, the blend of bravado and insecurity, compassion and contradiction, our three-dimensional coffee-guzzling grin-exchanging bodies spun free of the promotions and preludes of an online dating profile, hoping we have found someone who will care about our sweet and eccentric and terribly human selves.

Alexis and Drew will stay together for nine glorious and gut-wrenching months before they break up. That will have everything to do with a clash of social habits and personalities, but it will come after many shared pizzas and beers and mornings lingering in bed. It will come after more occasions for us to have coffee and tell sex jokes as they continue thumb-wrestling, giving each other sideways smiles, maintaining the firefly glow.

They will be in something that, at least for a time, I will see fit to call love.

Chapter 6

SEXY LIKE US

Expanding Notions of Disability and Sexuality through Burlesque Performance

After several months exploring the world of disability and sexuality, I figured that disability burlesque had to exist as well. Folks in the creative, subversive, and ever-expanding world of disability communities must have braided together the sexual strip and tantalizing tease with the joke, the gaff, the wink and bawdy nudge. This search sent me bounding across the internet once again, reading interviews and sending emails and then finding (dream of dreams) a theater company composed of professional and community actors with disabilities who had recently produced a show that included burlesque performances. I "attended" from six months and two time zones away, through the magic of a video recording sent to me by the artistic director of the company:

The theater lights darken, and the emcee rolls onto the stage. He's a young man wearing a white shirt, black pants, tie, and black top hat. He uses a power wheelchair due to cerebral palsy, and the audience cheers when he introduces himself as Edmond the Orgasmic. Edmond explains that the show they are about to view will be a "cabaret of carnal celebration" and "something truly astonishing, stupendous and spectacular! Something which many people would rather you didn't see, something so controversial it will make you scream in shock, something so astounding it will make you question the very nature of reality! Ladies and gentlemen: I give you, people with disabilities talking about sex!" His dramatic build-up to this "revelation" is greeted with laughter, yet as with many jokes in this performance, the punch line reveals the deeper truth of how people with disabilities often have their sexuality denied, dismissed, or otherwise derided in dominant culture. But the emcee, along with a cadre of other actors with disabilities, will spend the next hour dispelling those notions, an argument they perform with erotic flair.

This performance was part of *Sexy Voices*, a cabaret-style theater production based on the real-life experiences of the disabled performers who participated in conceiving, writing, and acting in the production. *Sexy Voices* was produced by Vancouver's Realwheels, a theater company with a mission to deepen the understanding of disability, and provide a platform for members of disability communities to express their political and personal concerns onstage. At times vibrant, poignant, and always though-provoking, *Sexy Voices* incorporates a sense of play that allows cast members to challenge dominant cultural conceptions of what it means to be disabled, what it means to be sexual, and what it means to "strip" layers from the body. *Sexy Voices* also invites audience members to stare at the actors, listen to their stories, and find shared understanding. "In many ways, we are sexy like you," the performers say. "Are you sexy like us? What haven't you stripped off and shown the world? What is your story?" The performance functions as a call to community and reveals disability and sexuality to be constructed categories that are in constant flux.

Mainstream media stories tend to adopt ableist attitudes that focus on the "inspirational quality" of disabled performers' work, their "exceptional" nature and "bravery." Yet by portraying disabled people as valiant sufferers, Kafer suggests these individuals are stripped of any other story, rendering the complexity of their struggles, relationships, and identity moot (2013, 91). This narrative also strips individuals of their sexuality, leaving them as two-dimensional figures whose only salient characteristic is disability. However, closely reading interviews and performances by disabled burlesque performers reveals that the art form presents a unique opportunity to (re)construct and convey a complex sexual identity and works against the idea of the desexualized disabled body.

Clare writes of how often disabled people are omitted from the sexual sphere, noting that while he doesn't want to be the subject of "leering," disabled people find themselves in a quandary since in "the absence of a sexual gaze of any kind directed at us—wanted or unwanted—we lose ourselves as sexual beings" (1999, 113). While being considered a sexual object can be confining and dehumanizing, Clare points out that its lack can be dehumanizing in other ways. *Sexy Voices* works against this ideology, deconstructing mainstream notions of sexuality and offering alternate models. The actors demonstrate how part of being a sexual subject can be desiring consideration as a sexual object. Interrogating different forms of sexuality and sexual expression through burlesque opens possibilities not only for disabled bodies, but also for all bodies to be "sexy like us." Through examining *Sexy Voices*, we can see how this theory may be enacted onstage.

I begin this chapter by discussing the history of burlesque, which started as a form of social critique and gender performance that assumed an increasingly risqué note during the turn of the twentieth century. Contemporary burlesque performers suggest their art form is a political and emancipatory practice that embraces all body types, yet I argue that not everyone has been allowed equal access to the burlesque stage. This problem is part of the larger issue of people with disabilities lacking access to performance venues, as I suggested in the previous chapter, and not being considered "fit" performers of sexuality. Some disabled performers and performance groups have pushed against that notion, yet burlesque performers with disabilities have often been cast in the media as more inspirational than sexual.

In the second section of the chapter, I examine Realwheels's performance of *Sexy Voices*, in which actors demonstrate how disabled bodies may be sexualized and sexual. While the performers' bodies can be read through a conventional heterosexual lens, they also queer sexual practice and expand the definition of what it means to be sexy. I use queer theorist José Muñoz's idea of disidentification to explore these moments since while he situates this theory in a queer and racial context, he also suggests it can be used by members of other minority communities to reinscribe meanings on images and objects. Through the burlesque performances in *Sexy Voices*, the disabled actors create spaces of (dis)identification, connecting with the audience through the revelation of story and skin, demonstrating how disabled bodies can be read as sexual in a range of contexts. Yet the production also raises issues regarding who feels comfortable telling their story and who may still be left out of the limelight when considering disabled sexual expression.

BURLESQUE, DISABILITY, AND PERFORMANCE

Burlesque started in the late 1860s as a type of comic stage show meant to challenge the political status quo. The first burlesque performers defined themselves as women who had the audacity to look back and "address the audience directly," in defiance of gender norms of the time (Wilson 2008, 21). These shows employed a "chaotic and nebulous combination of dancing, singing, minstrelry, witty repartee, political commentary, parodies of plays and scant clothing," and they "fulfilled a necessary transgressive function, which was to undermine hierarchy in terms of authority, gender, form, skill, theatrical distance, social decorum, and class" (Wilson, 18). Disability was invoked in the way performers were derided in media accounts as mentally ill, their performances pathologized as a means to discount them, similar to the way that suffragettes were discredited when campaigning for the right to vote (Baynton 2017, 24–26). Both performers and audience members were skewered in newspaper accounts as being prone to "dispossess themselves of their clothing . . . then follow a series of piercing screams called comic singing, distorted and incoherent ravings called puns, and finally, strong convulsions" (Allen 1991, 128). Depicted as disabled and dehumanized, the performers' behavior was considered a form of lunacy outside the bounds of proper comportment.[1]

Yet while much scholarship highlights how burlesque was focused around gender, class, and social change, we can't forget that at the turn of the century, minstrelsy was also a popular type of performance. Burlesque shows included stereotypes that were intended to make fun of "everyone," yet the caricatures they reproduced reaffirmed eugenic ideas about racial minority groups and often sexualized the "other."[2] Another phenomenon concurrent to the rise of burlesque was the spread of the freak show, a space in which racialized and gendered bodies were displayed (for a price) before gawking onlookers. These "performances" often featured individuals who we would now consider to have some form of disability, and the display of "deviant" bodies allowed ticket-buyers to be reassured of their normality.[3] Both burlesque and freak shows existed in an era in which bodies were increasingly being measured and evaluated by medical science and curious onlookers (Snyder and Mitchell 2006, 72).[4] While there was the possibility that audience members might also find spaces of identification with the so-called "freaks," it was ultimately a spectacle of devalued bodies.[5]

During the early twentieth century, burlesque performance focused increasingly on clothing removal and sexual allure, and less on the cross-dressing and joking behaviors of earlier burlesque. These shifts were reflected in the "Golden Age" of burlesque of the 1940s and 50s (Butler 2014, 46). This form of burlesque tended toward elaborate costuming and attention to choreography and the craft of the "tease." Performers emphasized the slow reveal, careful to control how much of their body they allowed the audience to see (Briggman 2009, 191). There was still a comic element to this performance as Rachel Shtier notes, "The striptease presented seduction, which is at its best a kind of interpretive art, like acting . . . [I]t made fun of our obsession with sex, which is what made reformers turn against it as much as the tendency to reveal flesh" (2004, 341).

As an art form, scholars suggest that contemporary burlesque has the potential to open new and different conceptualizations of sexuality for both performers and audiences. Jacki Wilson argues that through the exchanged look, performers can assert themselves as sexual beings and that burlesque may "widen the palette of erotic imagery . . . through unconventional skin and flesh, this desire to be desired, this insistence that they can be desired, both disruptively and disobediently plays up to narrowly defined 'ideals' and parodies 'fuckability'" (2008, 177).

Yet while burlesque has great communicative possibilities, the lack of diversity on the burlesque stage is troubling. Counter to Wilson's suggestion that burlesque embraces all bodies, some performers argue that race, class, gender, and body type still play a role in who is able to assume the stage.[6] This idea is corroborated by many disabled burlesque performers, a testament to the fact that not everyone can flaunt their fuckability.

Scholar and burlesque performer Sherril Dodds elaborates on this tension, noting that contemporary burlesque performances often work against narrow definitions of what kind of bodies should be considered sexy: "the overt display of 'imperfections,' such as sagging breasts and wobbly bellies, is embraced and applauded, the idealized and unattainable bodies of consumer capitalism are a rarity" (2013, 78). There is often an element of comedy and play in contemporary burlesque routines,[7] yet Dodds also notes that performers often employ a "nostalgic femininity," which doesn't seek new ways to be sexual (80). In short, while contemporary burlesque has maintained elements of humor and social commentary that were present in earlier versions, it has not gone far enough in its exploration of what alternate forms of sexuality and sexy bodies might look like, and worse, burlesque performance venues may have wittingly or unwittingly barred performers from the stage in an unwillingness to "read" them as sexual.

This deficit must be evoked when Wilson poses questions regarding liberation and exposure in erotic dance: "What is truly liberating about exposing oneself? Does this revelation of flesh equate with some kind of personal victory? Does flesh, the ability to dance naked, frolic nude, or strip in a public place make you free, give you real freedom?" (2008, 133). The answers to her inquiries are dependent on the performers and audience members, which leads to more questions: Who is revealing their body? Who is watching? Where and when is the person exposing themselves? Is it more or less of a "personal victory" or a "real freedom" when one is revealing a body that has often been hidden, desexualized, abjected? Does it matter whether that body is considered sexual and fuckable by the viewer, or is simply the opportunity to be seen an advancement toward liberation? If a performer embraces that chance, what will they reveal of their skin, their scars, their sexuality? How will they stare at the audience, and what kind of stare will be returned?

DISABILITY AND PERFORMANCE:
CONTEMPORARY BARRIERS

Due in part to the history of disabled bodies being stared at in entertainment and medical contexts, there is still tension around how people with disabilities are regarded in performance settings and everyday life. Disability scholar Carrie Sandahl notes that disabled actors are discriminated against throughout the entertainment industry, beginning with acting teachers who expect a "neutral" body that allows an individual to "disappear" into a role. This prejudice prohibits many talented actors with disabilities from entering the profession (Sandahl 2005, 257, 260). Elsa Henry, a burlesque performer and actor who uses a wheelchair, writes of difficulties she encountered being cast in stage performances or limited to certain roles: "I often just wanted to play someone without having to adapt it to myself. I've been witches, and I've been old women, and I have been the tortured and angry Betty Parris—but until burlesque, I never felt like I was playing a person I wanted to play" (2012). Her comments point to the fact that, in the theater arts, disabled people rarely have the opportunity to break cultural stereotypes related to disability. If they wish to have any role, sometimes they must be complicit in reinscribing ideas about disability that they'd rather reject. This sort of typecasting highlights the larger problem of ableist ideologies that assign negative qualities to disabled bodies, assuming that a "deformed" physical exterior must signal an equally "deformed" emotional interior (Snyder and Mitchell 2006, 18–19, 49).

But even performers with disabilities must be aware of maintaining inclusive practices. As Kuppers writes, organizers of dance and theater workshops for disabled individuals must be careful that no one is being left out "based on racial stereotypes, class, gender, economic access, [or] internalized ableism" since people may be "excluded from the norm" even within disability communities (2013, 4). Kuppers also cautions against any performance that is an "easy celebration [of disability] without grounding in lived reality" (153) or ignores how performaning is often physically or socially difficult if one has a disability (226–31). This complexity adds another layer to disability theater, seeking a position that will not be a spectacle of suffering or ignore the frailties of the human body.

Even after granting disabled performers access to the stage, we are left with the question of how these bodies will be regarded by audience members. While it is generally considered rude to stare at people with unconventional bodies, disabled performers demand the attention of eyes. Garland-Thomson discusses these complexities in her analysis of the stare, which she suggests "is distinct from the gaze which has been extensively defined as an oppressive act of disciplinary looking that subordinates its victim" (2009, 9). Unlike the gaze, the stare is a shared look between starer and stare, which Garland-Thomson suggests has the potential to create connections between people and lead to constructive reflection: "Triggered by the sight of someone who seems unlike us, staring can begin an exploratory expedition into ourselves" and ultimately help us to "rethink the status quo" (6). Yet as with any kind of look, the stare is ambiguous in its potential since we can't limit the types of gazes exchanged and messages received. Pairing an art form such as burlesque that is inherently sexual with a group of people who are often desexualized opens the door for a wide range of audience questions, interpretations, and explorations.

EXPANDING NOTIONS OF DISABILITY AND SEXUALITY

The cramped definition of what it means to be a sexual being in dominant culture is why many disability theorists have called for queering disabled sexuality and opening new ways for disabled people to explore sexual practice. Disability scholars Robert McRuer and Anna Mallow argue that we must consider disability and sexuality as "fluid" and "expansive" terms (2012, 13, 24). As an example, McRuer analyzes the work of performance artists Bob Flanagan and Sheree Rose, disability and BDSM activists who explored sexuality through their art. Flanagan had cystic fibrosis, and some of their performances involved Rose, his partner, giving him "a beating characteristic of their erotic and sexual practices together" (2006, 181–82). This treatment was "therapeutically useful" since it served to clear Flanagan's lungs, and McRuer suggests it was also "erotically satisfying for both participants" (182).

As Rose explains, while her intimate relationship with Flanagan included performative aspects, it also changed the meaning of his disability for both of them: "It transformed illness from something horrible and tragic into something else . . . He would write songs that said, 'If it wasn't for SM, I'd be dead. If it wasn't for Sheree, I'd be dead. She gave me all these extra years.' And it's true. He couldn't have died on me . . . As his mistress I would say, 'You are not going to die. How dare you?'" (Takemoto 2009, 105). Part of Flanagan's sexual submission to Rose was to keep living for their art, working with and against the pain of disability.[8] McRuer suggests that members of cystic fibrosis and BDSM communities found his performances particularly meaningful, since they dissolved the barrier between pain and pleasure and demonstrated how a perceived injury could also be intimate and have beneficial properties (2006, 182–84).

Other performance groups such as San Francisco–based Sins Invalid have worked to expand the meaning of beauty and sexuality for all bodies, arguing that disabled people, people of color, and queer people have often been excluded from this frame (Berne et al. 2018, 246). Sins Invalid co-founder and executive and artistic director Patricia Berne argues that performance can create a space in which people with disabilities may develop the confidence and esteem they require to guide them through difficult moments of social hatred and discrimination. Berne suggests that Sins Invalid's goal is to "create a space where someone is bathed in their own beauty, and they can use that in times when their beauty and existence are being threatened by the violence of oppression" (246). Scholar Shayda Kafai notes that Sins Invalid performances often focus on "crip beauty," an important aspect of their theater, since even disabled models often "replicate normative depictions of what our Western culture deems beautiful" (2018, 232). She suggests that crip beauty "urges that there is pleasure and eroticism in bearing witness to disability, in cultivating a space where bodyminds that are traditionally forced into invisibility can gather together . . . [reminding] us that disability is something to celebrate and not something to hide" (232).

Still other performers challenge notions of disability and sexuality in a more comic fashion, including Mat Fraser, who performs a "crip tease." During the routine, Fraser strips long dark pants, a jacket, and two prosthetic arms that he waves like pendulums in front of his body, swinging the limbs between his knees and tugging on them suggestively. After he has revealed shorter arms, he licks his fingers and uses them to slick back his hair, implying that his disability is much sexier than the artifice that "normalized" him ("Mat 'Seal Boy' Fraser"). Fraser comments that part of the aim of his art is to force the audience to look at disabled bodies, a complicated encounter that may both reinforce and break stereotypes (2013, 247). For several years he has performed in a Coney Island sideshow that he suggests:

> *comments on contemporary culture from the stance of a re-imagining of the Freak as a cultural commodity . . . [D]isabled people are coming to this art form as a way of expressing themselves in a performance arena that doesn't judge them automatically as lesser, other, and invalidated . . . Fraught with complications as it is, it is a refreshing alternative to liberal funded, box ticking confined Disability Arts work.* (2013, 247)

In short, even while the freak show venue is a complex space, it can still be one of display, reclamation, and liberation.

Kafer has also interrogated disabled sexuality through examining her conflicted thoughts on the relationship between female amputees and the devotee community. She admits that devotees' single-minded focus on amputations has made her suspicious of people she doesn't know, leading her to assume that if someone finds her attractive it is because of disability. She laments, "How disconcerting that I was so quick to buy into the ableist assumption that my impairments eclipse all other aspects of my life" (2012, 344–45). Kafer's reflections point to the complex relationship between sexuality and looked-at-ness, how it can be difficult to interpret the erotic stare since it's not easy to discern why someone finds an individual to be attractive.

Lehrer also notes complications around this sort of looking since some disabled people may become an inadvertent spectacle in public: "In the sidewalk mating dance we're winnowed out as undesirable breeders . . . It's a very sexual problem, this custody of the eyes. Because, after all, a lover's regard begins with a stranger's gaze" (2012, 236). There is a challenge to courting eyes if one has an unconventional body, begging the question of how we can find space for a different kind of stare, one that does not compel people with disabilities to slide into the background, but flaunt the self in all its fabulousness. As Garland-Thomson suggests, performing disability can redefine what it means to be disabled and inscribe new meanings on the disabled body (2009, 139). She argues that disabled performers can potentially change the conversations around disabled bodies and the taboo against looking at them: "By boldly inviting the stare in their performances, they violate the cultural prescriptions against staring, at once exposing their impairments and the oppressive narratives about disability that the prohibition against staring attempts to politely silence" (2005, 32).

DISABILITY BURLESQUE

My search for disabled burlesque performers yielded a range of newspaper and magazine articles, interviews, and videos. Perhaps the most interesting aspect of this process was noting the wide (but not unexpected) variety of perspectives that reporters, interviewers, and performers had toward burlesque and the display of disabled sexuality.

One young burlesque performer who has cerebral palsy and the stage name "Cerebral Pussy" entered the burlesque world when she was a college student. Burlesque helped her reframe CP in her own mind. She says, "The words 'cerebral palsy' used to make me cringe . . . The same thing often goes for sexual content. Cerebral Pussy lets things I was afraid to claim now define me" (Graves 2015). Burlesque gave her the opportunity to "play" with how she conceptualized of her disability and her identity as a sexual person, drawing on the notion that one can have a body that is both comic and sexy. She comments on this aspect of her performances, saying her goal is to "[make] a joke out of my body so that everyone knows it's okay to interact with disabled bodies as human beings who are ridiculous and have ridiculous needs and move ridiculous ways and are also really hot" (Graves 2015). In this way she expands the meaning of disability and sexuality to include the non-serious, embracing performance styles that are simultaneously silly, seductive, and sensual. Her routines are also a kind of "joke" on the audience in the way she desires to reshape thinking about disability. Cerebral Pussy muses, "any narrative that's ever about disability is like, 'Oh, the poor asexual disabled one who will never find a partner' . . . And I like to be able to like, really challenge that" (Graves 2015). Yet she also finds it difficult to interpret audience reaction to her performances. When people watch her, do they see a burlesque performer, a disabled performer, or something in-between, and how does that identification color their reaction to her work? Cerebral Pussy notes that audience comments have varied: "I get some people who are like, oh my god, that was so amazing, and I can't tell if their compliments are because they're kind of ableist and it was a 'that was so inspirational' kind of comment, or if they actually enjoyed it" (Graves 2015).

While Cerebral Pussy has found a space of liberation in performance, she has also encountered numerous physical and social impediments to performing, including problems finding accessible stages and willing promoters: "When I tell [venue owners] I'm a disabled burlesque performer, they're like 'Oh . . . Well . . . Send us some videos, and maybe we'll get back to you.' So mostly what I've relied on is word of mouth" (Graves 2015). While she doesn't say it outright, there is an implication that individuals who operate these venues subscribe to the ableist notion that disabled burlesque performers won't draw a crowd, produce a satisfying performance, or be truly sexy. Further, there may be a lack of interest on the part of club owners to accommodate the needs of disabled performers.

Her problem finding venues suggests a continued tension in the burlesque scene between performing for the self and performing for an audience, and furthermore, what kinds of audiences will be receptive to one's performance style. Even if a performer is allowed access to the burlesque stage, they may not be able to escape ableist ideologies. Mainstream media sources tend to cast people with disabilities as "inspiring," such as one British newspaper that featured a story with the headline "Brave Sheffield Woman Performs

Burlesque Routine in Wheelchair and Wearing Stoma Bag." The article emphasized her "exceptional" qualities with the opening line, "A brave Sheffield woman took to the stage in her wheelchair and wearing her stoma bag to perform a sexy burlesque routine" (2015).[9] Clare criticizes this kind of "supercrip" narrative as "[focusing] on disabled people 'overcoming' our disabilities. They reinforce the superiority of the nondisabled body and mind. They turn individual disabled people, who are simply living their lives, into symbols of inspiration" (1999, 2). Notably, the reporter failed to mention any aspect of the performance itself, instead focusing on the performer's physical condition, which included "chronic pain, mobility difficulties, internal bleeding, thrombosis and chronic fatigue." She is portrayed as a valiant sufferer, foregrounding the actual content of her performance.

Also troubling were comments from the performer herself, who said, "I also hope that anyone in the audience watching and thinking that they aren't attractive for whatever reason will see it and realise that this is someone who has physical deformities, but it's the confidence and the 'inner sexy' that comes out when you believe in yourself" ("Brave Sheffield Woman" 2015). This remark leads one to question why performers with "physical deformities" can't have a physical "outer sexy" as well as an emotional "inner sexy." Is there no way to look at disabled bodies not as "deformed," but as sexy in their own right?

The website 21st Century Burlesque, which features stories of interest to members of burlesque communities, has a similar "supercrip" spin in its introduction to an online issue featuring stories written by disabled burlesque performers. The website authors prefaced those narratives with this note at the top of the web page with Sweet Scarlett's story: "We let it be known that we were interested in speaking to anyone that would like to talk about their disabilities (or disaburlyties as we like to call them) . . . The stories we read were so honest and uplifting—we have dedicated a large portion of this issue to these brave women and we hope you enjoy and take comfort from their stories" (2008). Again, the performers are cast as "brave," while their tales are "uplifting" and can provide "comfort" to other (presumably TAB) performers. While the dancers are "outstanding" individuals for being disabled but performing anyway, there is an implicit message to TAB dancers that even if they become disabled, they should have the stamina to keep performing. As Kafer notes, the underlying ideology behind these kinds of "overcoming" narratives is that able-bodied people should simply power through any physical or emotional impairments they may experience (2013, 91–93).

In contrast to that introduction, the narratives by disabled performers reveal that burlesque has given them space to explore their creativity and sexuality. Sweet Scarlett notes that many burlesque venues are not accessible to her as an audience member because of her visual impairment and problems seeing in low light. At the same time, the stage adapts to her limited vision: "I can dance and move without hesitation . . . When performing I am not the timid girl with the cane (or without my cane and people just think I'm clumsy) I'm anyone I want to be. In some ways when I'm performing is the only time I don't have to worry about my sight" (Sweet Scarlett 2008). For her, the burlesque stage is a freeing space where she doesn't have to consider the physical limitations of her disability. She can perform a side of her personality that is sure and confident, and not worried about negative perceptions of others. Sweet Scarlett also indicates the ways in which public spaces can pose a challenge for people with disabilities, who must negotiate streets with canes and wheelchairs and service animals, revealing the ways in which physical environments can be disabling. The burlesque stage is free of the clutter that impedes her movements and her perceptions of self.

One burlesque performer who has successfully integrated disability into her routines is Caitlin Myers, who goes by the stage names "Jacqueline Boxx" and "Miss Disa-Burly-Tease." Myers has Ehlers-Danlos Syndrome which has led to chronic pain, but she admits she was reluctant to use a wheelchair even when her condition became so painful that it was difficult to dance while standing (Nelson 2015). Myers knew that using a wheelchair would mean performing her disability in a new way, and it took weeks for her to adjust to that idea. She was encouraged to do so by members of her burlesque troupe who suggested integrating the chair into performances. Myers eventually acquired a wheelchair, painted it gold, and added plush cushions and accents to make it look like a throne. She developed a routine to feature her chair and reframe her disability as having a fluid meaning. She says, "I was liberated by my chair . . . There are moments where my choreographed muscle movements mask my syndrome enough that it is no longer 'apparent' and it might be easy to dismiss any affiliation I might have with that limited signifier 'disabled.' My disability is always there, though, visible or not (Boxx 2016b). Myers's flexibility belies any discomfort she may be feeling, yet the centrality of the wheelchair to her performance inscribes her body as disabled. Her routines also twist the notion of how a wheelchair can be "used" not as a mobility device, but as an object of pride and a sex symbol.

Myers performs her routine "This Is My Throne" to the song "Royals" by Lorde (Boxx 2016a). At the start of her performance, she is lying on the floor, and seems to awaken as the song begins. She wears a loose white dress made of filmy material, her hair cut in a shoulder-length bob. Myers glances over her shoulder to a large gold cloth-covered object behind her and then peers back and forth from the object to the audience with wide-eyed wonder, scooting across the floor to get closer to the mysterious item. She continues to glance from object to audience, poking the gold cloth as if asking audience members to dare her to remove it; then she whips away this cover to reveal a wheelchair with brown cushions and gold accents on the frame.

Through this "tease," Myers invites the audience to join her in seeing the chair as intriguing. In the reveal, her wheelchair is integrated into "stripping" away layers, and the gold cloth and decorations suggest it is not only sexy, but something of value. Myers further sexualizes the chair by stroking it seductively and licking the frame, treating it as a sex toy. She slinks in front of the chair, spreads her legs in a suggestive straddle, and pushes herself upright and back to sit on the throne.

She shimmies her shoulders at the audience, stroking her hands up her breasts, then undoes the buttons on her tunic to reveal a black, red, and gold leotard. Myers sits sideways in her chair so her profile is to audience; then she pivots again, so she is lying backward in the chair with her head by the footrests and legs at the backrest. She opens her legs to hooted appreciation from audience members, pivots back around, slides the straps of her leotard off her shoulders, and reaches behind the top of the chair to grab a crown. She places the crown on her head before pulling down the top of her leotard to reveal her breasts, nipples covered by pasties. Myers crosses her legs and rolls offstage, marking the chair as sexual and functional, a throne from which she can seduce audience members.

Her body and the chair are cast as desirable through concealment and revelation, presenting them in ways that can be read as sexual though her tight costume and how she uses her wheelchair to erotically enable her performance, riffing on the idea of the "chair strip." This mobility device becomes instrumental to her performance of sexuality since the arms help her pivot and assume suggestive poses. While Myers's movements are fluid, the way she gets into the chair and leaves the stage suggests she may have problems standing and walking, so the chair both aids her performance and adds another layer of eroticism through the way she moves into and around it.[10] Her routine is also comic in the way it plays with revealing the unexpected and the image of innocence turned sexual. Myers changes from a young woman wearing white to a seductress clad in red and black, yet this only happens when she is seated in the wheelchair. Her performance is a double tease that plays with and complicates the meaning of disability and sexuality, revealing her hidden sensuality, how it can be enhanced by assistive devices, and that "innocent" disabled people have a sexual side that audience members likely don't expect.

The burlesque stage presents an opportunity for this kind of scopic discovery through prolonged looking, opening possibilities for disabled performers and audience members to begin a visual dialogue, and perhaps continue it beyond the bounds of the stage. We must allow for body variation in these venues, breaking down the notion of "fit" and "unfit" bodies and giving individuals the opportunity to recontextualize their bodyminds in and out of the limelight. These are also the goals that shaped the mission and message of *Sexy Voices*.

SEATED SEDUCTION FROM THE STAGE:
SEXY VOICES BY REALWHEELS

While Cerebral Pussy, Caitlin Myers, Sweet Scarlett, Elsa Henry, and other disabled performers have become part of the burlesque scene, many others in disability communities feel a similar need to make themselves understood as sexual beings. At the same time, it's difficult to locate supportive venues to express this identity onstage. This is why groups such as Vancouver's Realwheels serve a vital function. The managing artistic director of Realwheels, Rena Cohen, says that the organization was formed to give persons with disabilities an artistic voice and creative forum to express political and personal concerns. She explains, "the company was founded by James Sanders, who lives with quadriplegia." Following graduation from university, Sanders was not called for auditions, aside from a few roles in which he was asked to read the part of a disabled individual. Cohen says, "James founded Realwheels in response to those early, isolating experiences." She adds that the organization's goal "has been to build a more inclusive society by deepening understanding of the lived experience of disability. By virtue of casting James—a capable actor who also happens to be a wheelchair user—in lead roles, we began fulfilling our mandate without fixating on disability as the narrative driver."

Realwheels produces professional and community theater, and *Sexy Voices* was launched as one of their Wheel Voices community projects. As Cohen notes, "We attract people seeking performance-based artistic and social outlets. There's a gap in opportunities for people with disabilities to participate in theater projects, and a parallel gap in in opportunities to project a sexual identity."[11]

Cohen suggests that while performing can be a liberating experience, allowing actors to experience a community of like-minded and sometimes similarly-embodied individuals, the performance space has limitations. The charged and sensitive subject matter of *Sexy Voices* meant not all members of local disability communities, nor past contributors, felt comfortable participating. For some, this was due to a history of sexual abuse. Cohen was attuned to this issue, explaining, "Theater-based experiences are often therapeutic by nature, but the tools we were bringing to this creative process weren't going to provide the level of care needed in this case. You create a safe space for people to work and to feel supported, but ultimately, ours isn't a therapeutic process, it's an artistic process." This facet of the performance cannot be overlooked, since disabled people have been victims of sexual abuse or made to feel sexual shame, often at the hands of health care providers (Siebers 2008, 146–47). When considering disability and sexuality, this victimization must not be disregarded, especially since it is still rampant today.

Cohen emphasizes that the performance was designed to be multifaceted and capitalize on the performers' strengths, stories, and performance styles to capture a wide spectrum of disability experiences. She reflects that the mixture of humorous, poignant, and painful stories created a richer end product that "gives the audience a full experience in seventy minutes with fifteen people, trying to be as true as possible to the voices of those who are participating. Some lead with their humor, some lead with their sexuality, some lead with other things."

A number of theater and performance groups across the United States, Great Britain, and Canada feature performers with disabilities, yet not all have addressed issues of disabled sexuality, and even fewer have done so with the comic twist that was incorporated into *Sexy Voices*. I "attended" the performance through a video recording that was made during one the four nights the show played in Vancouver. According to Cohen, audiences were composed of both TAB and disabled members, who enjoyed the performance with relish (as evidenced by the volume of laughter and applause).

In addition to its humorous and poignant take on sexuality and disability, *Sexy Voices* represents a vital part of disability culture because of the nature of its creation process. As Cohen emphasizes, the individuals who wrote and performed in the show were not professional actors, but community members who wanted to tell their stories. Returning to the question of who has access to the stage, however, it is important to note that these actors needed the time, confidence, energy, and emotional readiness to discuss the weighty matters of disability and sexuality.[12] These factors suggest how the commitment to engaging in stage performance is no small task, especially considering the stamina required to see such an endeavor through from beginning to end.

Sexy Voices is composed of fifteen segments, in which several distinct themes and social messages are conveyed through costuming, spoken dialogue, musical selections, gesture, and ways the disabled actors display and conceal their bodies. These performances ask audience members to connect with the performers through the stare and through stories that suggest how all bodies are subject to change and loss. In this manner, *Sexy Voices* explores the sexualities of many different body types through the inventive and often comic lens of disability culture.

READING DISABLED BODIES AS SEXY BODIES

The costuming, movements, and language in *Sexy Voices* represents disabled bodies as sexy bodies, drawing on dominant cultural signs of sexuality and fuckability. Many of the performers dress in black and red, erotic hues that can represent passion and sophistication. Most of the female actors wear revealing clothing that recalls the glamour and sparkle of the Golden Age of burlesque, with long flowing dresses, evening gloves, and feather boas.

Sexuality is also performed through striptease, though many of the performers strip in adaptive ways that are designed to work while seated in a wheelchair. Several use black handkerchiefs or scarves to cover their bodies or legs and are easy to remove during the tease. The wheelchair strip works against the stereotype of the inert or passive disabled woman "confined" to a wheelchair and juxtaposes what Garland-Thomson calls "to-be-looked-at [and] not-to-be-looked-at [creating] a stareable scene" (2009, 157). In the context of *Sexy Voices*, there is not only the invitation, but the insistence that audience members stare at disabled bodies.

Some would suggest that stripping, regardless of the location of the performance and the nature of the bodies being revealed, results in a sexual objectification that is far from liberating. While burlesque dancers may counter this argument by saying they are in control of their performance and exercise agency as sexual subjects, Clare asserts that being considered a sexual object is more complex than it might seem. He writes, "Sexual objectification is totally intertwined with sexuality. How are our sexual desires expressed and represented? What are the differences between wanted and unwanted sexual gaze? When does that gaze define our sexualities for us, many times in degrading and humiliating ways? And when does that gaze help us create ourselves as sexual beings?" (1999, 111). Clare recognizes that while this gaze can be dehumanizing, it also has the potential to be constructive in terms of marking an individual's sexuality and fuckability.[13] As Cohen notes, many of the actors in *Sexy Voices* were compelled to become part of the performance because of their desire to project themselves as sexual subjects and objects. *Sexy Voices* points to how dressing oneself for objectification can be a form of asserting agency since performers wear clothing that is usually considered off-limits for disabled people in dominant culture. People who use wheelchairs should not wear feather boas and tight dresses, but more conservative attire, or perhaps shapeless hospital gowns that conceal their figure and potentially their desire, restricting them to the role of medical subject (though as I note in chapter 4, Brown's blog suggests how this image can be sexualized as well). By rejecting limitations on how their bodies should be costumed and ways they can perform, these actors expand the definition of what a sexy and fuckable body might look like and ways it might move, complicating the meaning of disability and entwining it with one of desirable and desiring individuals.

SEXUAL OBJECTIFICATION AND REVISING OBJECT MEANINGS

Many of the performances in *Sexy Voices* play with how sexuality can be enacted, incorporating burlesque and bawdy humor in the process. The final musical number is one of the most comic and memorable. Parodying the song "You Can Leave Your Hat On" by Joe Cocker, the cast instead sings "You can leave your bag on." The company of fifteen actors wears plastic urinary drainage bags draped around their necks like scarves, or waves the bags over their heads as a burlesque performer might wave a long glove they had just removed. Usually this kind of bag would symbolize a disability as something embarrassing that should be hidden, but in the finale, the bag is recontextualized as an erotic object a lover should display.

The song was also rewritten to be sung to a person who is a wheelchair user. As the male actor (who uses an electric wheelchair) croons, "Baby tilt back your chair, yeah, tilt back your chair, do figure eights in your chair," a female actor rolls to the center of the stage and does a wheelie and then figure eights. The singer continues, "Show me your drain bag, yeah show me your drain bag, then come back and spin your chair." In this rendition, disability is defined as sexy in that a disabled person becomes the erotic object of a serenade. During the song, another female actor uses her drainage bag to give a male actor a sexy spanking in middle of the stage, while the singer directs, "Show me that beautiful bag, stroke that bag for me." The bag is eroticized through being compared to sexualized parts of the body, such as breasts, thighs, or hips, that should be touched as part of foreplay.

While using humor to change the meaning of disability, and the drain bag is meant to take some of the stigma out of needing to wear one, the performance also makes the drain bag and disability a sexual focal point. The audience cannot avert their gaze from something that is generally not seen as "appropriate" for public viewing. In this way, the musical number upends the divide between sexual intimacy and the intimacy found in medicalized spaces. What is a more intimate act than being willing to show someone your drain bag as a means of sexual connection, embracing the body and all its various fluids? By the end of this segment, if the drain bag does not look "normal" to audience members, at least it has been potentially inscribed with a meaning that is sexy and comic and doesn't simply connote the inability to control one's bladder. The drain bag becomes something that may be revealed in the "strip" before sex, and thus the performance is one way of responding to Siebers's call to rethink disabled sexuality and "[broaden] the definition of sexual behavior" (2008, 136). Besides being repurposed from a medical device to a potential sex toy, the drain bag can also be read as intimate because its revelation suggests that the lovers are comfortable with their bodies and don't need to conceal them. In this absence of shame, the drain bag can even be read as "hot" because it is connected so closely with the intimate workings of the body and the many ways that lovers can embrace their vulnerabilities.

Sexy Voices reinscribes meanings to disability-related objects at several points during the performance, giving those items a new interpretation and emphasizing the many ways disabled people can assert their identity as sexual subjects and objects because of, and not in spite of, disability. This process engages with what José Muñoz terms disidentification. He uses this concept specifically to explore the presentation of queerness onstage and how queer people can be depicted as complex individuals who have agency (1999, 1). But in expanding this form of resistance to be employed by other minority groups, Muñoz writes that disidentification has powerful social potential: "To disidentify is to read oneself and one's own life narrative in a moment, object, or subject that is not culturally coded to connect with the disidentifying subject" (12). This definition suggests possibilities for the pairing of disability and sexuality, since part of disidentification means "expanding and problematizing identity and identification, not abandoning any socially prescribed identity component" (Muñoz 29). Such an idea is enacted in *Sexy Voices* when a disabled person's possible dependency on the bag is expanded and embraced as an erotic and playful sexual enhancement. Muñoz writes, "Disidentification is about recycling and rethinking encoded meaning," and individuals in marginalized groups can use the "code of the majority . . . as raw material for representing a disempowered politics or positionality that has been rendered unthinkable by the dominant culture" (31). In the context of *Sexy Voices*, the urine bag becomes a potent symbol for "recycling" an aspect of disability that many TABs in the dominant culture would rather not consider, an object that should not be mentioned in polite conversation, much less flaunted.

Muñoz further suggests that the stage can become a place for marginalized persons to present and perform agency and even reinvent stereotypes so they become a means for self-creation (1999, 1, 4). While the performers in *Sexy Voices* are clearly playing with different means of disability identity formation, Muñoz also admits, "Disidentification is not always an adequate strategy of resistance" since minorities sometimes have to "follow a conformist path if they hope to survive a hostile public sphere." Yet disidentification can "[work] within and outside the dominant public sphere simultaneously" in the way it conveys messages (Muñoz 5). Communities can be selective about when they employ these strategies and gauge audience appropriateness accordingly. By showing how medical objects can be eroticized, not only do disabled people assert their sexuality, but they also complicate the meanings of both disability and sexuality through posing new ways for bodies to be viewed as sexual objects. The drain bag suggests how disabled bodies can be eroticized though accessories that may accompany disability, not because these objects connote helplessness, but because they suggest a shared intimacy and expand the definition of what it means to have intimate relations.

Disidentifications can also be tied to a camp sensibility since camp performances tend to speak to audiences of insiders that "get" the joke. Camp focuses on the appearance of people and objects, so it is up to audience members to realize the significance of the performance lies in things not seen. Disability scholar Cynthia Barounis suggests that Mat Fraser's performance of a dandy is a type of "crip camp" based on a dandy's "ostentatious adornments," but Fraser's character has another level of meaning because of "the body that lies beneath" this costume (2013, 309). In this context camp humor becomes a kind of inside joke. Barounis notes that camp has been used by queer activists in "performing with irreverent zeal stereotypes that had historically been a source of shame and stigma, these artists and activists exposed the artifice of those representations while at the same time taking up a powerful anti-assimilationist stance" (310). In revealing and claiming the stereotype, the activists can shape their own kind of sexuality. Camp is neither inside nor outside a culture but rests on its borders, an appropriate space for the sexualized drain bag. Not all audiences will "get" camp humor, or all the facets of comedy in *Sexy Voices*, but that may not be the point of camp. At its heart, camp is an insider type of humor that presents a way to form one's identity, while refusing to accept how one may be defined by others.

IDENTIFYING WITH DISABILITY NARRATIVES

Several actors in *Sexy Voices* tell stories related to sexuality and negotiating the world with a changeable body. Some of these narratives are poignant and painful, while others have a humorous twist, but the act of telling invites the audience to find a space of identification with the experiences of the teller. One such narrative is a poem titled "Ditty to My Left Titty," performed by a gray-haired female actor. She uses an electric wheelchair and wears a black sequined dress and black lace shawl around her arms and shoulders. Her performance is overtly dramatic, as she recites the poem in a booming voice and parodies the grand lady of the stage. Her wide gestures are an occasion for comedy as she begins by announcing, "Ditty to my left titty," raising her hand and then gripping her breast. She peers down the neckline of the dress and says, "It's still there." The audience laughs at the one-liner, but the joke has a serious side as it recalls women who have had breast cancer and needed to have one or both breasts removed. It is with a sense of nonchalance that she performs this "breast check," though the idea of making sure her breast is still present suggests that she might not be surprised if it had gone missing. While she may not be ready to join Audre Lorde's army of one-breasted women (1997, 14–15), it seems like she might be willing to do so if the occasion arose.

The rest of the poem speaks to the (mis)adventures the speaker and her body have had over the decades. She relates to the audience, "Oh such a pity that you're no longer pretty / Life for you has been rather shitty. / But for my adventurous lifestyle, I'll make no excuse." She goes on to recount various escapades with her lovers, sexual and otherwise, until concluding with an address to her breast: "Cancer took a big bite out of you, / and a stroke put us in this chair, / but you, sweet titty, have always been there, / proud, strong, and loved beyond compare." The audience laughs throughout her performance, and while the speaker presents herself as the dramatic object of the joke with her multiple misfortunes, she is also funny and resilient despite cancer's life-threatening implications. She creates a potential space of identification with audience members, inviting them to recognize parts of her story as familiar. Perhaps they have had breast cancer or know someone who has. Perhaps they have been in similar accidents. Perhaps they simply understand the perils of the aging body. Her story is one that complicates the meaning of disability by expanding it beyond a specific group of people to show how it is part of the aging process and the story of many bodies, ones that have adventures, acquire disabilities, and continue to revel in their sexuality while recognizing that it is ever-shifting. This story also suggests how disability and sexuality exist in tandem as people age, defying the dominant cultural notion that there comes a point in life at which people shouldn't consider themselves to be sexual subjects (or at least not tell others about it).

In allowing her body and sexual self to change, the actor embodies McRuer and Mallow's call to think expansively and inclusively about disability and sexuality. Because disability incorporates the idea that bodies are not static, it can make room for a sexual identity that is likewise open to redefinition. Her embodiment of disability also upends the notion of the aging body as desexualized. She is not passive and quiet, but sensual and sassy, embracing her body (and her left titty) with all its war wounds and collected memories. Despite, or perhaps because of, her adventures, she has a sense of kinship toward her body as part of her lived experience, as opposed to feeling alienated from it due to limitations and losses. That intimate connection with one's embodied self can be its own potent form of sexuality, another way that her story expands the definition of what it means to be sexy to include embracing and celebrating the self as an unabashedly sexual being.

SEXUAL PLAYFULNESS, EXPERIMENTATION, AND OBJECTIFICATION

While aspects of disability can be physically and emotionally challenging, the lives of disabled people do not always have to be treated with an air of seriousness. One example of a particularly playful and erotic performance in *Sexy Voices* features a young woman actor wearing a black dress and black leather leggings who uses an electric wheelchair. She begins this segment with the line, "Dear accessibility devices, how many wild and kinky adventures have we had together?" and continues by explaining how her "sleek and sexy black and red wheelchair has taken me for all kinds of rides." The audience is treated to intimate details as she explains how she did reverse cowgirl sex in her chair and "crashed into a wall because I forgot to turn the power off." During this story, a male actor sits in her chair, and she sits on top of him as they mime intercourse. While the actor makes herself and her partner the butt of the joke for crashing into a wall, they are also cast as sexual subjects, and she makes herself a gleeful target of envy since the sex was so hot that they literally "lost control." In this segment, wheelchairs become not merely mobility devices but a means to enable sexual intercourse (similar to Brown's poem in chapter 4).

After the erotic pantomime, the male actor removes his shirt to reveal leather straps across his chest, a kind of bondage gear. This performance takes increasingly kinky turns as the female actor assumes the role of the dom, explaining how she uses her dressing stick as a spanking toy that leaves red welts. To demonstrate, she slaps the male actor's rear. Both actors walk to another corner of the stage, and he sits in a chair while she straddles him, explaining how she tied her boyfriend to her shower chair and screwed him while gripping the side bar to give her leverage. She says, "It was the hottest shower I ever had" and then praises her long-handled reacher, which pinches tits and asses, eliciting audience laughter as she pretends to twist the tits of her male partner. This section of *Sexy Voices* makes it easy to imagine the entertainment and eroticism disabled people could find in BDSM communities. While such environments may seems to be a paradoxical space for disability, which is often linked to physical pain, in this case the pain is recast as desirable and leading to erotic pleasure, much like McRuer describes of Flanagan and Rose's performances.

During this section, there is a dual performance occurring behind opaque screens, as other actors are silhouetted "performing" sex acts, while moaning, yelping, and shrieking. When the female actor mentions her sexy ergonomic cane, which can be used for spankings, behind one screen, the silhouette of a male actor holds a cane at crotch level and unfolds it (to audience laughter) while a female actor oohs and ahs. She then turns around and offers her bottom to be spanked by the phallic symbol. The use of screens recalls a kind of tease from burlesque shows of the 1910s in which women would get undressed behind a screen onstage, either for a bath or before bed. While the audience only glimpses shadows, it isn't difficult to imagine more intimate details (Wilson 2008, 244). Featuring wheelchair users behind screens frames their bodies erotically, to be read as something the viewer desires to see. Instead of keeping disabled people out of the picture, they become integrated into the sexy play of revelation and concealment.

This performance offers a titillating argument to counter the idea of disabled people as sexually disinterested and expands the notion of sexual practice by suggesting that disabled sex can be even hotter and kinkier because of the range of accessibility devices that may be repurposed as sex toys. The segment reveals the humor and creativity of disability cultures in changing the meaning and function of those devices so they enable and enhance sexuality. Not only does this part of the show portray disabled people as sexually interested, but it also shows them as creative instigators who are more than happy to take the lead in sex play. This section also queers sexuality, expanding the bounds of the "norm" to include different forms of intimate play and bodies that do not fit the normative definition of sexuality but prove themselves to be eminently fuckable. The repurposing of assistive devices also engages in disidentification since a disabled person's need for long-handled reachers and shower grip bars is embraced and redefined as erotic. The performers take what were representations of dysfunction and twist them into highly functional and fun sex toys. By showing how these objects can be eroticized, disabled people assert themselves as active sexual subjects and also show how sexual spaces can be more vibrant if they do not take themselves too seriously or remain static. *Sexy Voices* suggests that people should not be afraid to be inventive in expressing their sexual side, an idea that recalls Gurza's invitation for disabled people to be "devious with our devices." One should not limit the ways in which these aids could function in daily life, including to enable and enhance one's sexual subjectivity.

(RE)DEFINING DISABLED SEXUALITY FOR THE SELF

Sexy Voices reveals that disability is in part a social construction, yet the performances also highlight the reality of living with impairment and the challenges of (re)shaping one's identity as a sexual subject. One segment features a female actor dressed as a mermaid, who glides along the stage in an electric wheelchair. Her hair is long and aqua-tinged, and her body is swathed in green and black shawls and a black robe. She explains the journey of negotiating a new impairment, saying, "For the first time after my accident, on the beach to hear the waves rolling. Taking steps without falling in the parking lot feels like climbing Mount Everest without an oxygen mask." Her voice is choked during a few lines of the performance, likely due to the impact of relating her story onstage. This expression of emotion recalls Clare's reflections on the barriers posed by disability, noting that while there are many cultural obstructions to access for disabled people, there are also "real lived physical limitation[s]" that can be posed by environmental factors (1999, 4–5).

The mermaid explains how she reassured herself by saying, "You're a superstar. I love you. Breathe in, my love." The sound of the waves is calming; she feels peace and strength; and in the water her body is free; she can dive. The mermaid glides her chair around the stage, flipping her tail to a flowing piano glissando, music that mimics the fluidity of her movements as she finds a space of comfort. She pauses to wave the ends of her scarves and begins to remove them, draping the shawls over the sides of her wheelchair. She also takes off her long black gloves, the audience hooting in appreciation when it becomes clear she is doing a wheelchair strip, an erotic performance that goes beyond the expected bump-and-grind. The strip is an invitation for audience participation since as the mermaid unties the belt around her black shawl, someone yells encouragement. She points a flirting finger at them, smiling as she turns her chair away from the house, removing the black shawl that covered the top part of her body. The audience cheers as she turns back around, ending the performance clad in her shimmering tail and matching green bikini top, her shoulders and arms bared, body no longer weighed down by shawls and scarves. She glides offstage, still waving her tail.

This narrative can be read as a story about returning to a beloved place with a new kind of body and using that space to help gain a level of ease with the self. The performance involves an emotional and physical stripping of weights and suggests how the process of coming to understand a different embodied identity can be sexy. Through relating her narrative and stripping off visible layers, the audience understands that the mermaid is stripping off emotional layers that have prevented her from embracing herself. She also finds a freedom with her body in the water that she could not find in the parking lot since land is inhospitable to her legs. In the ocean, she can explore the abilities and sensuality of this different form. She removes the darkness that shrouded her, and the audience can stare, validate, and appreciate her sexuality. They cheer her revealing of skin and story as two kinds of baring of self that complement each other and construct the disabled body as sexually, culturally, physically, and psychologically complex. Further, this section suggests how telling personal stories can be an intimate act, expanding notions of sexual behavior to include a "sexy" sharing of thoughts and ideas (McRuer and Mallow 2012, 12), including personal and sexual yearnings and vulnerabilities that can be integrated into one's identity.

This performance also opens the definition of what it might mean to "recover" or "rehabilitate" from an injury. The segment does not suggest that the mermaid should try to walk—in fact it dwells on the idea that walking takes great effort—but through staying in her chair she demonstrates a fluidity of motion that suits her body, and is smooth and sexual. The goal is not to "liberate" her from the chair, but to show that there are environments in which her body can find a good "fit." The mermaid costume further widens the meaning of disability, by suggesting that different body types can be beautiful in their own right and have their own way of embodying sexuality. While the performance ends with a sexy and satisfying "reveal" for the audience, it is important not to ignore that her body will continue to face cultural and physical barriers—she is still a mermaid, with all the joys and frustrations that will entail, but she has expanded her personal definition of sexuality and found an environment where she can thrive in her own skin. The reaction of the audience is equally important since in this space they become a community to look at and validate her display of disabled sexuality with shouts of appreciation. Audience members recognize the sensuality of the strip, but some may also applaud the intimacy the mermaid has found with herself in connecting anew with her sexual side. In cheering alternate forms of fuckability, audience members integrate themselves into the performance by appreciating sexuality in its many incarnations.

INTEGRATING WAYS OF MOVING INTO
SEXUAL OBJECTIFICATION

As in the case of the wheelchair strip, one way in which the actors of *Sexy Voices* cast themselves as sexual objects is through integrating movements specific to disability into erotic performances. This is true of a female actor who sings "Turn Me On" while dancing in a manual wheelchair. She wears high black boots and a knee-length black dress with feathery shoulder straps and has strings of lights wrapped around the base and sides of her wheelchair. The lyrics include the lines "Switch me on, turn me on," which she sings while gliding back and forth across the stage, pivoting her chair from one side to the other to physically enact the "switch" and "turn." She also does a striptease during her performance, removing black cloths from her lap to reveal a shorter dress.

Stylistically, the routine draws inspiration from Golden Age burlesque shows, in which performers integrated dance into their routines to compliment the tease. Similar to Myers, the actor sexualizes her wheelchair as a key part of her performance, both in the way she uses it to move around the stage and how it adds glitter to her dance. The strings of lights connote femininity in their shine, and her smooth glides and hand gestures also gender her as feminine. As Clare suggests, we tend to connect gender to movement, though this proves limiting to disabled people since "the mannerisms that help define gender—the ways in which people walk, swing their hips, gesture with their hands . . . are all based upon how nondisabled people move" (1999, 112). Clare notes that people who need assistive devices may not be read as moving like a real "woman" or "man," yet through her wheelchair decoration, manipulation, and gesture, this actor suggests how her body can be read as gendered (and feminine) through swiveling her wheels instead of hips and gliding in a seductive way that asks the audience to view her as a sexual subject and object. Similar to how the drain bag was recast as an object that enhances sexuality, her wheelchair becomes a vehicle (literally and metaphorically) to add to her erotic appeal.

A second performance in which movement is comically integrated into one's sexuality is the poem "The Midnight Coffee Bar." The verse is performed by a male actor dressed in a black suit and hat, who uses an electric wheelchair. While the poem has the same meter and cadence as Poe's "The Raven," instead of lamenting love lost, he explains an encounter with a sexy young woman at a coffee shop. When the actor describes seeing her wink and approach him and his tray, a female actor wearing a short black dress dances next to him, swiveling her hips beside his chair and tray that holds a coffee mug and pastry plate. Her movements suggest that she considers him a possibility for seduction, and he responds accordingly, telling her, "You can nibble/upon my roll . . . she took it in her fingers nicely and labored long to lick the icing." The audience laughs as the female actor lifts a long pastry from his tray and licks it suggestively. He continues the coffee shop innuendo, saying, "I dove upon her steaming muffin, for all the pleasure it would bear . . . I savored heavily filling inside her, a taste of cherry apple cider." The female actor faces him, her back to the audience while she swishes her hips. The male actor loses words for a moment when she stands beside his chair, still gyrating suggestively while he says, "As she . . . as she . . . as she . . . " The audience chuckles as it is apparent his train of thought has gone off the tracks; then he admits a crowd had gathered in the coffee shop to watch their "interactions." When they realize they have an audience, the pair separates, but for the coffee shop paramour it has been a successful encounter.

This performance is notable since the erotically charged poem is inscribed by a (suave, sexy, available, desirous) disabled speaker, but at the same time disability is never referred to in the spoken dialogue. The wheelchair functions as a prop in its own right, and becomes a sexual object as much as its occupant since the female actor moves around and beside it in a sensual fashion. While both the speaker and dancer make themselves sexual subjects and objects through their shared attentions, it is important to note that the poem could have been spoken by any actor. This potential flexibility is key since it contextualizes the man in the wheelchair as being like any other person who would go out to a late-night coffee shop and be considered a viable partner by an attractive young person. Disability is central to the performance since it is visually foregrounded, but then it fades into the background, suggesting that disabled individuals can have the same (pastry-themed) desires as TABs and be considered sexual partners just as readily. Along these lines, these performances imply how devices such as wheelchairs can add to rather than detract from the gendering of people with disabilities, again making disability a site of eroticism rather than being detrimental to one's identity and sexual self.

FROM MEDICAL TO (QUEER) SEXUAL
SUBJECT AND OBJECT

While some of the stories in *Sexy Voices* focus on personal narratives of (re)defining one's sexuality, others convey the ways that cultural attitudes and institutions oppress disabled people and have turned them into medical objects. Many of the segments in *Sexy Voices* are comic, yet given the wide variety of disability experiences represented in this performance, it is important to note that several are poignant rather than humorous. One of the most emotionally affective is "Ten True Things People Have Said about My Life," a narrative told by a female actor who uses an electric wheelchair. She is short, with bright red hair and curled fingers. Her arms and legs are bare, and her torso is covered in black scarves that crisscross her chest.

The first part of her narrative focuses on the medical, scientific, and legal oversight she's been subjected to over several years, making it evident that her body is constantly being judged and evaluated as a medical as opposed to sexual object. In the first scene, she is observed by three people, two others who use wheelchairs and one standing, all of whom write on notepads. The standing actor wears a hat and long gray coat and holds a pointer he uses to gesture to her body. The dialogue is recorded and played over loudspeakers, seeming to come from everywhere and nowhere. A male voice describes the young woman's limited motion and how her joints are "decimated." He says, "Show them how much she can move it . . . ten degrees, being generous . . . And the deformities! Just look at the sunken jaw, sloped shoulder, the crisscrossed toes. Textbook JRA." The actor removes one of the black handkerchiefs from her chest. In this medicalized space that mimics a teaching hospital, she is a subject for study and part of what Clare suggests is a scientifically sanctioned "freak show," blending a prying gaze with the search for diagnosis and medical cure (1999, 83–84). Referred to in the third person, she is regarded as a specimen and not a human being.

In the next scene, a male actor crouches in front of the young woman as if taking her picture, while an older female actor in a motorized wheelchair plays the part of a reporter. Over the loudspeaker, a female voice says she has been called "the million-dollar girl" because she has two million dollars in parts. "How does that make you feel?" the voice asks. The young woman removes two more black handkerchiefs, further exposing her body. The insinuation of the reporter's comments is that she is not a person but a price tag, someone whom society is compelled to keep alive, though she is possibly a waste of resources. Shouldn't she feel guilty for having that much money spent on her? The costs speak to the way rehabilitation practices aim to "fix" disabled bodies so they are "perfect," an impossible goal of the medical model of disability (Longmore 2003, 1). This segment is also a reference to the television series *The Six Million Dollar Man*, about an injured astronaut turned cyborg superhero, whose prosthetics give him exceptional physical abilities ("Six Million Dollar Man").[14] The implicit message is that if bodies can be made more able and "useful" through technology, they are worthy of the expense, but simply keeping people alive and able to function is economically questionable.

The third scene imitates a courtroom setting, with a male actor in a motorized wheelchair playing a lawyer. He gestures to the audience, while a male voice intones that a man paid another partygoer to perform sex acts on a disabled girl, which is the reason for the trial. The female actor removes another black handkerchief, revealing that her body is crisscrossed with thin beige straps. This segment evokes shame on many levels: the shame of being considered so sexually unattractive that someone would have to be paid to perform sex acts on the individual in question; the shame of having those acts spoken about in public; and the shame that such an act is considered criminal since either no one should be performing sex acts on that person, or they were a victim of a sex crime and could not fight back. Any of these scenarios would lead to additional trauma when the matter was discussed before judge and jury. The female actor doesn't speak, so much of the texture of this story remains a secret. The audience doesn't know if the act was consensual, or whether she enjoyed it. Her voice and reaction are left out as immaterial to the crime, symbolizing the way that many disabled people have likewise gone unheard, even in matters that had great personal importance to them and their emotional and physical welfare.

In the next episode, a female actor playing a nurse rolls onstage in an electric wheelchair, while a female voice tells the young woman that if she doesn't gain motion she's grounded to the hospital for the weekend, no birthday party. "Maybe when I come back next week you'll show progress," the voice says before the nurse rolls offstage. This monologue speaks to the medical model of disability, which suggests that the disabled body itself is the "problem," and it must be treated through therapy or other medical procedures (Kafer 2013, 6). As this section of the performance suggests, if the patient doesn't meet the expected rehabilitation goals, they are "not trying hard enough" and must be punished. No one questions the standard of what her body "should" be able to do or suggests these standards may be arbitrary and unattainable; she is simply blamed for a supposed lack of effort and told she will face further isolation if she doesn't comply. In none of these segments is she asked or able to respond to the individuals giving her orders or diagnoses; she is simply expected to be a complicit object and meet the standards of the TAB world.

At the end of this scene, the actor takes off the last handkerchief, leaving her naked except for the beige straps, and black pasties on her breasts. In "stripping" off the handkerchiefs this performance is both erotic and devastating, leaving her unshielded and vulnerable as opposed to sexual. Her body and her story represents the ways disabled people have so often been medicalized, scrutinized, denigrated, made to perform, and treated as deviant, inhuman, and passive objects. They are not given a voice, suggesting that what they think doesn't matter, or no one cares to hear it. The straps can also be read to connote a kind of bondage in the way she is bound by the expectations of others. (At the same time, bondage can take on a wide variety of meanings from oppressive to erotic, depending on the context. The next section of this performance provides a queer way to read these bindings.)

This segment of *Sexy Voices* places the disabled body in spaces where it is perhaps most expected by TAB audience members—in hospital scenes, news reports, and economic contexts based on the cost of care. But these moments also destabilize the meaning of disability in their visual representation of this dehumanization. After taking off the handkerchiefs, it is clear how her body and personhood have been left radically exposed. The act of stripping makes her body a sexual object while it is simultaneously commodified, medicalized, and shamed, drawing the stares of audience on a number of seemingly contradictory levels. Audience members may also imagine the deep humiliation and larger stories lying just under the surface of these sparse sentences of dialogue since they can glimpse only a hint of her shame and anger as the actor looks back at them. In dramatizing these episodes onstage, the segment brings to light the constant indignities people with disabilities have endured over the decades. Even in denying the disabled actor a voice, silently presenting the spectacle from her point of view gives symbolic and wrenching resonance to these episodes in disability history that have been repeated over and over.

DISABILITY COMMUNITIES QUEERING
AND VALIDATING SEXUALITY

One of the most important messages that *Sexy Voices* imparts is the way that disability communities can serve as vital support networks. While the first half of "Ten True Things People Have Said about My Life" is emotionally devastating, the second half is erotic and affirming, as the actor is saved by the voices of friends and lovers who regard her as a whole human being, and a sexual one.

This section begins with a second female actor approaching the first and standing beside her wheelchair as a female voice says, "I want to get to know your body, what hurts and what feels good." A third female actor using an electric wheelchair joins the pair and strokes the first actor's arm as a female voice says, "I bought this for our bath. When I smell you in class we'll smell like the same soap." A male actor walks onstage and crouches in front of her, mirroring the pose of the man who was taking pictures of her in the first segment but putting her feet on his shoulders as if preparing to perform oral sex. A man's voice talks about being sexual and how it might work. Another female actor walks behind her and kisses her neck, while a female voice says, "I love the taste of you." This section of the performance revels in the closeness and pleasures of the body, the gentle and loving caress, the erotic gaze that is desiring and not punitive, exploring how sensuality and sexuality can be queered and expanded in the intimacy of touch, but also making it clear that the actor is desired and desirable.

By the end of this scene, she is surrounded by seven people who represent a community that loves and cherishes her. A song plays in the background with the lyrics, "Her love keeps me warm, / I don't want to change." Two actors use the beige straps that bind her body to lift her out of her wheelchair and hold her aloft for a few moments before setting her down again, the straps perhaps representing ties that bind her to a community through her body, as opposed to oppressing her because of it. It is this community that changes her body from a research object, commodity, and sign of social deviance, to a sexual subject and object who is active and validated with caresses and loving voices.

Disability is also sexualized by highlighting the variations in sexual culture and demonstrating how eroticism and intimacy can be queered, fluid, and not limited in possibilities. The scene expands sexuality to include intimate touch and other forms of contact, and the spoken dialogue highlights the way that all the senses can be integrated into sensual experiences, presenting a wide range of options to enjoying the sexual side of the self and others. Equally powerful is the fact that this gender queer celebration enfolds the young woman in a larger community, including more people than those who were monitoring and disciplining her body in the first half of this segment.

The performance suggests that the female actor is unafraid to reveal her body as a sexual object for the stare. Despite the emotional abuse she has suffered, she greets onlookers' eyes with boldness, anger, and defiance: *If you want to look at me, here I am, and dammit, I'm sexy.* She has not been shamed into hiding from the stare of the audience, members of which have now regarded her body within medical, legal, economic, and erotic contexts. As Garland-Thomson suggests, often people are reluctant to reveal their bodies for fear of being looked at intently, but if bodies remain covered there is no way to invoke the productive stare and have people of different body types recognize each other as human (and in this case, sexual) beings (2009, 159).

Using a community focus, this segment suggests possibilities for a wide variety of sexual relationships. In revealing the support structures that groups of individuals create for each other, *Sexy Voices* points to ways these networks can help redefine, reiterate, and reinforce what it means to be intimate, have a sexual identity, and find pleasure in being considered a sexual being by others. Through (re)shaping sexual practice in a multiplicity of ways, such communities can help individuals find physical and emotional satisfaction as active sexual subjects and desired objects.

SEXY AS WE WANNA BE (SUBJECT TO TERMS AND CONDITIONS)

By expanding and complicating the meanings of disability and sexuality, and inviting the audience to find spaces of identification with disabled actors, *Sexy Voices* enacts a critique of dominant ideologies that desexualize disability and disabled people. The performance asks audience members to stare at disability in a productive way that can move individuals toward a recognition of body variation and vulnerability. In embracing this variability as sexy, audience members may be able to identify ways they can be fluidly "sexy like us," as opposed to disabled people adopting dominant cultural notions of sexuality. As Clare argues, disabled people must be aware of the "dangers of accepting beauty and sexuality as defined exclusively by nondisabled people, by straight people, by white people, by rich people, by men. Let us remember disabled bodies in all their variety" (1999, 116).

The bodies in this performance are often inscribed as sexy in ways that reflect dominant cultural expectations—through the costuming, the striptease, the shimmy that recalls older burlesque shows—yet those symbols are important in allowing the audience to read these bodies as sexy, and allowing the actors to announce themselves as sexual subjects. As Muñoz suggests, we cannot escape the web of cultural symbols in which we are caught, yet we can play with those symbols and "recycle" their meanings (1999, 31). This flexibility may be a strength and weakness of these performances, which is why it is important that *Sexy Voices* incorporates a wide range of bodies, voices, settings, and tone, from steamy showers to coffee shops, and from sensual and silly to stark and serious. *Sexy Voices* fulfills Clare's call for "images—honest, solid, shimmering, powerful, joyful images—of crip bodies and sexuality" (1999, 117). There is an invitation to dance, to join kinky sex games, to understand love and intimacy in its many and varied forms, and to embrace a fluid kind of sexuality that makes room for all bodies and types of sexual expression.

By finding sparks of sexual liberation and oppression in a multiplicity of stories, stereotypes may be supported, broken down, or twisted around, but by the end of the production, it is apparent that disability isn't just one story, it is many.

EPILOGUE

It took a year of increasingly blurry vision in my left eye for me to consent to one then two appointments with an ophthalmologist—more lights, dilation, and corneal pictures. She says my shadowed world is due to my weird cornea. Probably. Unless it's due to my cataract, which is there but small, though a small cataract in the right place could create a lot of distortion. The ophthalmologist describes my cornea as "a little weird, but not too weird" and repeats my optometrist's suggestion to try a very large contact. It will bend light into my eye at a different angle, resolving some of my astigmatism, unless it doesn't, at which point I will need to speak with a surgeon about making very small, very specific holes in my lens.

I don't want my eye to go under the knife, or laser, or any small-hole-making device. I just want to keep reading.

Haller and Ralph suggest that some comics and cartoonists with disabilities are moving toward a kind of humor that doesn't focus on disability, but on disabled people as folks who can be joke-tellers or the butt of the joke, shifting emphasis off the body as benefit or bane to simply one of many forms of being (2003). While disabled comics still shape some of their material around their status as cultural outsiders, they can also "[joke] about their unique problems in terms of situations everyone encounters, [and] connect with their audiences" (Reid, Stoughton, and Smith 2006, 633). But how to enhance, expand, expedite this cultural change from being people with disabilities to just people—family, friends, lovers, coworkers? Perhaps it still depends on the audience of watchers and readers and listeners, all spiraling off the same story into their own spaces of association, imagination, memory.

We never know which crumbs of words, images, scents. or sounds will spark a connection. This is why it's crucial for comics, artists, storytellers, performers, to keep molding models of disability experience, reshaping meanings. It is through those creative connections and reconfigurations that we can lose lingering labels such as "the disabled," "the blind," "the Deaf," as if these folks weren't part of "we" and "us." I don't mean this to be an erasure of difference, a devaluing of the groups where people find cultural bonds, or an attempt to iron specifics from stories and replace them with a universal "We'll all be disabled someday" because all bodies are not experienced in the same way physically or emotionally (Kafer 2013, 11–12). I simply mean (and many people have sung and signed and stamped this song) that we need to learn how to delight in difference, realize the richness that flows from a plurality of perspectives.

Community translates to holding out a hand, a smile, a phrase, a scent that connects us in sameness and difference; the pride, the pain, the multiple prescriptions, the pairs of reading glasses, the pairs of prosthetic legs. Along with an army of one-breasted women we will raise a brigade of wheelchair users, a band of people with white canes, an armada of those who are Deaf or hearing-impaired, marching down the streets with others willing to make their disability visible on big brilliant buttons: Depression, Fibromyalgia, Diabetes. We can fill those Times Square screens with the words of those typing from home, joining the parade: Autistic, Anxiety, Chronic Fatigue Syndrome. Multiple Chemical Sensitivity. Bodies, words, identities, written and shouted and felt in pavement vibrations.

The only certainty in such complex communities is disagreement if we should embrace a humor that integrates or a humor that separates and marks people as different, insiders and outsiders. Yet this doesn't have to be an either/or equation if there is room for inside jokes, rants, giggles, situations understood only by those in the know, who smile or grimace or laugh out loud. As Kuppers suggests, being part of a community is to "understand that solidarity can be found—precariously, in improvisation, always on the verge of collapse" (2013, 109). Jokes sit on that line, where a guffaw could easily turn into a groan. Isn't that where we often find the most delight, in fragile comedy that may or may not spin a smile?

This is also why it's important to play with performance spaces, the varied and virtual venues where disabled people can invite others to listen to their stories, laugh at leglessness, join them in mosh pits and at bars or in threads of typed conversations. This is why it's important that conversations multiply, branch, blossom, suggest ways to open spaces of possibility, batter down barriers, not think outside the box but bust it apart, or perhaps just take down one wall.

It's through forming these connections that people with disabilities can collectively promote positive disability futures (Kafer 2013, 2) and the benefits of interdependence. As Mairs writes, "I view my life less as a contest than as a project, in which others must participate if it is to prosper" (1996, 71). She emphasizes the need to remember that our lives are collaborations, our performance of self ever-shifting, and there are many ways of nurturing those social bonds, from giving baths to giving stories, from helping someone eat to having the grace to be helped (82–83). Sometimes it's only through the balm of a joke, the stab of laughter, that I'm allowed to remember my frailties, shove the weight of autonomy off my body, ask my partner to please read the label since the type is too small. As many times as I remind myself that independence is a fiction, it's one of my favorite stories.

I like my optometrist and ophthalmologist, but after weeks of appointments and fittings for the very large contact, I realize no one has told me what's wrong. My eye is strange, or aging, or maybe both, but we skipped the diagnosis and moved straight to treatment.

"May I ask a macro question?" I say to my optometrist at the latest appointment. "What's happening with my eye, and is it going to keep happening?"

"What we think right now," he says, opening with the dose of uncertainty I should have expected, "is that your cornea has always been a little weird. I'm a preemie, too, and my corneas are also a little weird, but I haven't needed to get surgery. The thing that's changing isn't your corneas, but the shape of your lens because of the cataract. Your vision is being affected by your cornea, even though it wasn't before."

So my eye is a little weird, and getting older, as happens to all bodies. But I have the means to go to a doctor—two doctors—and figure out what's wrong. Or probably wrong. For one of the first times in my life, my sight has made me feel disabled, but I'm in a culture, a place, a time, a profession, where I'm accustomed to using my vision to read. And read. And read.

Like everything else, this contact won't be covered by insurance. My optician says he's tried this game before—the insurance company will say my problem can be corrected with glasses, and skirt out of paying for the contact or fitting appointments.

When my optician quotes me a price for the out-of-pocket expense, both my eyes get huge (or I imagine the right one does in solidarity with the left). He reminds me this cost includes follow-up appointments—there could be several—and both contacts.

"I only need one contact, remember?" I say.

"Oh," he says, "that's right." He quotes a new figure. I laugh.

"Is this your usual marketing tactic?" I ask. "Over-quote the price, then say, 'Oh wait, it'll only be this much,' so I'll say 'Wow, that's a lot cheaper!'"

He laughs with me. I decide to call this my disability benefit. Sometimes being half-sighted has perks. Just one prescription lens in my glasses! Just one contact! It's so economical!

When I tell one of my friends this story, she's aghast that insurance won't cover the contact. I shrug. Vision insurance is usually horrible. But I have my disability benefit!

I tell Drew the story since he's wrangled with insurance companies about wheelchairs for years. He bursts out laughing because he's just started working for an insurance company.

"We help a lot of people," he says. "And we're bastards."

I tell my story, and tell my story, and tell my story to various friends, amazed that everyone doesn't find the situation patently hilarious. Disability benefits! Get it?

Disability scholar and memoirist Kenny Fries writes of how Charles Darwin hoped that people would evolve to be more sympathetic and realize that helping others meant they would likewise receive assistance when needed (2007, 162). But who remembers that Darwin predicted a move toward interdependence as a mark of a higher consciousness, the mode of philosophy he hoped we would find, understanding that such relationships benefit humanity? Darwin didn't invent the term "survival of the fittest"— that was philosopher Herbert Spencer. Instead, his work was about shift, about change, about survival of the flexible (Fries 2007, 82). As Fries notes, mutability can be another form of "disability benefit" since "What we learn by adaptability may tell us more about the natural ways in which all of us can best flourish in an increasingly interdependent, complex, and confusing world" (180). How telling that Western culture, based on an ideology of autonomy, would choose to mishmash that message, deride the idea of disability rather than delve into its potential.

Learning how to use a prosthetic, even a tiny one, is a pain in the rear. Pretend you have one sighted eye. Pretend that sighted eye doesn't like to have anything touch it, a natural defense response that has been ingrained over decades to protect itself from harm. Pretend you must convince your eye that this (expensive) huge contact will (hopefully) make everything better, but the prescription plastic disc has to be suctioned to your eye for sixteen hours a day.

My eye shuts to the possibility.

This will not be fun.

My mother, who is a glasses-wearer but was part of the first generation of hard contact users, is sympathetic to my plight. She becomes my cheerleader as I learn how to balance the centimeter-and-a-half wide concave contact on my index and middle fingers, fill it with saline solution, and hold my eyelids open with my right hand while I try to put the contact on my eye with my left hand. It's a slippy, drippy, expletive-soaked process as my damp eyelid snaps shut again and again until my eye is ringed red. How many gallons of saline do I spill? Will this ever work? Minutes spin into hours. When I manage to get the contact on, too often it slides off center and I can't see where it went. I'm supposed to take the contact out with a device that looks like a tiny white plunger, but how to remove it when I can't see it?

I keep thinking, This could be worse. *I keep thinking,* If this works, you'll be able to see better. *I keep thinking,* At least you're able to afford this prosthetic that may be as close to a cure as you'll get for now. *I keep thinking,* You don't want more reading headaches.

I need to become accustomed to seeing under water, the task I'm asking my eye to perform when I slip on the saline-filled contact. How do swimmers do it?

I give myself a break from the contact. I putter around the kitchen. Then . . . inspiration? Innovation? Desperation? I fill the bowl of the contact with saline, balance it on the tiny white plunger, sit on the closed toilet and hold the contact to my eye, keeping my eyelids pried open, the water too cold as I feel the tiny herk and jerk of my facial muscles, the flinch and flex and flutter. My eyelids get tired. Achy. I stop.

Perhaps this is what happens with most prosthetics: You pay too much. You want the cure to come faster. The acclimation period is miserable. You wonder if it's worth it.

After living with a certain kind of body long enough, it's difficult to remember what life was like before or after. The rhythm may start to feel like what always was, even if that's just another soothing story. We reshape our days, our routines, to fit our form. As Harriet McBryde Johnson writes of the assistance she needs to get ready for the day, "I sometimes think how strange it would be to do these morning things in solitude as nondisabled people do, and to regard, as many of them do, a life like mine as a dreadful and unnatural thing. To me it is natural to feel the touch of washcloth-covered hands on flesh that is glad to be flesh" (2006, 251). This kind of interdependence can be another form of intimacy, another form of trust, remembering the many ways we are in other people's hands. Yes, we must not forget that it can be a space of abuse and danger, but it can be one of pleasure as well.

I read my mother's journal, the one she kept during the year after my birth, when I was tiny and tentative. During my first two months, it was a daily dance on the line between life and death. Her writing is the same neat cursive with which I'm familiar, but the story fills in emotional cracks I hadn't known existed. The nights she cried. Her fear when she and my dad discovered I had retinopathy of prematurity. Her anxiety that the vitrectomy to preserve the sight in my right eye had less than a fifty percent chance of working. Her sadness when it didn't succeed.

Such a different narrative than the one I'm accustomed to, the one in which I've always been blind in one eye. I want to hug my young mother, the person in the story, and tell her everything will be okay, you'll just have to yell at me to look both ways eight times before I cross the street. I won't lament the possibility that my life could have taken a different shape.

My mother also writes of my first prosthetic, the plastic cover my ophthalmologist wanted me to wear over my right eye so that my skull would grow to have eye sockets that were the same size. I didn't like the prosthetic then, either, and managed to keep taking it out though I wasn't even a year old. My parents never figured out how I performed that operation with my tiny fingers, but now I send sympathy to my much smaller self. Convincing my body to be patient with a prosthetic isn't much easier the second time around. I know my body is malleable, mutable, adaptive, though reminding myself of that fact doesn't make the process easier.

When Perillo begins to make peace with her status as a wheelchair user and stops looking for the magical treatment that will dissolve her MS, she discovers that she "[feels] unburdened, lighter, strangely giddy as I float" (2009, 141). Through resisting her impulse to be healed, she finds a kind of intimacy in allowing her body to do as it will: "There is an erotic component to the surrender—it comes from the self relinquishing control, throwing itself away. That body is offered to whatever seizes possession of it—whether the seizer be disease or time or a human lover" (141). Sometimes it's easier to give up the fight, loosen our grip on one sense of self and allow another side of our identity to make itself at home.

But it can be difficult not to prolong the battle, clinging to a particular iteration of one's bodymind, aware of the psychological and social repercussions of letting go when dominant society still refuses to embrace variability in so many realms. While Shuttleworth calls for opening the definition of what constitutes sexuality and sexual identity for people with disabilities, he admits that many of the men he spoke with who had CP didn't want to rewrite all sexual social norms. They desired romantic relationships, to be considered sexual beings, and for prospective partners not to dismiss them out of hand (2012, 66).

Remarkable how simple it is, and yet how complex, to float appreciation of variability and sexuality into everyday life as Mairs suggests, to see a body often enough that it slides into one's frame of reference as expected, looking just as it should. This takes less effort than one might expect, yet why is it so difficult? Is it simply as Garland-Thomson suggests, the task of extending that first curious stare to hold another's attention and start the scopic dialogue (2009, 87–89)? As Lehrer notes, we must remember the potential for shift in ways of seeing, and how "a lover's regard begins with a stranger's gaze" (2012, 236).

Enough with my dallying details. Sometimes I get the contact in, but it slips off center. Other times the contact is centered, but with a pesky air bubble trapped in the middle that makes the world even blurrier than usual. It takes two months before I'm able to get the contact in correctly every time, my body having lowered its defenses or simply acquiesced to this prosthetic. Yes, the world is somewhat resolved; I can see people more clearly down the hall, though there are still three moons clustered in the sky. Maybe I'll always glimpse the moon in triplicate. I don't mind.

I need new glasses with plain lenses to protect both my eyes from the poking things of the world. It's a necessary protection, and after years of being a glasses-wearer, my face looks wrong without wire frames.

Wearing my new contact and polycarbonate lenses, I invite Eric to meet me and two friends at a coffee shop on a Saturday morning. We're armed with laptops and writing projects. Eric says he'll be there around eleven, and at eleven-thirty I wonder if he's been delayed. I frown at my laptop screen, struggling with another disobedient sentence, when I hear a voice from the void on my right: "Any time now." I turn to see Eric grinning at me, as are my two other friends. Who knows how long he's been sitting there staring at me, but wheelchair users can be stealthy as anything.

"You're an asshole," I say before hugging him. We all laugh.

In expanding the meanings of disability, humor, and sexuality, not everyone will want to smash all the molds. But that doesn't stop us from embracing flux and fluidity. Being "sexy like us" leaves space for individuals to experiment with femininity, masculinity, and queer spaces that do not abide by rote rules of either/or. Being "sexy like us" demolishes definitions of intimacy, of what it means to have a sexual encounter, of what shapes a bodymind to be attractive, mixing the physical and emotional, the spiritual and the seductive, the humorous and the heart-wrenching.

Is it sexy to strip off my sight? On TV and in the movies, taking your glasses off means a hot night, but I need that little plunger to get the contact out. Maybe if the operation were performed by my partner? Is a blurrier world a sexier world?

Will the moment be ruined if we drop the contact on the floor (as I have done many times) and spend countless minutes hunting for it with our rears in the air (as I have done many times), or could crawling on the rug with a flashlight searching for a tiny plastic disc constitute foreplay?

Drew tells me (after a not terribly scientific experiment) that he had more Tinder hits when he didn't include a picture of himself in his wheelchair. Without the visual cue, however, he's not sure how to bring up the chair later on, in midconversation with an interested potential date. We don't know how to feel about his data.

No, that's a lie. We're sad.

Drew is charismatic, a people person, a thoughtful guy. He's just a few months into his job as an insurance agent and tells me that his wheelchair is the best gimmick ever. It says, You need insurance. You never know what could happen to your fragile body. But I'm not sitting at home feeling sorry for myself. Want to see my rock-climbing gear in the back of my van? *Drew wouldn't be the first person to tell you he was a supercrip, but he'll admit it grudgingly and concede that maybe he needs more insurance due to his hobbies.*

In joking with disability, having vibrant disability communities, and valuing disability as a political identity, we must also remember that is a privilege given to a few people in first world countries, and not a bond shared worldwide.[1] There is great diversity within international disability communities, and as disability scholar Eunjung Kim writes, we must respect the variability of disability experiences. Kim suggests, "This appreciation of difference is required to avoid another trap: that of assuming the universal characteristics of disability insofar as everyone with a disability is believed to go through the same experiences wherever they are located" (230). Moving forward, we must continue (re)shaping disability studies to examine global disability communities and inequalities, disability due to violence and war and the many ways bodies are political instruments with a multiplicity of meanings, separations, and unities. These are spaces that further complicate the definition of disability and adaptation, of humor than hangs on the edge of truth and taste, of sexualities affirmed and denied, in the constant conversations on appreciating and celebrating all types of bodyminds.

While I'm battling my contact, I hear a story on the radio about a seven-day clinic in Ethiopia where ophthalmologists perform thousands of cataract surgeries, some on people who have been blind for years due to clouded lenses. Hundreds of patients are scheduled every day for the four-minute surgery, and they and their families camp in the clinic's courtyard with tents and blankets.

It only costs four dollars to buy one of the new plastic lenses, which I imagine cupping their eyes gently after the milk-white lens is removed. The patients' eyes are bandaged afterward, and a family member leads them back to the courtyard to rest. Every morning, the doctors remove those bandages to see how the patients are healing and check for possible infections. In the new light everyone blinks and laughs and cries and dances. Family members explain that the blind people couldn't farm, and the chickens took their food, but now they can return to the rhythms of their old life ("4-Minute Surgery" 2018). It's another space in which it's difficult to sport disability pride and adapt to a world with less sight. I sit with my own plastic lens, pile of books, and reading glasses, returning to my rhythms of writing and teaching, still not wanting to be "cured" of my blind eye, but admittedly pleased to settle back into my kind of normal. For now.

I know my story isn't over.

NOTES

INVITATION/INVOCATION: FOR WORDS

1. See Gibley 2016 for a discussion of the movie *Me before You*, and the anger it ignited in disability communities. The film is based on a novel about a disabled man who is a wheelchair user and decides to end his life so he can leave money to his TAB lover. Disabled activists decried the way the book and film devalued the lives of people with disabilities. Also see *Million Dollar Baby* 2005 for a statement by the Disability Education Rights & Defense Fund regarding the harmful attitudes about disability conveyed in this film. The movie follows the story of an aspiring boxer who becomes disabled after an injury and asks her coach to end her life rather than continue to live as a quadriplegic.

CHAPTER 1: THE FUNNY, THE FRAUGHT, AND FORMS OF FOREPLAY

1. See Baynton 2017 for a discussion of judgments on disability and bodily fitness and how they shaped the American public perception of otherness; see Minch 2013 for an exploration of the connections between nationalism and disability among Mexican Americans and Mexican immigrants; and see Brownsworth 1999 for a discussion of the stigmatization and medicalization of queer identities.

2. As Kafer notes, the acronym TAB, or temporarily able-bodied, is "intended to remind nondisabled people that the abled/disabled distinction is neither permanent nor impermeable" (2013, 25).

3. The word "bodymind" implies a connectedness between body and mind. As Margaret Price notes, "mental and physical processes not only affect each other but also give rise to each other—that is, because they tend to act as one, even though they are conventionally understood as two—it makes more sense to refer to them together, in a single term" (2015, 269). In my use of the term, I also take inspiration from Eli Clare, who writes that he uses the word to, "[follow] the lead of many communities and spiritual traditions that recognize the mind and body not as two entities but as one, resisting the dualism build into White western culture" (2017, xvi).

4. See Samuels 2014 for a discussion on disability and race as identities that individuals assume they should be able to judge visually.

5. For more on the ambivalent nature of the stare, see Siebers 2008, 99.

6. For more on intentional and unintentional iterations of passing, see Brune and Wilson 2013.

7. For a discussion of gender as performance, see Butler 1988; for a discussion of the "mirroring body" and health as imitation and performance see Frank 2013, 43–46; for a discussion of normality as social construction and a definition of the "normate" see Garland-Thomson 1996, 8–9.

8. I take inspiration for this idea from Eli Clare's *Brilliant Imperfection* (2017) and his insistence on exploring the gray areas surrounding disability and cure without providing solutions, instead choosing to dwell in complexity.

9. For stories of individuals who sought experimental treatments for disability when standard medical cures failed, see Skloot 1996, 19–33, 93–101; and Perillo 2009, 32–44.

10. In the title of Galloway's book, the word "deaf" is intentionally in lower case to signify that Galloway does not consider herself to be culturally Deaf. As she notes, "If you are deaf of deaf—a deaf person born to deaf parents—and your language is Sign and the company you keep is primarily deaf, you are Deaf with a capital *D*." Since Galloway developed her hearing loss slowly and mostly associated with people who were not Deaf, she is part of "the little-*d* deaf" community (2009, 78)

11. For more on power imbalances between authors and subjects with disabilities, see Couser 2003, 29–38.

12. Ironically, Burcaw reinforces the idea of disability drift when he pretends to be intellectually disabled on a video chat call with his friend Jon and a teenage girl. Burcaw and Jon try to make the girl feel sorry him and show him her breasts, claiming it will be his "only chance" since he's intellectually disabled. The boys balk when she takes off her shirt, and Burcaw feels a great deal of remorse at his masquerade: "I don't know if it gets worse than that in terms of exploiting a disability . . . we decided we were the worst people on earth" (2016, 118–21). Burcaw realizes that using his disability as a practical joke was doing violence to the young woman, and taking advantage of the pity TABs may have for people with disabilities. It's not clear, however, if he also understands how his joke was doing violence to people with intellectual disabilities.

13. For more on disability acquired through traumatic experiences such as war, racial violence, or other systems of oppression, see Siebers 2010, 37–38; Garland-Thomson 2009, 126–28, Barker 2017, 105–6, and Schalk 2017, 141.

14. See Rowden 2009 for a discussion of how blind Black musicians have been labeled as musical savants, jazz geniuses, and saintly gospel singers. See Metzel 2011 for a discussion of how dominant American culture has equated mental illness and blackness since the time of slavery, promoting the stereotype of the dangerous Black man.

15. See Erevelles and Minear 2017, 388–93.

16. For a discussion on the difficulty of talking about physical disability and discomfort in public, see Finger 1993, 33, 80.

17. For a discussion on the complex relationships between disability identity, pride, and pain, see Kuppers 2013, 95.

18. Kuppers writes of the varying opinions among members of disability cultures regarding engagement with dominant (ableist) society. She notes that many disabled

people "live in definitional hybridity and hold multiple perspectives on segregation and inclusion, on radical assertion of difference as positive value versus the need to catch an accessible bus . . . Living disability culture means code-switching" (2013, 18).

19. For more on disabled women being steered away from pregnancy or condemned for the decision to have children, see Mairs 2002; Jamison 1996, 189–91; Kafer 2013, 76–82; Clare 1999, 113.

20. For more on the anxieties people may feel about their disability precluding a sexual relationship, see O'Brien 1990; Nolan 2013, 8, 139, 148; Shuttleworth 2012; Burcaw 2016, 69–74; Sienkiewicz-Mercer 1996, 86–89, 188–90, 219–22.

21. Examples of disability studies texts with elements of autobiography include Kafer's "Desire and Disgust" and *Feminist, Queer, Crip*; Clare's *Exile and Pride* and *Brilliant Imperfection*; McRuer's *Crip Theory*; Nakamura's *A Disability of the Soul*; Linton's *My Body Politic*; Longmore's *Why I Burned My Book*; Kuppers's *Disability and Community Performance*; and Siebers's *Disability Theory*.

22. See Nakamura's discussion of her reluctance to admit her own struggles with depression when studying people with mental disabilities (2013, 17–22). For a discussion of doctors' reluctance to be treated for mental disabilities such as depression, see Jamison 1996, 200–8.

CHAPTER 2

1. For more on the political and theoretical uses of the term "crip," see Kafer 2013, 13–16; McRuer 2006.

2. While some people in disability communities prefer this kind of "person-first" language, Bolt notes that the phrase is problematic for others since "the preposition *with* implies that people carry, or are accompanied by, disabilities, meaning that environmental factors are intrinsically ignored" (2013, 27).

3. This word is a slur used against people with intellectual disabilities, which I have generally chosen to replace when quoting material. In this instance, however, I have decided to leave the quotation unchanged since it suggests why the word has acquired a negative connotation.

4. Also see Kleege's remarks on how being called "visually challenged" is part of "the current mania to stick a verbal smiley face on any human condition that deviates from the perceived norm" (1999, 9–10).

5. This name may be a reference to a 1999 episode of the television show *Family Guy* titled "A Hero Sits Next Door." When Peter's character meets an athlete who is a wheelchair user, he says, "Holy crip, he's a crapple" ("Hero Sits Next Door").

6. Simi Linton's memoir *My Body Politic* (2007) serves as an interesting contrast to Perillo's experiences. Linton explains her adjustment to becoming a quadriplegic wheelchair user in her early 20's and how the process was eased when she found friends in disability communities and started working for disability rights.

7. This comment references the television show *Glee*, in which an able-bodied actor portrayed a character who was a wheelchair user. This character rejected his identity as a person with a disability and wanted to use his legs again. Several episodes of *Glee* upset

members of disability communities for this reason, as well as the fact the show did not include an actor who was disabled ("Glee" 2009).

8. "Lady Gaga Opens Up about Her Struggles with Pain Disorder Fibromyalgia." Billboard.com, 17 Nov. 2017, billboard.com/articles/columns/pop/7964732/lady-gaga -opens-up-fibromyalgia-pain.

MEDITATION 2: ON BLINDNESS

1. See "How COVID-19 Impacts" (2020) for a discussion of the emotional toll the COVID-19 pandemic has taken on people with disabilities, including the fear that they may be denied care if there are not enough resources to treat everyone with the virus. See "As Hospitals Fear" (2020) for the story of a young woman in Oregon who had cerebral palsy and quadriplegia and was hospitalized during the pandemic. Medical staff tried to pressure her and her caregiver to agree to a do not resuscitate (DNR) order, with the implication that she didn't deserve that level of care. She later died from pneumonia.

2. See Davis 2017, 7–8, and Silberman 2016, 109–39 for more on the eugenics movement, the involuntary sterilization of people with disabilities, and the systemic killing of disabled people by the Nazis in WWII. Also see Clare's discussion of the Carrie Buck case that was brought before the Supreme Court (2017, 103–12).

CHAPTER 4: COMICALLY CRIPPING SEX IN THE VIRTUAL PUBLIC

1. See www.andrewgurza.com/about.

2. See www.andrewgurza.com/homepage.

3. See deliciouslydisabled.blogspot.com/2015/03/deliciously-disabled-dalliances-how -to.html.

4. See www.andrewgurza.com/blog/2016/10/31/accessing-anal-how-to-make-anal -sex-accessible-to-the-boy-in-the-chair.

5. See www.andrewgurza.com/blog/2016/10/1/deepthroating-while-disabled-the -symbolism-importance-and-realities-of-oral-sex-as-a-queer-cripple. Gurza reflects that his first attempt at oral sex when he was nineteen did not work well, even though his partner was positioned so Gurza had an "all access pass to him and his cock."

6. I take inspiration for this title from Berlant and Warner's essay "Sex in Public" (2010), which advocates for the creation of queer counterpublic spaces that "support forms of affective, erotic, and personal living that are public in the sense of accessible, available to memory, and sustained through collective activity" (2612). While their essay focuses on physical neighborhoods, I want to expand that idea to online neighborhoods and push the idea of accessibility.

7. See www.andrewgurza.com/blog/2017/6/11/queer-and-cripple-in-the-6ix.

8. See www.andrewgurza.com/blog/2017/1/23/the-reveal-narrative. Gurza reflects on the "unexceptionality" of disabled sexuality and the need to fit disabled sexuality into mainstream sexual culture.

9. A. K. Morrissey contests the connection between sexuality and full personhood, noting that we must not devalue people who are asexual, or assume that asexuality is a "pathology" (2017, 166, 172–73)

10. See crookedlunch.wordpress.com/2013/10/08/always-already-why-you-cant-crip-cyberspace/.

11. Carrie Sandahl defines "cripping" as a rhetorical tactic that "spins mainstream representations or practices to reveal able-bodied assumptions and exclusionary effects" (2003, 37).

12. See Parsloe's (2015) discussion of online communities among people on the autism spectrum, and Miller's (2017) discussion of online communities among queer college students with disabilities.

13. Ellis and Kent note that while Facebook has allowed many people in disability communities to connect with each other, the platform has also been criticized for its lack of accessibility since it relied on captcha that were difficult for people with visual impairments to use (2013, 99–101).

14. Sundquist, Josh. 2010–19. "Costumes." Joshsundquist.com, joshsundquist.com/amputee-halloween-costumes.

15. Mandeville Sisters. 2015. "I Ate My Hand for Halloween." YouTube, 15 Oct., www.youtube.com/watch?v=Wpkt0r4y7WM.

16. See @blonion, *Twitter*, 16 Aug. 2016, 8:30 a.m., https://twitter.com/blonion/status/765526145026629634.

17. See @blonion, *Twitter*, 17 Sept. 2017, 11:39 a.m., https://twitter.com/blonion/status/905817702194864128.

18. See @blonion, *Twitter*, 9 May 2016, 3:15 p.m., https://twitter.com/blonion/status/729751581701234688.

19. Johnson notes that while running for political office, prospective voters stare at her chair while pretending not to look at it, referring to her instead as "the lady with the cool earrings" (2006, 76).

20. See fukability.blogspot.com/2013/10/disability-feminism-selective-abortion.html.

21. See fukability.blogspot.com/2013/07/moving-in-non-normative-ways.html.

22. See fukability.blogspot.com/2013/09/feminist-critique-of-guinness-ad.html.

23. See fukability.blogspot.com/2014/12/im-part-of-top-25-people-to-watch-in.html.

24. See fukability.blogspot.com/2016/01/lgbti-disability-forum-2015-its-time-to.html.

25. See fukability.blogspot.com/2014/11/queer-writing-unconference-my.html.

26. See fukability.blogspot.com/2016/03/on-radio-talking-disability-sexuality.html.

27. See fukability.blogspot.com/2012/08/do-you-have-sex-in-my-wheelchair.html.

28. See fukability.blogspot.com/2012/08/sex-toys-for-fun-loving-krips.html.

29. See fukability.blogspot.com/2012/09/i-must-not-find-medical-profession-sexy.html.

30. See deliciouslydisabled.blogspot.com/2015/03/deliciously-disabled-disrobed-when-i-am.html.

31. See www.andrewgurza.com/homepage.

32. See www.andrewgurza.com/blog/2017/3/12/harnessing-my-sexuality-as-a-queer-cripple-becoming-my-super-sexy-self.

33. See www.andrewgurza.com/blog/2017/2/7/boys-in-chairs-that-time-i-couldnt
-masturbate-by-myself-anymore.

34. See deliciouslydisabled.blogspot.com/2015/05/touch-me-how-experience-of-touch
.html.

35. See deliciouslydisabled.blogspot.com/2015/03/deliciously-disabled-dalliances-how
-to.html.

36. See deliciouslydisabled.blogspot.com/2015/04/doing-it-deliciously-disabled-style.html.

37. See www.andrewgurza.com/blog/2016/9/9/test-two.

38. See www.andrewgurza.com/blog/2017/1/23/the-reveal-narrative.

39. See www.thatgirlinthewheelchair.com/p/about.html.

40. See www.thatgirlinthewheelchair.com/2013/10/obligatory-halloween-post
-featuring.html.

41. See www.thatgirlinthewheelchair.com/2016/09/i-survived-fashion-is-for-every
-bodyand.html.

42. See www.thatgirlinthewheelchair.com/2015/07/clean-pioneer-disability-romance
.html.

43. See www.prettycripple.com/about/#.Wt5195ch3b1.

44. See www.prettycripple.com/?s=style+crush#.WCvxBcnmK00.

45. See www.prettycripple.com/nyfw-time-sketch-boobs/.

46. This shirt is reminiscent of Dave Chapelle's comedy skit "It's a Wonderful Chest,"
in which a woman with large breasts is convinced not to have breast reduction surgery.
The sketch plays on the idea that men and women accept their roles as starers and starees,
while highlighting the performativity of gender and gender roles (Cumbo 2009, 49).
Scholar Andrea Cumbo argues "the ability to laugh is an act of power, the very thing that
is often stripped from women when they become 'object,'" so finding this sketch funny
may be empowering (49). This episode also highlights "the objectification of women" and
makes it an object of mockery (50).

47. See www.prettycripple.com/tag/wheelchair-barbie/#.WCvvGsnmK00.

48. See www.andrewgurza.com/blog/2017/8/14/working-as-a-queer-cripple-my
-feelings-around-presenting-sex-disability-and-queerness.

49. See www.andrewgurza.com/blog/2017/6/11/queer-and-cripple-in-the-6ix.

CHAPTER 5: "MY OTHER RIDE IS MY VIBRATOR": SEX, DISABILITY,
AND THE EMANCIPATORY POTENTIAL OF JOKES

1. See Lehrer for a discussion of how this prohibition was re-created at the school she
attended, where disabled children were not allowed to have sex education classes even
when they were adolescents (2012, 240).

2. For more on the nexus of disability, eugenics, and disabled people being viewed as
unfit to reproduce, see Davis 2017, 8; Snyder and Mitchell 2006, 19; Mairs 2002, 160.

3. For a discussion on how disabled men have historically been considered sexually
deviant and as sexual predators, see Jarman 2012b, 92, 95.

4. The original version of this joke, and others in this chapter that refer to people with
dwarfism, use the "m-word." I have chosen to replace this word since it is "considered a

derogatory slur" by advocacy organizations such as the Little People of America ("LPA Issues Statement" 2015).

5. For an exploration of Keller's sexual otherness and how her sexuality was considered a taboo subject during her lifetime, see Nielsen 2004, 40, 128–33.

6. As Muñoz suggests, members of minority communities can use disidentification strategies to refashion "damaged stereotypes" as "powerful and seductive sites of self-creation" (1999, 4). If crutches are extensions of the body, what sexual sensations could they create when rubber together? At the same time, this reading requires an audience who can appreciate the subversive sexual possibilities and "get" that aspect of the joke.

7. For a critique on how the subject of whiteness was discussed and avoided in the comedy of Dave Chapelle and became a problematizing issue, see Gogan 2007, 80–84.

8. See Metzl 2011 for a discussion of how black males have been historically stereotyped in American culture as mentally disabled.

9. Richard Corliss writes of how Williams hid his depression through comic performance when he was with others, though when he was alone or with one other person, his deep sadness was more apparent (2014, 52).

10. The original version of this joke, and others that refer to people with intellectual disabilities, use the "r-word," which I have chosen to replace since it is a derogatory slur.

11. The telethon was long protested by many disabled people and advocacy organizations, who argued the MDA infantilized the people it was supposed to "help." Jerry Lee Lewis is famed for writing a particularly offensive essay that appeared in *Parade Magazine*, suggesting he would rather be dead than disabled. See H. Johnson's protest of the MDA telethon, 2006, 47–75; Clare's critique of the MDA telethon, 1999, 105–7; and M. Johnson's recounting of disability activism against the MDA telethon 2004b.

12. See Kafer 2012, 336.

13. Gilbert notes that male comics use similar personas as female comics, though they employ the libidinous "stud" instead of "bawd," the surly "rebel" instead of "bitch," and the depressed "loser" instead of "whiner" (2004, 134).

14. For discussions on the damaging effects of labels such as the "r" word, see Clare 2017, 42; Siebers 2008, 103.

15. For more on the way prosthetics may "overwhelm" the disabled body so other people focus on the prosthetic and not the person, see Perillo 2009, 66; and Siebers 2008, 109–10.

16. Henderson notes that what is considered an "ugly" smell is culturally determined, giving the example that bathing too frequently was considered a problem in decades past (2015, 148). In this case smelling like a stripper is cast as degrading, suggesting the women are "dirty" and their paramours do not wish to be reminded of their activities with such ladies.

17. Along similar lines, Linton reflects on feeling conflicted about being singled out as a wheelchair user at a James Brown concert, since she was allowed in first and later received a kiss from Brown. She writes that she felt welcomed, not patronized or demeaned, but she often decides whether to accept such favors based on the degree of "pleasure" and "compromise" (2007, 105–7).

18. Mairs writes of feeling like her body is "a guttering candle in a mound of melted wax, or a bruised pear." At the same time, she realizes that many women are not content with their bodies and become determined to reshape them (1996, 54–55).

19. For more on the paradoxical stereotypes of blind women as desexualized, sexually sensitive, and grateful for any sexual attention they receive, see Kleege 1999, 23.

20. The YouTube page on which this video is posted includes a note that Devin was a man in the audience who had been heckling the comics all night, so this comment was a jab aimed at him.

21. For more on the sterilization of people with disabilities, see Clare's discussion of the Carrie Buck case (2017, 106–9) and Desjardin's discussion of parents of intellectually disabled people in Canada who try to convince their children to be sterilized and avoid the risk of pregnancy (2012, 80).

22. As Kuppers notes of the diverse goals within disability communities, "Some disabled people aspire to a liberal ideal of equality for all, a subsumption into a society that makes space for them . . . But some disabled people have . . . a radical understanding of disability culture, as a segregated/separated entity that either rejects or enhances the 'ordinary.'" (2013, 17).

23. See Mintz's reflections on how disabled women have problems being taken seriously as mothers since they are often viewed and treated as children in dominant society (2007, 144–54), yet some have found ways of cooperative parenting that expand the definition of what it is to mother (162).

CHAPTER 6: SEXY LIKE US: EXPANDING NOTIONS OF DISABILITY AND
SEXUALITY THROUGH BURLESQUE PERFORMANCE

1. See Lewis 2017 for a discussion of how individuals have been labeled "mad" after disagreeing with the dominant political and social ideologies of the time.

2. See Allen for a discussion of the 1895 World's Fair and the White City, which featured a display of individuals who hailed from different countries. Among these exhibits were persons from Algeria who performed traditional dance. American audiences were fast to read their hip-swiveling movements as sexually charged. Several dancers were hired to stay in America following the World's Fair and perform in New York City. While this so-called "cooch dance" proved very popular, the dancers were taken to court and "convicted of immoral conduct." Despite this legal reprimand, "cooch" dancing found a home on the burlesque stage (1991, 225–30).

3. For a discussion on the social dynamics of normality and the freak show, see Clare 1999, 71–74. For a discussion of gender, race, and the enfreakment of bodies in sideshows, see Garland-Thomson 1996, 50–79.

4. See Snyder and Mitchell 2006, chapter 2, for a discussion of race, disability, and eugenics practices.

5. Garland-Thomson argues that some audience members may have found a space of identification with the so-called freaks due to disability resulting from factory accidents (1996, 65).

6. See Disman 2014 for a profile of gender queer burlesque troupe Unapologetic Burlesque.

7. Dodds describes a "voluptuous" burlesque performer who does a "teddy bear strip," which begins with the performer bouncing to the stage in a huge plush teddy bear

costume and "[easing] off the big fluffy suit to reveal a long silver dress," the plush costume being a play on sexy teddy lingerie (2013, 78).

8. For more on the intimate relationship between Bob Flanagan and Sheree Rose, see Takamoto's interview with Rose. Even though Rose had to face Flanagan's mortality, she notes he gave other people the opportunity to think more deeply about death and the illness of loved ones through his art (2009, 108).

9. Mairs suggests that people call her "brave" since "admiration, masking a queasy pity and fear, serves as a distancing mechanism." Her comment implies the individuals in question don't want to feel too closely aligned with someone who has a disability (1996, 32).

10. For other explorations of crip dancing, see Clare 2017, 135. Also see Linton's description of a bubble wrap and light stick dance party at a wedding for two wheelchair users (2007, 128–30) and a dance party at a disability conference in which one man performs an "overtly sexual" tongue dance (153–54).

11. For a discussion of the problems with nondisabled actors playing people with disabilities in movies, see Siebers 2008, 115. For a discussion of the barriers disabled people face in the performance arts, see Smith 2005, 81. Also see Lamm's description of how she found burlesque performance to have a liberatory function: "It was kind of a shock for me, trying to quickly change my attitude from 'I'm not really disabled and even if I am, nobody notices,' to 'I am a foxy one-legged dyke, and you will love it, or else'" (1999, 160).

12. For a discussion of how race, gender, education, and leisure time affect who is able to perform burlesque, see Dodds 2013, 85.

13. Clare notes that arguments against the sexual objectification of women do not take into account bodies that are often desexualized, and therefore "[fail] to understand the complicated relationship between the self as subject and the self as object," as well ways to find "pleasure" in one's body as sexual subject and object (1999, 114).

14. *The Six Million Dollar Man* aired as a television series from 1974 through 1978. Through using technologically advanced bionic limbs and other parts, the protagonist was granted better vision, speed, and strength than any other human and thus had superior crime-fighting ability ("Six Million Dollar Man").

EPILOGUE

1. See Kim for a discussion of political disability identity as a privilege (2017, 18).

WORKS CITED

"A 4-Minute Surgery That Can Give Sight to the Blind." 2018. *NPR*, 22 Feb., www.npr.org
/sections/goatsandsoda/2018/02/22/577602059/the-miracle-of-cataract-surgery-the
-blind-can-see-again.

Albrecht, Gary L. 1999. "Disability Humor: What's in a Joke?" *Body & Society*, vol. 5, no. 4,
pp. 67–74. doi.org/10.1177/1357034X99005004007.

Allen, Robert C. 1991. *Horrible Prettiness: Burlesque and American Culture*. UNC Press.

"Apparalyzed—Forums." Apparalyzed.com, n.d., www.apparalyzed.com/forums. Accessed
19 Mar. 2016.

"As Hospitals Fear Being Overwhelmed By COVID-19, Do The Disabled Get The Same
Access?" 2020. *NPR*, 14 Dec., https://www.npr.org/transcripts/945056176.

Bamberg, Michael. 2005. "Narrative Discourse and Identities." *Narratology Beyond
Literary Criticism: Mediality Disciplinarity*, edited by Jan Christoph Meister, Tom
Kindt, and Wilhelm Schernus, Walter de Gruyter, pp. 213–37. doi.org/10.1515
/9783110201840.213.

Barker, Clare. 2017. "Radiant Affliction: Disability Narratives in Postcolonial Literature."
The Cambridge Companion to Literature and Disability, edited by Clare Barker and
Stuart Murray, Cambridge UP, pp. 104–18.

Barker, Nicole. 2014. "'What Will You Gain When You Lose?': Disability Gain, Creativity, &
Human Difference." *Serendip Studio*, https://serendipstudio.org/oneworld/identity
-matters-being-belonging-becoming/%E2%80%9Cwhat-will-you-gain-when-you
-lose%E2%80%9D-disability-gain.

Barounis, Cynthia. 2013. "Why So Serious? Cripping Camp Performance in Christopher
Nolan's *The Dark Knight*." *Journal of Literary and Cultural Disability Studies*, vol. 7,
no. 3, pp. 305–20. doi:10.3828/jlcds.2013.26.

Barrick, Mac. 1980. "The Helen Keller Joke Cycle." *The Journal of American Folklore*,
vol. 93, no. 7, pp. 441–49. doi.org/10.2307/539874.

Baynton, Douglas. 2017. "Disability and the Justification of Inequality in American
History." *The Disability Studies Reader*, 5th ed., edited by Lennard Davis, Routledge,
pp. 17–34.

Bell, Chris. 2017. "Is Disability Studies Actually White Disability Studies?" *The Disability
Studies Reader*, 5th ed., edited by Lennard Davis, Routledge, pp. 406–15.

Bell, Chris. 2012. "Introduction: Doing Representational Detective Work." *Blackness and
Disability: Critical Examinations and Cultural Interventions*, edited by Chris Bell,
Michigan State UP, pp. 1–8.

Berlant, Lauren, and Michael Warner. 2010. "Sex in Public." *The Norton Anthology of Theory and Criticism*, 2nd ed, W. W. Norton, pp. 2600–2615.

Berne, Patricia, et al. 2018. "'Beauty Always Recognizes Itself': A Roundtable on Sins Invalid." *WSQ: Women's Studies Quarterly*, vol. 46, no. 1 & 2, pp. 241–50. doi.org /10.1353/wsq.2018.0002.

Bolt, David. 2013. *The Metanarrative of Blindness: A Re-Reading of Twentieth Century Anglophone Writing*. U of Michigan P.

Boxx, Jacqueline. 2016a. "Jacqueline Boxx—This is my Throne GBE." *YouTube*, 16 Feb., www.youtube.com/watch?v=2V5NWk_W8MY&list=PLxCljYSCgBoHBKHL4AZYDY Ma2TgMxVo9U&index=42.

Boxx, Jacqueline. 2016b. "What My Use of a Wheelchair 'Means' as Miss Disa-Burly-Tease." *Pin Curl Magazine*, 25 Jan., http://pincurlmag.com/what-my-use-of-a-wheel chair-means-as-miss-disa-burly-tease.

"Brave Sheffield Woman Performs Burlesque Routine in Wheelchair and Wearing Stoma Bag." 2015. *The Star* [Sheffield, UK], 20 Dec., www.thestar.co.uk/news/brave -sheffield-woman-performs-burlesque-routine-in-wheelchair-and-wearing-stoma -bag-1-7637830.

Briggman, Jane. 2009. *Burlesque: A Living History*. Bear Manor Media.

Brosh, Allie. 2013. *Hyperbole and a Half*. Simon & Schuster.

Brown, Jacki Jax. 2012–2017. *Fukabilty: Disability & Sexuality*. http://fukability.blogspot.com/.

Brownsworth, Victoria. 1999. "Introduction." *Restricted Access: Lesbians on Disability*, edited by Victoria Brownsworth and Susan Raffo, Seal Press, pp. xi–xxii.

Bruener, Ally. 2011. "Ally Bruener comedy set." *YouTube*, uploaded by Bailey Nance, 2 Jan., www.youtube.com/watch?v=7FKWfru29d8.

Brune, Jeffrey, and Daniel Wilson. 2013. "Introduction." *Disability and Passing: Blurring the Lines of Identity*, edited by Jeffrey Brune and Daniel Wilson, Temple UP, pp. 1–12.

Burbach, Harold J., and Charles Babbitt. 1993. "An Exploration of the Social Functions of Humor Among College Students in Wheelchairs." *Journal of Rehabilitation*, Jan./Feb. /March, pp. 6–9.

Burcaw, Shane. 2016. *Laughing at My Nightmare*. Square Fish.

Butler, Alexis. 2014. "Re-Vamping History: Neo-Burlesque and Historical Tradition." *Canadian Theater Review*, vol. 158, pp. 44–47. doi.org/10.3138/ctr.158.009.

Butler, Judith. 1988. "Performative Acts and Gender Constitution: An Essay in Phenomenology and Feminist Theory." *Theater Journal*, vol. 40, no. 4, pp. 519–31. doi. org/10.2307/3207893.

Canguilhiem, George. 2008. *Knowledge of Life*, translated by Stefanous Geroulanos and Daniela Ginsberg, Fordham UP.

Cavett, Dick. 2014. "Boxing the Black Dog." *Time*, 14 Aug., time.com/3110838/boxing-the -black-dog/.

Clare, Eli. 2017. *Brilliant Imperfection: Grappling with Cure*. Duke UP.

Clare, Eli. 1999. *Exile and Pride*. South End Press.

Cohen, Rena. Personal interview. 9 Feb. 2017.

Coleman-Brown, Lerita. 2017. "Stigma: An Enigma Demystified." *The Disability Studies Reader*, 5th ed, edited by Lennard Davis, Routledge, pp. 146–56.

Corker, Mairian. 1999. "'Disability' The Unwelcome Ghost at the Banquet . . . and the Conspiracy of 'Normality.'" *Body & Society*, vol. 5, no. 4, pp. 75–83. doi.org/10.1177/135 7034X99005004008.

Corliss, Richard. 2014. "The Heart of Comedy." *Time*, 25 Aug., pp. 42–54.

Couser, Thomas. 2009. *Signifying Bodies*. U of Michigan P.

Couser, Thomas. 2003. *Vulnerable Subjects: Ethics and Life Writing*. Cornell UP.

Cox, Peta. 2013. "Passing as Sane, or How to Get People to Sit Next to You on the Bus." *Disability and Passing: Blurring the Lines of Identity*, edited by Jeffrey Brune and Daniel Wilson, Temple UP, pp. 99–110.

Crawford, Mary. 2007. "Only Joking: Humor and Sexuality." *Sexuality, Society, and Feminism*, edited by Cheryl Travis and Jacquelyn White, American Psychological Association, 2000, pp. 213–36.

Cumbo, Andrea. 2009. "The Comedian Is a 'Man': Gender Performance in the Comedy of Dave Chappelle." *The Comedy of Dave Chappelle: Critical Essays*, edited by K. A. Wisniewski, McFarland and Company, pp. 47–59.

D'aoust, Vicky. 1999. "Complications: The Deaf Community, Disability, and Being a Lesbian Mom—A Conversation with Myself." *Restricted Access: Lesbians on Disability*, edited by Victoria Brownsworth and Susan Raffo, Seal Press, pp. 115–23.

Davis, Lennard. 2017. "Introduction: Disability, Normality, and Power." *The Disability Studies Reader*. 5th ed., edited by Lennard Davis, Routledge, pp. 1–14.

Desjardins, Michael. 2012. "The Sexualized Body of the Child: Parents and the Politics of 'Voluntary' Sterilization of People Labeled Intellectually Disabled." *Sex and Disability*, edited by Robert McRuer and Anna Mallow, Duke UP, pp. 69–88.

"Disabled." *Morticom Hilarious and Obscene Disabled Jokes*. Morticom.com. n.d. morticom.com/jokesdisabled.htm. Accessed 5 May 2016.

Disman, Adriana. 2014. "The Politics of Burlesque: A Dialogue among Dancers." *Canadian Theater Review*, vol. 158, pp. s1–s16. doi.org/10.3138/ctr.158.001b.

Dodds, Sherril. 2013. "Embodied Transformations in Neo-Burlesque Striptease." *Dance Research Journal*, vol. 45, no. 3, pp. 75–90. doi.org/10.1017/S0149767713000016.

Dolmage, Jay. 2014. *Disability Rhetoric*. Syracuse UP.

Dundes, Alan. 1987. *Cracking Jokes: Studies of Sick Humor Cycles and Stereotypes*. Ten Speed Press.

Elder, Sean. 2015. "Wait, There's More." *Newsweek*, 3 April, pp. 58–60.

Ellcessor, Elizabeth. 2016. *Restricted Access: Media, Disability, and the Politics of Participation*. New York UP.

Ellis, Katie, and Mike Kent. 2013. *Disability and New Media*. Routledge.

Elman, Julie. "What Is the Accessible Date Assignment?" *Cripping the City*. n.d., disability .sexuality.blogspot.com/p/accessible-dates. Accessed Feb. 5, 2022.

Erevelles, Nirmala, and Andrea Minear. 2017. "Unspeakable Offenses: Untangling Race and Disability in Discourses of Intersectionality." *The Disability Studies Reader*, 5th ed, edited by Lennard Davis, Routledge, pp. 381–95.

Ferrari, Fabrizio. 2015. "'Illness Is Nothing but Injustice': The Revolutionary Element in Bengali Folk Healing." *Journal of American Folklore*, vol. 128, no. 507, pp. 46–64. doi .org/10.5406/jamerfolk.128.507.0046.

Finger, Anne. 1993. *Past Due: A Story of Disability, Pregnancy, and Birth*. Seal Press.

Foy, Jennifer. 2015. "Fooling Around: Female Stand-Ups and Sexual Joking." *The Journal of Popular Culture*, vol. 48, no. 4, pp. 703–13. doi.org/10.1111/jpcu.12222.

Frank, Arthur. 2013. *The Wounded Storyteller: Body, Illness, and Ethics*. 2nd ed., U of Chicago P.

Fraser, Mat. 2013. "Cripping It Up." *Journal of Visual Art Practice*, vol. 12, no. 3, pp. 245–48.

Fraser, Mat. 2012. "Mat 'Seal Boy' Fraser Burlesque Performance." *YouTube*, uploaded by Michel Evans, 12 Jan., www.youtube.com/watch?v=XMO9VR6y6BI.

Fries, Kenny. 2007. *The History of My Shoes and the Evolution of Darwin's Theory*. Carroll & Graf.

Freud, Sigmund. 1960. *Jokes and Their Relation to the Unconscious*. Translated by James Strachey, W. W. Norton and Co.

G. Nina. 2015. "Sex and the Stuttering Woman." *YouTube*, 4 Nov., www.youtube.com/watch?v=0dmvK1TM9vc.

G. Nina. 2012. "See What Happens When You Heckle a Female Stuttering Comedian Part 2." *YouTube*, 3 Apr., www.youtube.com/watch?v=7S_uuTRMsBE.

Galloway, Terry. 2010. *Mean Little deaf Queer: A Memoir*. Beacon Press.

Garland-Thomson, Rosemarie. 2017. "Integrating Disability." *The Disability Studies Reader*, 5th ed., edited by Lennard Davis, Routledge, pp. 103–16.

Garland-Thomson, Rosemarie. 2009. *Staring: How We Look*. Oxford UP.

Garland-Thomson, Rosemarie. 2005. "Dares to Stares: Disabled Women Performance Artists and the Dynamics of Staring." *Bodies in Commotion: Disability and Performance*, edited by Carrie Sandahl and Philip Auslander, U of Michigan P, pp. 30–41.

Garland-Thomson, Rosemarie. 2002. "The Politics of Staring: Visual Rhetorics of Disability in Popular Photography." *Disability Studies: Enabling the Humanities*, edited by Rosemarie Garland-Thomson, Brenda Jo Brueggemann, and Sharon L. Snyder, Modern Language Association, pp. 56–75.

Garland-Thomson, Rosemarie. 1996. *Extraordinary Bodies: Figuring Physical Disability in American Culture and Literature*. Columbia UP.

Gibley, Ryan. 2016. "'I'm Not a Thing to Be Pitied': The Disability Backlash against Me Before You." *The Guardian*, 2 Jun., www.theguardian.com/society/2016/may/25/disability-rights-campaigners-protest-at-premiere-of-me-before-you.

Gilbert, Joanne. 2004. *Performing Marginality: Humor, Gender, and Cultural Critique*. Wayne State UP.

"'Glee' Wheelchair Episode Hits Bump with Disabled Actors." 2009. *Access*. NBC Universal, 10 Nov., accessonline.com/articles/glee-wheelchair-episode-hits-bump-with-disabled-actors-78536/#d9gexrlKCxqAUscL.99.

Gogan, Brian. 2009. "Laughing Whiteness: Pixies, Parody, and Perspectives." *The Comedy of Dave Chappelle: Critical Essays*, edited by K. A. Wisniewski, McFarland and Company, pp. 72–83.

Goffman, Erving. 2017. "Selections from *Stigma*." *The Disability Studies Reader*, edited by Lennard Davis, 5th ed, Routledge, pp. 133–44.

Goffman, Erving. 1967. *Interaction Ritual*. Aldine Publishing Company.

Goffman, Erving. 1956. *The Presentation of Self in Everyday Life*. Doubleday.

Graves, Cassidy Dawn. 2015. "An Interview with Disabled Burlesque Performer Cerebral Pussy." *NYU Local*, 5 Oct., nyulocal.com/an-interview-with-disabled-burlesque -performer-cerebral-pussy-edad68fdef81#.i4pngqp7u.

Gurza, Andrew. 2017–2019. *Disability After Dark*. andrewgurza.com/home.

Gurza, Andrew. 2015. *A Dose of Deliciously Disabled.*, http://deliciouslydisabled.blogspot.com/.

Gwaltney. John. 1970. *The Thrice Shy: Cultural Accommodation to Blindness and Other Disasters in a Mexican Community*. Columbia UP.

Haller, Beth, and Sue Ralph. 2003. "John Callahan's Pelswick Cartoon and a New Phase of Disability Humour." *Disability Studies Quarterly*, vol. 23, no. 3/4.

Hayles, N. Katherine. 1999. *How We Became Post Human: Virtual Bodies in Cybernetics, Literature, and Informatics*. U of Chicago P.

Healey, Devon. 2017. "Eyeing the Pedagogy of Trouble: The Cultural Documentation of the Problem-Subject." *Canadian Journal of Disability Studies*, vol. 6, no. 1, pp. 85–103. doi.org/10.15353/cjds.v6i1.334.

Health Equity Institute. 2013. "(Sex)abled: Disability Uncensored." *YouTube*, 7 Aug., www .youtube.com/watch?v=qA02oShNQr8.

"Helen Keller." *Jokeped*, Jokepad, n.d., jokeped.com/category/53/Helen-Keller. Accessed 5 May 2016.

Henderson, Gretchen. 2015. *Ugliness: A Cultural History*. Reaktion Books.

Henry, Elsa S. 2012. "Self Casting & Burlesque." *Feminist Sonar*, 10 Sept., feministsonar .com/2012/09/self-casting-burlesque.

"A Hero Sits Next Door." *International Movie Database*, www.imdb.com/title/tt0576911/. Accessed 11 Jan. 2021.

"How COVID-19 Impacts People with Disabilities." 2020. *American Psychological Association*, 6 May, www.apa.org/topics/covid-19/research-disabilities.

Jamison, Kay Redfield. 1996. *An Unquiet Mind: A Memoir of Moods and Madness*. Vintage.

Jarman, Michelle. 2012a. "Coming Up from Underground: Uneasy Dialogues at the Intersections of Race, Mental Illness, and Disability Studies." *Blackness and Disability: Critical Examinations and Cultural Interventions*, edited by Chris Bell, Michigan State UP, pp. 9–30.

Jarman, Michelle. 2012b. "Dismembering the Lynch Mob: Intersecting Narratives of Disability, Race, and Sexual Menace." *Sex and Disability*, edited by Robert McRuer and Anna Mallow, Duke UP, pp. 89–107.

Johnson, Harriet McBryde. 2006. *Too Late to Die Young: Nearly True Tales from a Life*. Picador.

Johnson, Jeffrey. 2008. "The Visualization of the Twisted Tongue: Portrayals of Stuttering in Film, Television, and Comic Books." *The Journal of Popular Culture*, vol. 41, no. 2, pp. 245–61. doi.org/10.1111/j.1540-931.2008.00501.x.

Johnson, Mary. 1994a. "Sticks and Stones: The Language of Disability." *The Disabled, the Media, and the Information Age*, edited by Jack Nelson, Greenwood Publishing Group, pp. 25–42.

Johnson, Mary. 1994b. "A Test of Wills: Jerry Lewis, Jerry's Orphans, and the Telethon." *The Ragged Edge: The Disability Experience from the Pages of the Disability Rag*. Avocado Press, pp. 120–30.

Jones, Kimmie. 2010–2017. *That Girl in the Wheelchair*, thatgirlinthewheelchair.com/.

Jones, Lizard. 1999. "From Each . . . To Each." *Restricted Access: Lesbians on Disability*, edited by Victoria Brownsworth and Susan Raffo, Seal Press, pp. 48–56.

Kafai, Shayda. 2018. "Reclaiming and Honoring: Sins Invalid's Cultivation of Crip Beauty." *WSQ: Women's Studies Quarterly*, vol. 46, nos. 1 & 2, pp. 231–35. doi.org/10.1353/wsq.2018.0018.

Kafer, Alison. 2013. *Feminist, Queer, Crip*. Indiana UP.

Kafer, Alison. 2012. "Desire and Disgust: My Ambivalent Adventures in Devoteeism." *Sex and Disability*, edited by Robert McRuer and Anna Mallow, Duke UP, pp. 331–54.

Kafer, Alison, and Eunjung Kim. 2017. "Disability and the Edges of Intersectionality." *The Cambridge Companion to Literature and Disability*, edited by Clare Barker and Stuart Murray, Cambridge UP, pp. 123–38.

Kim, Eunjung. 2017. *Curative Violence: Rehabilitating Disability, Gender, and Sexuality in Modern Korea*. Duke UP.

Kleege, Georgina. 1999. *Sight Unseen*. Yale UP.

Kuppers, Petra. 2013. *Disability Culture and Community Performance: Find a Strange and Twisted Shape*. Palgrave/MacMillan.

Kuusisto, Steve. 1998. *Planet of the Blind*. Delta.

Lamm, Nomy. 1999. "Private Dancer: Evolution of a Freak." *Restricted Access: Lesbians on Disability*, edited by Victoria Brownworth and Susan Raffo, Seal Press, 1999, pp. 152–61.

Legman, Gershon. 1968. *Rationale of the Dirty Joke*. Grove Press.

Lehrer, Riva. 2012. "Golem Girl." *Sex and Disability*, edited by Robert McRuer and Anna Mallow, Duke UP, pp. 54–68.

Lewis, Bradley. 2017. "A Mad Fight: Psychiatry and Disability Activism." *The Disability Studies Reader*. 5th ed., edited by Lennard Davis, Routledge, pp. 103–16.

Lewis, Katherine Reynolds. 2015. "Why Schools Over-Discipline Children with Disabilities." *The Atlantic*, 24 Jul., theatlantic.com/education/archive/2015/07/school-discipline-children-disabilities/399563/.

Linton, Simi. 2007. *My Body Politic*. U of Michigan P.

Longmore, Paul. 2003. *Why I Burned My Book and Other Essays on Disability*. Temple UP.

Lorde, Audre. 1997. *The Cancer Journals*. Special edition, Aunt Lute Books.

Lorde, Audre. 1982. *Zami: A New Spelling of My Name*. The Crossing Press.

"LPA Issues Statement to Abolish the "M" Word." 2015. *Little People of America*, Sept., https://www.lpaonline.org/the-m-word.

Lyle, Monique L., and Stacy Simplican. 2015. "Elite Repudiation of the R-Word and Public Opinion about Intellectual Disability." *Intellectual and Developmental Disabilities*, vol. 53, no. 3, pp. 211–27. doi.org/10.1352/1934-556-53.3.211.

MacPherson, Hanna. 2008. "'I Don't Know Why They Call It the Lake District, They Might as Well Call It the Rock District!' The Workings of Humor and Laughter in Research with Members of Visually Impaired Walking Groups." *Environment and Planning D: Society and Space*, vol. 26, pp. 1080–95. http://dx.doi.org/10.1068/d2708.

Mairs, Nancy. 2002. "Sex and Death and the Crippled Body: A Meditation." *Disability Studies: Enabling the Humanities*, edited by Rosemarie Garland-Thomson, Brenda Jo Brueggemann, and Sharon L. Snyder, Modern Language Association of America, pp. 156–70.

Mairs, Nancy. 1996. *Waist-High in the World*. Beacon Press.

Manderson, Lenore, and Susan Peake. 2005. "Men in Motion: Disability and the Performance of Masculinity." *Bodies in Commotion: Disability and Performance*, edited by Carrie Sandahl and Philip Auslander, U of Michigan P, pp. 230–42.

Martinez, Francesca. 2012. "Francesca Martinez on Russell Howard's Good News Best Of." *YouTube*, uploaded by Rick B, 18 Dec., www.youtube.com/watch?v=pYqcql8wSho.

McKenzie, Judith Anne. 2013. "Disabled People in Rural South Africa Talk about Sexuality." *Culture, Health, and Sexuality*, vol. 15, no. 3, pp. 372–86. doi.org/10.1080/13691058.2012.748936.

McRuer, Robert. 2017. "Compulsory Able-Bodiedness and Queer/Disabled Existence." *The Disability Studies Reader*, edited by Lennard Davis, 5th ed, Routledge, pp. 396–405.

McRuer, Robert. 2010. "DISABLING SEX: Notes for a Crip Theory of Sexuality." *GLQ: A Journal of Lesbian and Gay Studies*, vol. 17, no. 1, pp. 107–16. doi.org/10.1215/10642684-2010-021.

McRuer, Robert. 2006. *Crip Theory: Cultural Signs of Queerness and Disability*. New York UP.

McRuer, Robert, and Anna Mallow. 2012. "Introduction." *Sex and Disability*, edited by Robert McRuer and Anna Mallow, Duke UP, pp. 1–34.

Metzl, Jonathan. 2011. *The Protest Psychosis: How Schizophrenia Became a Black Disease*. Beacon Press.

Michalko, Rod. 2002. *The Difference That Disability Makes*. Temple UP.

Miller, Ryan A. 2017. "'My Voice Is Definitely Strongest in Online Communities': Students Using Social Media for Queer and Disability Identity-Making." *Journal of College Student Development*, vol. 58, no. 4, pp. 509–25. doi.org/10.1353/csd.2017.0040.

"Million Dollar Baby Built on Prejudice about People with Disabilities." 2005. *Disability Education Rights & Defense Fund*, 13 Feb., dredf.org/2005/02/13/million-dollar-baby-built-on-prejudice-about-people-with-disabilities/.

Minch, Julie Avril. 2013. *Accessible Citizenships: Disability, Nation, and the Cultural Politics of Greater Mexico*. Temple UP.

Mintz, Susannah. 2007. *Unruly Bodies: Life Writing by Women with Disabilities*. New edition, U of North Carolina P.

Morrissey, A.K. 2017. "Remedial Asexuality: Sexualnormativity in Health Care." *The Remedy: Queer and Trans Voices on Health and Health Care*, edited by Zena Sharman, Arsenal Pulp Press, pp. 165–74.

Mossman, Mark. 2002. "Visible Disability in the College Classroom." *College English*, vol. 64, no. 6, pp. 645–59. doi.org/10.2307/3250769.

Muñoz, Jose. 1999. *Disidentifications: Queers of Color and the Performance of Politics*. U of Minnesota P.

Nakamura, Karen. 2013. *A Disability of the Soul: An Ethnography of Schizophrenia and Mental Illness in Contemporary Japan*. Cornell UP.

Nario-Redmond, Michelle, Dobromir Gospodinov, and Angela Cobb. 2017. "Crip for a Day: The Unintended Negative Consequences of Disability Simulations." *Rehabilitation Psychology*, vol. 62, no. 3, pp. 324–33. doi.org/10.1037/rep0000127.

Nayar, Pramod. 2014. *Posthumanism*. Polity Press.

Nelson, Adiba. 2015. "She's Sitting Pretty." *3 Story Magazine*, 3 Story Media, May, www.3storymagazine.com/burlesque-in-a-wheelchair.

Nielsen, Kim. E. 2004. *The Radical Lives of Helen Keller*. NYU Press.

Nolan, Christopher. 2013. *Under the Eye of the Clock*. Arcade Publishing.

O'Brien, Mark. 1990. "On Seeing a Sex Surrogate," *The Sun*, May, www.thesunmagazine .org/issues/174/on-seeing-a-sex-surrogate.

O'Connell, Michael. 2012. "Michael O'Connell at Flappers Comedy Club." *YouTube*, uploaded by AmericasComedy, 28 Nov., www.youtube.com/watch?v=1AiPnJokjtI.

O'Connell, Michael. 2010. "Michael O'Connell at Tommy T's Comedy and Dinner Theater—01/05/10." *YouTube*, 20 Jan., www.youtube.com/watch?v=71rJInBrz8c.

Parsloe, Sarah. 2015. "Discourses of Disability, Narratives of Community: Reclaiming an Autistic Identity Online." *Journal of Applied Communication Research*, vol. 43, no. 3, pp. 336–56. doi.org/10.1080/00909882.2015.1052829.

Patsavas, Alyson, and Eva Egermann. 2019. "Crip Magazine: An Archive of Pain." *Disability Arts Online*, 6 Sept., https://disabilityarts.online/magazine/opinion/crip -magazine-an-archive-of-pain/.

Perillo, Lucia. 2009. *I've Heard the Vultures Singing: Field Notes on Poetry, Illness, and Nature*. Trinity UP.

Pinker, Stephen. 1994. "The Game of the Name." *New York Times*, 5 Apr., www.nytimes .com/1994/04/05/opinion/the-game-of-the-name.html.

Price, Margaret. 2015. "The Bodymind Problem and the Possibilities of Pain." *Hypatia*, vol. 30, no 1, pp. 268–84.

Price, Margaret. 2011. *Mad at School: Rhetorics of Mental Disability and Academic Life*. U of Michigan P.

Quayson, Ato. 2017. "Aesthetic Nervousness." *The Disability Studies Reader*, edited by Lennard Davis, 5th ed, Routledge, pp. 219–31.

Quiram, Polly, and Antonio Capone, Jr. 2007. "Adult ROP: Late Complications of Retinopathy of Prematurity." *Retinal Physician*, Jun., www.retinalphysician.com /issues/2007/june-2007/adult-rop-late-complications-of-retinopathy-of-pr.

Reid, D. Kim, Edy Hammond Stoughton, and Robin M. Smith. 2006. "The Humorous Construction of Disability: Stand Up Comedians in the United States." *Disability & Society*, vol. 21, no. 6, pp. 629–43. doi.org/10.1080/09687590600918354.

Rixon, John. 1998. "Tasteless Helen Keller Jokes." *alt.tasteless.jokes*. Google Groups, 12 Aug., groups.google.com/forum/#!topic/alt.tasteless.jokes/tvIELEyo6NI.

Robillard, Albert B. 1999. "Wild Phenomena and Disability Jokes." *Body & Society*, vol. 5, no. 4, pp. 61–65. doi.org/10.1177/1357034X99005004006.

Rosen, S.L. 1994. "Survivor." *The Ragged Edge: The Disability Experience from the Pages of the Disability Rag*. Avocado Press, pp. 19–21.

Rosqvist, Hanna Bertilsdotter. 2012. "The Politics of Joking: Narratives of Humour and Joking among Adults with Asperger's Syndrome." *Disability & Society*, vol. 27, no. 2, pp. 235–47.

Rowden, Terry. 2009. *The Songs of Blind Folk: African American Musicians and the Cultures of Blindness*. U of Michigan P.

Sache, Jes. *Crooked Lunch*. 2011–2016, crookedlunch.wordpress.com/.

Samuels, Ellen. 2017. "My Body, My Closet: Invisible Disability and the Limits of Coming Out." *The Disability Studies Reader*, edited by Lennard Davis, 5th ed., Routledge, pp. 343–59.

Samuels, Ellen. 2014. *Fantasies of Identification: Disability, Gender, Race*. New York UP.

Samuels, Ellen. 1999. "Bodies in Trouble." *Restricted Access: Lesbians on Disability*, edited by Victoria Brownsworth and Susan Raffo, Seal Press, pp. 192–200.

Sandahl, Carrie. 2005. "The Tyranny of Neutral: Disability and Actor Training." *Bodies in Commotion: Disability and Performance*, edited by Carrie Sandahl and Philip Auslander, U of Michigan P, pp. 255–68.

Sandahl, Carrie. 2003. "Queering the Crip, or Cripping the Queer? Intersections of Queer and Crip Identities in Solo Autobiographical Performances." *GLQ, A Journal of Gay and Lesbian Studies*, vol. 9, nos. 1–2, pp. 25–56.

Schalk, Sami. 2017. "Interpreting Disability Metaphor and Race in Octavia Butler's 'The Evening and the Morning and the Night.'" *African American Review*, vol. 50, no. 2, pp. 139–51. doi.org/10.5040/9781350079663.ch-004.

Schmiesing, Ann. 2014. *Disability, Deformity, and Disease in the Grimms' Fairy Tales*. Wayne State UP.

Sexy Voices. 2016. Directed by Rachel Peake, Realwheels Theatre.

Shakespeare, Tom. 1999. "Joking a Part." *Body & Society*, vol. 5, no. 4, pp. 47–52. doi.org/10.1177/1357034X99005004004.

Shapiro, Joseph. 1994. *No Pity: People with Disabilities Forging a New Civil Rights Movement*. Broadway Books.

Shteir, Rachel. 2004. *Striptease: The Untold History of the Girlie Show*. Oxford UP.

Shuman, Amy. 2011. "On the Verge: Phenomenology and Empathic Unsettlement." *Journal of American Folklore*, vol. 124, no. 493, pp. 147–74. doi.org/10.5406/jamerfolk.124.493.0147.

Shuttleworth, Russell. 2012. "Bridging Theory and Experience: A Critical-Interpretive Ethnography of Sexuality and Disability." *Sex and Disability*, edited by Robert McRuer and Anna Mallow, Duke UP, pp. 54–68.

Shuttleworth, Russell, and Helen Meekosha. 2017. "What's So Critical about Critical Disability Studies?" *The Disability Studies Reader*, edited by Lennard Davis, 5th ed., Routledge, pp. 175–94.

Skloot, Floyd. 1996. *The Night-Side: Chronic Fatigue Syndrome & The Illness Experience*. Story Line Press.

Siebers, Tobin. 2017. "Disability and the Theory of Complex Embodiment: For Identity Politics in a New Register." *The Disability Studies Reader*, edited by Lennard Davis, 5th ed., Routledge, pp. 313–32.

Siebers, Tobin. 2010. *Disability Aesthetics*. U of Michigan P.

Siebers, Tobin. 2008. *Disability Theory*. U of Michigan P.

Sienkiewicz-Mercer, Ruth, and Steve Kaplan. 1996. *I Raise My Eyes to Say Yes*. Whole Health Books.

Silberman, Steve. 2016. *Neurotribes: The Legacy of Autism and the Future of Neurodiversity*. Penguin Random House.

"The Six Million Dollar Man." *NBC*, www.nbc.com/the-six-million-dollar-man. Accessed 11 Jan. 2021.

Smith, Owen. 2005. "Shifting Apollo's Frame: Challenging the Body Aesthetic in Theater
    Dance." *Bodies in Commotion: Disability and Performance*, edited by Carrie Sandahl
    and Philip Auslander, U of Michigan P, pp. 73–85.

Snyder, Sharon, and David Mitchell. 2017. "Narrative Prosthesis." *The Disability Studies
    Reader*. 5th ed., edited by Lennard Davis, Routledge, pp. 204–18.

Snyder, Sharon, and David Mitchell. 2006. *Cultural Locations of Disability*. U of Chicago P.

Solomon, Andrew. 2001. *The Noonday Demon: An Atlas of Depression*. Scribner.

Sweet Scarlet. 2008. "Disaburlyties: Sweet Scarlet." *21st Century Burlesque.com*, 1 Nov.,
    www.21stcenturyburlesque.com/disaburlyties-sweet-scarlet/.

Takemoto, Tina. 2009. "Love Is Still Possible in This Junky World: Conversation with
    Sheree Rose about Her Life with Bob Flanagan." *Women & Performance: A Journal of
    Feminist Theory*, vol. 19, no. 1, pp. 95–111. doi.org/10.1080/07407700802655588.

Tammet, Daniel. 2006. *Born on a Blue Day: A Memoir*. Free Press.

Titchkosky, Tanya. 2017. "Life with Dead Metaphors: Impairment Rhetoric in Social
    Justice Practice." *The Disability Studies Reader*, edited by Lennard Davis,
    5th ed, Routledge, pp 269–81.

Trethewey, Natasha. 2019. "A Public Reading." The Phi Beta Kappa Visiting Scholar
    Program and the University of Missouri Creative Writing Program Visiting Writer
    Series, University of Missouri, 19 Apr., Memorial Union, Columbia, MO. Guest
    Lecture and Reading.

Truchan, Magdalena. 2013–2020. *Pretty Cripple*, www.prettycripple.com/.

True, Gala. 1998. "Introducing the Patient's Voice: An Applied Folklore Approach."
    Journal of Folklore Research, vol. 35, no. 3, pp. 223–39.

Vaughn, Mya, et al. 2015. "Women with Disabilities Discuss Sexuality in San Francisco
    Focus Groups." *Sex Disability*, vol. 33, pp. 19–46. doi.org/10.1007/s11195-014-9389-x.

Vidali, Amy. 2010. "Seeing What We Know: Disability and Theories of Metaphor." *Journal
    of Literary & Cultural Disability Studies*, vol. 4, no. 1, pp. 33–54. doi.org/10.1353
    /jlc.0.0032.

W., Penn. "Jokes About the Disabled & People in Wheelchairs." *Tetraplegic Living: My
    Life in a Wheelchair*. TetraplegicLiving.com. n.d., www.tetraplegicliving.com/jokes.
    Accessed 5 May 2016.

Walker, Alice. 1983. *In Search of Our Mothers' Gardens: Womanist Prose*. Harcourt.

Wallach, Greg. 2009. "Fuck the Disabled." *YouTube*, 24 May, www.youtube.com
    /watch?v=M_VvygUaEiQ.

Wallach, Greg. 2008. "About to Eat Cake." *YouTube*, 6 Nov., www.youtube.com
    /watch?v=_969XrYeuw4.

Watermeyer, Brian, and Leslie Swartz. 2016. "Disablism, Identity and Self: Discrimination
    as a Traumatic Assault on Subjectivity." *Journal of Community & Applied Social
    Psychology*, vol. 26, pp. 268–76. doi.org/10.1002/casp.2266.

Waxman, Barbara Faye. 1994. "It's Time to Politicize Our Sexual Oppression." *The Ragged
    Edge: The Disability Experience from the Pages of the Disability Rag*. Avocado Press,
    pp. 82–87.

"WheelchairJunkie.com—Forums." *Mark E. Smith's WheelchairJunkie.com*,
    WheelchairJunkie.com. n.d. Accessed 19 Mar. 2016.

White, Tracie. 2007. "Eye Diseases Changed Great Painters' Vision of Their Work Later in Their Lives." *Stanford Report*, 11 Apr., news.stanford.edu/news/2007/april11/med -optart-041107.html.

Williams, Brad. 2014. "Brad Williams Likes the Sex Story." *YouTube*, uploaded by Flappers Comedy Club—Burbank, 1 Nov., www.youtube.com/watch?v=PHL60TUwxCw.

Wilson, Jacki. 2008. *The Happy Stripper: Pleasures and Politics of the New Burlesque*. I.B. Tauris.

Wisniewski, K. A. 2009. "Introduction." *The Comedy of Dave Chappelle: Critical Essays*, edited by K. A. Wisniewski, McFarland and Company, pp. 1–13.

INDEX

144–54, 184; educational function of, 67, 72, 74, 79–80, 84–88, 170–73; Helen Keller, 146–47, 153–54, 184; as learned practice, 76; on masturbation, 182–83; minister, 161–64; misogynistic, 146–51, 164–67; multiple interpretations of, 14–15, 45, 68, 73–74, 76–78, 80–84, 144–45, 153–56, 158–85; on obesity, 164–67; penis, 148–53, 158, 161–64, 177–78, 182–83; as political tool, 12, 14, 17–18, 22; queer, 158–64; rape, 146, 149–51; sex worker, 151–53, 171–74; and social change, 25, 67, 143–44, 185; TABs as butt of, 80–81, 87–88, 159–64, 171–73, 177–78, 180–81; untold, 27, 156–57; vibrator, 180
Jones, Kimmie, 122–28

Keller, Helen, 146–47, 153–54, 183–85; sex jokes about, 146–47, 153–54, 184; as sexual symbol, 184; as target of sexual violence, 146–47

Lewis, Jerry, 241n11

Mandeville sisters, 104
Martinez, Francesca, 182–83
masquerade, disability, 8, 16
masturbation, 116–17; jokes on, 182–83
McBryer, Jackson, 167–68
mermaid, as symbol of disabled sexuality, 215–17
message boards, 38–55
metaphors: blindness as, 59; disability as, 136–41
Monet, Claude, 29
mosh pits, 78–79
Muscular Dystrophy Association: campaigning against, 14; telethons, 158–61
Myers, Caitlin, 204–6

naming, as political tool, 33–37, 49, 55–56
narratives: overcoming, 83, 129–30, 203; positioning, 69–89; prosthesis, 139–40

personal: as activism, 67, 69–70; by disabled people, 18, 71–91, 212–13, 215–17; as emotional striptease, 215–17; and forming community, 206–7, 212–13, 217, 222
Nina G., 175–79

obesity, jokes about, 164–67
O'Connell, Michael, 168–74
online community, 11, 38–55, 100–135; access problems to, 104–5; danger in, 105

pain, xiii, 22, 46, 117, 137–38, 199, 214–16; as erotic, 199, 214
penis: bikini top, 131–32; jokes, 148–53, 158, 161–64, 177–78, 182–83
performances: of high value status, 9, 12, 108; of identity, 9, 11, 65, 107
by people with disabilities: actors, 193–95, 198, 206–24; burlesque, 193–97, 200–224, 243n11; comics, 67–68, 71, 76, 80–81, 90, 142–44, 154–86, 225; denied access to stage, 156–57
persons with dwarfism: as libidinous, 151–52, 164–67; as unfit sex partners, 151–52
pickup lines, 118–19
prosthetic, 227–31; as expensive, 227; in Halloween prank, 82–83; left at school, 76–77

queerness: access to spaces, 101–2, 135; and disability, 20–21, 96, 99–103, 108–22, 134–35, 156, 158–64, 222–23; and sex jokes, 158–64; and sexuality, 99–103, 108–22, 210–11, 222–23

race: and disability, 20, 94, 97, 140, 156; and education, 94; and sexuality, 242n2
racism, 20, 94, 97, 140, 156
rape jokes, 146, 149–51
Realwheels, 194–95, 206–8

retinopathy of prematurity, 3, 7, 230
rhizomatic model of disability, 117
romance novels: with Stephen Hawking,
    168; Westerns, 127–28
Rose, Sheree, 199–200

sex, as story material, 164–65
    and toys, 112, 209–11; accessibility
        devices as, 110–11, 214–15
    workers: assisting disabled people,
        190–91; as dirty, 152–53, 172–73,
        241n16; jokes about, 151–53, 171–74
sexuality: and ableism, 120–21, 194, 201–2;
        and aging, 188, 212–13; and amputees,
        105, 108, 201; and cerebral palsy,
        100–102, 115–16, 160, 167–68, 182–83,
        187, 201–2, 230; definition of, 24,
        110–22, 184–86, 205, 209–24, 230–32;
        and interdependence, 12, 24, 112,
        115–22; and intimate touch, 117–18,
        190–91, 222; and jokes, 142–86; and
        personhood, 102; and queerness,
        99–103, 108–22, 210–11, 222–23; and
        race, 242n2; as shifting, 212–13; and
        stutters, 175–79; wheelchairs enhanc-
        ing, 114–15, 119, 121–22, 181, 205, 208,
        213–19
Sexy Voices, 193–95, 206–24
Sins Invalid, 200
sitpoint theory, 70–71
staring: as creative act, 11, 198–99, 223; as
        erotic, 201, 208, 231; at people with
        disabilities, 7–8, 11, 107, 126–27, 131,
        198–99, 201, 208
stud persona, 165, 167
stuttering, 175–79
Sundquist, Josh, 104
supercrip, 83, 203
Sweet Scarlett, 203–4

TABs (temporarily able bodied), 235n2; as
    butt of jokes, 80–81, 159–64, 171–73,
    177–78, 180–81; as entitled, 46, 87–88
Tatas Tee, 131
Truchan, Magdalena, 128–34

urinary drainage bag, as erotic prop, 209–11

vibrator jokes, 180
violence, 20, 140; emotional, 219–21;
    horizontal, 17, 120, 172, 236n12; sexual,
    113, 146–50, 207, 220
visual impairment, 3–8, 10, 17–19, 21–23,
    28–31, 57–64, 73–76, 79–80, 93–98,
    137, 152–54, 225, 227–31; and burlesque
    performances, 203–4

Walker, Alice, 97
walkies, 45–46
Wallach, Greg, 158–64
wheelchairs: and basketball, xii, 13, 15–16,
    139, 190; dancing in, 205, 209, 217–18,
    243n10; as encompassing identity,
    9, 107; handles as breasts, 169–71;
    and identity presentation, 109–10,
    114–16, 122–24, 129–30; lap dances in,
    172–73; sex in, 110–11, 213; and sexuality,
    114–15, 119, 121–22, 181, 205, 208, 213–19;
    striptease in, 204–5, 208, 215–21
wheelchair users: as burlesque perform-
    ers, 203–6, 208–9, 212–21; as comics,
    168–74, 179–82; and dating profile
    pictures, 189; jokes told by, 13–14, 15,
    17, 78–79, 84–86, 168–74, 179–82; as
    parking enforcement officials, 45;
    as sexually promiscuous, 179–82; as
    targets of sexual violence, 146–48
white privilege, and comedy, 156
Williams, Brad, 164–67

ABOUT THE AUTHOR

Photo by Tristan Palmgren

Teresa Milbrodt's critical work has appeared in the *Journal of Literary and Cultural Disability Studies*, *Disability Studies Quarterly*, *Western Folklore*, and the *Journal of Creative Writing Studies*. Milbrodt is the author of three short story collections: *Instances of Head-Switching*, *Bearded Women: Stories*, and *Work Opportunities*. She has also published a novel, *The Patron Saint of Unattractive People*, and a flash fiction collection, *Larissa Takes Flight: Stories*. Her fiction, creative nonfiction, and poetry have appeared in numerous literary magazines. She holds an MFA in creative writing and a MA in American culture studies from Bowling Green State University and a PhD in English with emphases in creative writing and disability studies from the University of Missouri. She is an assistant professor at Roanoke College in Salem, Virginia, where she lives with her partner Tristan Palmgren. Milbrodt believes in coffee, long walks with her MP3 player, and writing the occasional haiku.

www.ingramcontent.com/pod-product-compliance
Lightning Source LLC
Chambersburg PA
CBHW030350270326
41926CB00009B/1044